Encoded Archival Description Tag Library

Version 2002

Prepared and Maintained by the
Encoded Archival Description Working Group
of the Society of American Archivists
and the
Network Development and MARC Standards Office
of the Library of Congress

Chicago

Encoded Archival Description Tag Library, Version 2002

EAD Technical Document No. 2

This tag library represents version 2002 of the Encoded Archival Description Document Type Definition (DTD), released in August 2002. It supersedes the Version 1.0 tag library published in 1998.

The SAA Encoded Archival Description Working Group is responsible for updating and editing the EAD DTD (EAD Technical Document No. 1) and tag library.

The Network Development and MARC Standards Office of the Library of Congress serves as the maintenance agency for online EAD documentation, including storage and delivery of electronic files and maintenance of the EAD web site, located at *http://lcweb.loc.gov/ead/*.

Available from: **The Society of American Archivists**
527 S. Wells Street, 5th floor
Chicago, IL 60607-3922 USA

312/922-0140
Fax: 312/347-1452
info@archivists.org
www.archivists.org

ISBN 1-931666-00-8

Table of Contents

Preface

The Society of American Archivists Encoded Archival Description Working Group[1] is pleased to bring you EAD 2002, the second full version of the encoding standard for archival finding aids. This version represents a truly international collaboration in the continued development and maintenance of EAD.

In 2000 the International Council on Archives Committee on Descriptive Standards published the second edition of the General International Standard Archival Description (ISAD(G)). One of the guiding principles of EAD is to maintain compatibility with ISAD(G). Many of the suggestions submitted to the Working Group in late 2000 and early 2001 reflected changes needed to maintain that compatibility; they have been accommodated in this version through the addition of new elements and/or attributes or through clarification of existing element and attribute definitions. Experimentation with EAD internationally, particularly recent tests in France and Germany, has shown that EAD is applicable to a variety of descriptive practices but also has indicated the need for structural changes. Some of the more significant changes are as follows:

There are two new elements in the Descriptive Identification of the Unit <did>: Language of the Material <langmaterial>, and Material Specific Details <materialspec>. Replacing the LANGMATERIAL attribute in <archdesc> and <c>, the <langmaterial> element makes it possible to provide intelligible information about language(s) to the end user. Information such as scale for technical drawings and maps and playing time for sound recordings can be expressed in <materialspec>, expanding EAD's applicability beyond "traditional" archival materials.

Archival Description <archdesc> (and therefore all components) also has some new elements. Location of Originals <originalsloc> parallels the originals/copies aspect of Alternative Form Available <altformavail>. Physical Characteristics and Technical Requirements <phystech> accommodates the new ISAD(G) rule 3.4.4, and indicates whether there are unusual physical aspects or if special equipment is needed to access the materials. Legal Status <legalstatus>, a new subelement of <accessrestrict>, replaces the former LEGALSTATUS attribute on <archdesc>.

A new subelement in the <profiledesc> header element, Descriptive Rules <descrules>, accommodates the new ISAD(G) element 3.7.2 to provide the descriptive code used to create the finding aid.

---

[1] At the time of this revision members of the Working Group were: Randall Barry (Library of Congress Network Development and MARC Standards Office), Catherine Dhérent (Archives de France), Michael Fox (Minnesota Historical Society), Tim Hutchinson (University of Saskatchewan), Kris Kiesling (University of Texas at Austin), William Landis (University of California, Irvine), Gavan McCarthy (University of Melbourne), Daniel Pitti (University of Virginia), Merrilee Proffitt (Research Libraries Group, *ex officio*), Lydia Reid (National Archives and Records Administration), and Meg Sweet (Public Record Office).

Structural changes have also been implemented in EAD 2002. Administrative Information <admininfo> and Adjunct Descriptive Data <add> have been "unbundled," i.e., the elements that were formerly nested within these two elements are now available directly in <archdesc> and <c>. While they provided a useful grouping tool at the highest level of description, frequently the need to open, for example, <admininfo> to use <accessrestrict> at the component level simply created tagging overhead. It should be noted that the use of <admininfo> and <add> is being deprecated by the Working Group (see Appendix B). This means that the Working Group recommends discontinuing their use because this structure will be eliminated in a future version of EAD. To facilitate grouping of elements on an as-needed basis, another new <archdesc> element has been created, Description Group <descgrp>. <descgrp> can be used to bundle most of the structural elements (except <did> and <dsc>), enabling archivists to group them logically at a given level of description.

EAD 2002 presents a host of new attributes, and most of the semi-closed lists of attribute values have been eliminated. In most cases, the semi-closed lists were very Anglo-centric and inhibited international adoption of EAD (e.g., the list of controlled vocabulary thesauri for the SOURCE attribute). It will now be the responsibility of individual repositories to use consistently the code lists and terminology recommended by national practices.

Finally, archivists persuasively articulated the need for certain elements and attributes in places where they weren't available in EAD version 1.0. As a result, <title> is now available in <indexentry>, and "singlequote" and "doublequote" have been added as values for the RENDER attribute, in addition to other improvements.

The Working Group gratefully acknowledges all who took the time to contribute to this version of EAD. EAD is stronger for your attention and interest! In addition, we extend our deep appreciation to the National Historical Publications and Records Commission, which has provided funding to support Working Group meetings.

Like many efforts of its kind, most of the work of bringing EAD 2002 to fruition was shouldered by a small group of dedicated souls. I'd like to extend my personal thanks to Daniel Pitti at the University of Virginia for once again revising the DTD (and revising…and revising…), to Michael Fox of the Minnesota Historical Society for writing definitions of new elements and attributes and for drafting a conversion script and testing the new DTD, to Tim Hutchinson of the University of Saskatchewan for careful proofreading, and to Merrilee Proffitt of the Research Libraries Group and Bill Landis of the University of California at Irvine for gathering and parsing the examples.

KRIS KIESLING
Chair, EAD Working Group

Tag Library Conventions

The EAD Elements section of the tag library contains descriptions of 146 elements, which are arranged alphabetically by their tag names. The Index by Element Name (Appendix D) makes it possible to locate those elements with tag names that might be hard to find alphabetically. For example, the index entry for Conditions Governing Use points to the tag name <userestrict>. The Index by Element Name also serves as a concise, easily browsable list of all EAD elements.

The EAD Elements section presents information for each element as shown in Figure 1. Some of a DTD's specialized terminology is explained on the following pages as a reminder of basic SGML/XML conventions involved in encoding documents with EAD.[2]

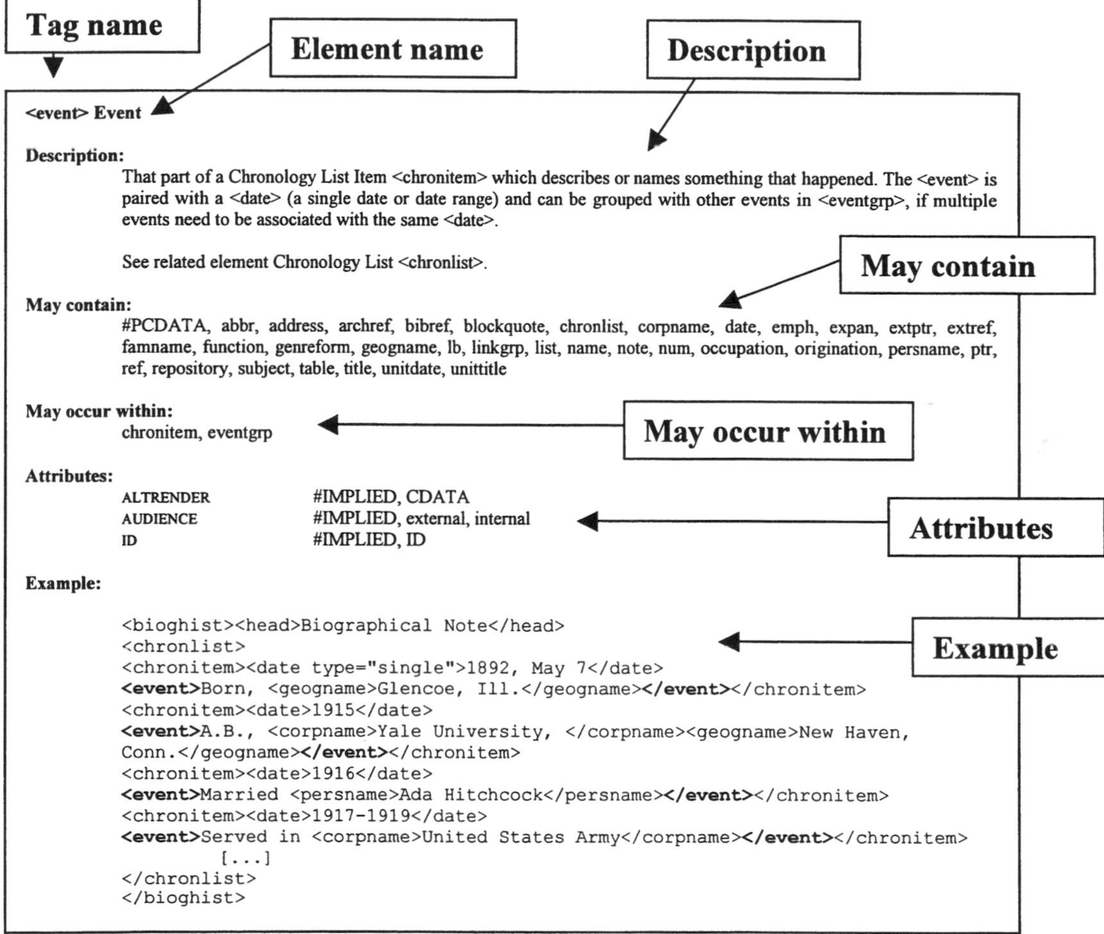

<event> Event

Description:

That part of a Chronology List Item <chronitem> which describes or names something that happened. The <event> is paired with a <date> (a single date or date range) and can be grouped with other events in <eventgrp>, if multiple events need to be associated with the same <date>.

See related element Chronology List <chronlist>.

May contain:

#PCDATA, abbr, address, archref, bibref, blockquote, chronlist, corpname, date, emph, expan, extptr, extref, famname, function, genreform, geogname, lb, linkgrp, list, name, note, num, occupation, origination, persname, ptr, ref, repository, subject, table, title, unitdate, unittitle

May occur within:

chronitem, eventgrp

Attributes:

ALTRENDER	#IMPLIED, CDATA
AUDIENCE	#IMPLIED, external, internal
ID	#IMPLIED, ID

Example:

```
<bioghist><head>Biographical Note</head>
<chronlist>
<chronitem><date type="single">1892, May 7</date>
<event>Born, <geogname>Glencoe, Ill.</geogname></event></chronitem>
<chronitem><date>1915</date>
<event>A.B., <corpname>Yale University, </corpname><geogname>New Haven,
Conn.</geogname></event></chronitem>
<chronitem><date>1916</date>
<event>Married <persname>Ada Hitchcock</persname></event></chronitem>
<chronitem><date>1917-1919</date>
<event>Served in <corpname>United States Army</corpname></event></chronitem>
        [...]
</chronlist>
</bioghist>
```

Figure 1. Layout of element descriptions

[2] For basic information about SGML and XML and pointers to additional sources, consult the XML Cover Pages at http://www.oasis-open.org/cover/.

This section also includes the three elements that occur in the EAD Group DTD: <eadgrp>, <archdescgrp>, and <dscgrp>. The EAD Group DTD allows several EAD-encoded finding aids to be combined into a single document and uses many EAD elements.

Tag Name:

Short, mnemonic form of the element name that is used in the machine-readable encoded document. The tag name is the first word at the top of the page. Tag names appear between angle brackets, e.g., <archdesc>, except in the listings under "May occur within" and "May contain," and are always in lowercase.

Element Name:

Expanded version of the tag name which more fully describes the element's meaning. The full name of the element is usually a word or phrase that identifies the element's purpose. In the tag library, the element name follows the tag name on the page defining that element and appears with initial capital letters, e.g., <archdesc> Archival Description.

Description:

The first paragraph of the description defines the element by drawing from terminology in archival glossaries, basic dictionaries, and data dictionaries such as ISAD(G), MARC21, the *Categories for the Description of Works of Art*, and the Text Encoding Initiative DTD.[3] Any additional paragraphs describe how the element is used, differentiate it from similar elements, point out useful attributes, provide an illustrative example, or direct the reader to related elements. Stock phrases are used to suggest the kind of element being discussed. "Wrapper element" indicates an element that cannot contain text directly; a second, nested element must be opened first. Wrapper elements designate sets of elements that comprise a distinctive section of a finding aid, for example, the Descriptive Identification <did>. "Generic element" refers to elements common to many kinds of documents that contain information that does not specifically relate to the structural parts of a finding aid, e.g., <address> and <date>. "Formatting element" indicates elements that can be used to invoke special character or text presentation, such as block quotes, chronologies, and emphasis. When an element is required, that fact is also stated. Specific ISAD(G) data elements and/or MARC

---

[3] International Council on Archives. *ISAD(G): General International Standard Archival Description*, 2nd ed., adopted by the Committee on Descriptive Standards, Stockholm, Sweden, 19-22 September 1999 (http://www.ica.org/eng/mb/com/cds/descriptivestandards).
Categories for the Description of Works of Art. (Santa Monica, Calif.: Getty Information Institute, http://www.getty.edu/research/institute/standards/cdwa/).
Library of Congress. *MARC21 Format for Bibliographic Data*. (Washington, D.C.: Library of Congress, 2001.
(http://lcweb.loc.gov/marc/bibliographic/ecbdhome.html).
The Text Encoding Initiative is an international research project that has developed an encoding standard for a wide range of document types in the domain of humanities computing (http://www.tei-c.org/).

fields that relate to a given element are provided when applicable. For information on specified sequences of elements, consult the DTD itself. For example, you may wish to check the list of subelements in an XML authoring program or DTD visualization tool.

May contain:

Identifies what may occur within the element being defined. Elements are listed in alphabetical order by tag name. Elements may be empty (e.g., containing only an attribute); or they may contain text (called #PCDATA); other elements; or a mixture of text and other elements.

The abbreviation #PCDATA (parsed character data) means that text content is allowed directly inside of an element, but the text cannot include characters that would be interpreted by a parser as action codes. For example, a left angle bracket has to be represented as the character entity reference `⟨` so that it is not misinterpreted as the start of an element name.

The list of nested elements usually includes more elements than are generally needed, because similar elements sharing the same content model travel together as a group. This is a device to ease the authoring of a DTD and to aid machine processing of encoded documents. For example, once one reference element such as <ref> is listed under May contain, all the reference elements appear, including <archref>, <bibref>, <extptr>, <extref>, and <ptr>, even though the simple internal <ref> element is the most likely choice in a particular context.

May occur within:

Identifies all of the parent elements within which the described element may appear, listed in alphabetical order by tag name. This information conveys the sense of where and how often an element is available throughout the DTD. Definitions for parent elements may provide additional information about an element's usage.

Attributes:

Identifies all attributes that can be associated with an element. Attributes are represented in lowercase letters in XML coding, but the EAD Tag Library uses the convention of SMALL CAPITAL letters to distinguish attributes from elements within the tag library context. See the EAD Attributes section of the tag library for definitions and additional information.

Examples:

Most element descriptions include a tagged example to indicate how attributes and elements can be used together. Most of the examples are taken from real finding aids; others have been specially constructed for the tag library. The examples illustrate any required sequences of elements, as in the case of subelements within the <eadheader>, or required attributes such as LEVEL in <archdesc>. In other cases, the examples are intended simply to show what is possible. Some examples have elipses, either between or within elements, where other elements or text have been omitted. Some elements have multiple examples—one may show very dense markup that uses numerous attributes while another may illustrate a minimalist approach to the markup. Either approach is valid in EAD, and it is up to the repository to determine the optimal level of markup based on institutional resources and/or consortial guidelines.

EAD Attributes

Introduction

Attributes are associated with most of the elements contained in EAD. These attributes reflect named properties of an element and may take on different values, depending on the context in which they occur. In order to set one or more attributes, an encoder should include the name of the attribute(s) within the same angle bracket as the start tag, together with the value(s) to which the attribute(s) is/are to be set. That is,

```
<[tag] [attribute]="[value]">
```

or

```
<[tag] [attribute1]="[value1]" [attribute2]="[value2]">
```

For example:

```
<unitdate type="inclusive">1937-1992</unitdate>
```

or

```
<origination label="Creator:">Kenny, Elizabeth</origination>
<unittitle encodinganalog="MARC 245" label="Title:">Elizabeth
Kenny Papers</unittitle>
```

Most attributes are optional and of the type called #IMPLIED. Three attributes are flagged as #REQUIRED, and two are #FIXED.

#IMPLIED	The attribute is not required. If no attribute value is specified, a processing program may infer a value.
#REQUIRED	The attribute must be specified within the start tag for the element, e.g.: `<archdesc level="recordgrp">`
#FIXED	The attribute has only one possible value which is specified by the DTD.

The value of attributes may be constrained by the DTD using specific attribute type values. For example, "id" attribute is of type ID, which constrains its value to a string beginning with an alphabetic character. An "id" value must be unique within the EAD instance within which it occurs, that is, no other tag in the entire document can have the same "id" value. Most EAD attributes are of type CDATA, which means that any text characters may be used.

CDATA:	Character data. No markup is recognized within a CDATA value except for character references. If the characters < (less than), > (greater than), & (ampersand), ' (apostrophe), or " (quotation) are used, they must be escaped using a character reference.
ENTITY:	The name of a nonparsed entity that has been declared in the declaration subset of the document. For example, the ENTITYREF attribute must contain the name of an entity that has been declared in the declaration subset. Processing software can use the reference to the nonparsed entity to display the entity in the body of the text or in a new window.
ID:	Unique identifier. For example, most elements have an ID attribute, so that a unique code can be established for and used to refer to that specific element. The content of the ID attribute is of the type called "id." Parsers verify that the value of attributes of type "id" are unique. ID attribute values must begin with an alpha, not numeric, character, either upper or lowercase, and may contain a . (period), : (colon), - (hyphen), or _ (underscore), but not a blank space. See also attributes of type "idref."
IDREF:	ID reference value; previously entered ID of another element. For example, the <container> element has a PARENT attribute that can only be an "idref," which means it has a reference to a valid ID in another element.
IDREFS:	List of ID reference values.
NMTOKEN:	A name token, which can consist of any alpha or numeric character, as well as a . (period), : (colon), - (hyphen), or _ (underscore), but not a blank space. A number of attributes in EAD where a character string from a code list is to be used are NMTOKEN.
NMTOKENS:	List of name tokens.

When the EAD DTD limits attribute values to a few choices, those values are declared in the DTD as part of what is known as a closed list, or technically, a name-token list. For example, the values of the attribute AUDIENCE are limited to either "external" or "internal." Some attributes are associated with semi-closed lists. Such lists include those values believed to be the most useful in many contexts. Since the DTD creators could not anticipate all useful values for an attribute of this type, the list permits, by means of another attribute, the ability to provide an alternative value. For example, the <dsc>

element includes several display types in a semi-closed list. Setting the TYPE attribute to "othertype" makes it possible to specify in a separate OTHERTYPE attribute display types that are not in the semi-closed list for TYPE. The definitions for some values in the closed and semi-closed lists appear below.

The following is a complete list of all the attributes that occur in EAD, and some discussion of how they may be used. Attributes that are used for linking and for tabular display are defined in separate lists that follow the General Attributes list.

General Attributes

ABBR	An abbreviation for a word or phrase that is expressed in an expanded form in the text; used for searching and indexing purposes. Available only in the <expan> element.
ACTUATE	see Linking Attributes
ALIGN	see Tabular Display Attributes
ALTHEAD	An alternative short form of the heading element <head> that might be used, for example, to create a running header.
ALTRENDER	The content of the element should be displayed or printed differently than the rendering established in a style sheet for other occurrences of the element. See also RENDER.
ARCROLE	see Linking Attributes
AUDIENCE	An attribute that helps control whether the information contained in the element should be available to all viewers or only to repository staff. Available for all elements except line break <lb>. The audience attribute can be set to "external" in <archdesc> to allow access to all the information about the materials being described in the finding aid, but specific elements within <archdesc> can be set to "internal" to reserve that information for repository access only. This feature is intended to assist application software in restricting access to particular information by explicitly coding data that is potentially sensitive or may otherwise have a limited audience. Special software capability may be needed, however, to prevent the export of an element marked "internal" when a whole finding aid is displayed in a networked environment. Values are: • external (default value) • internal
AUTHFILENUMBER	A number that identifies the authority file record for an access term drawn from that authority file. If this attribute is used, the SOURCE attribute should also be used to identify the authority file.
CALENDAR	System of reckoning time, such as the Gregorian calendar or Julian calendar. The value "gregorian" is the default. Available in <date> and <unitdate>.

CERTAINTY — The level of confidence for the information given in a <date> or <unitdate> element. For example:

```
<date certainty="approximate">1920</date>
```

CHAR — see Tabular Display Attributes

CHAROFF — see Tabular Display Attributes

COLNAME — see Tabular Display Attributes

COLNUM — see Tabular Display Attributes

COLS — see Tabular Display Attributes

COLSEP — see Tabular Display Attributes

COLWIDTH — see Tabular Display Attributes

CONTINUATION — For ordered lists, i.e., those with a TYPE attribute of "ordered," and optionally with a NUMERATION attribute, the CONTINUATION attribute specifies whether the list numeration is to continue with the numeration of the preceding list or start over. If this attribute is not present, starting over is implied. Values are:

- continues
- starts

COUNTRYCODE — A unique code for the country in which the materials being described are held. Codes are to be taken from ISO 3166-1 *Codes for the Representation of Names of Countries*, column A2. Available in <eadid> and <unitid>.

COUNTRYENCODING — The authoritative source or rules for values supplied in the COUNTRYCODE attribute in <eadid> and <unitid>. Available only in <eadheader>, the COUNTRYENCODING attribute should be set to "iso3166-1."

DATECHAR — Term characterizing the nature of dates, such as dates of creation, accumulation, or modification. Available only in <unitdate>.

DATEENCODING — The authoritative source or rules for values provided in the NORMAL attribute in <date> and <unitdate>. The DATEENCODING attribute should be set to "iso8601."

General Attributes

ENCODINGANALOG

A field or element in another descriptive encoding system to which an EAD element or attribute is comparable. Mapping elements from one system to another may help build a single user interface that can index comparable information in bibliographic records and finding aids. The mapping designations may also help a repository harvest selected data from a finding aid to build a basic catalog record. When possible, subfields as well as fields should be specified, e.g., subfields within MARC fields. If the RELATEDENCODING attribute in <ead>, <eadheader>, or <archdesc> is not used to identify the encoding system from which fields are specified in the ENCODINGANALOG attribute, then include the system designation in ENCODINGANALOG.

Example:

```
<origination><corpname encodinganalog="MARC
110">Waters Studio</corpname></origination>
```

or

```
<archdesc relatedencoding="MARC"><origination>
<persname encodinganalog="100$a$q$d$e"
source="lcnaf">Waters, E. C. (Elizabeth Cat),
1870-1944, photographer</persname>
</origination></archdesc>
```

ENTITYREF

see Linking Attributes

ERA

Period during which years are numbered and dates reckoned, such as A.D. or C.E. The value "ce" is the default.

EXPAN

The full form of an abbreviation or acronym in an element's text; used for indexing and searching purposes. Available only in the <abbr> element.

FINDAIDSTATUS

The extent to which the encoded finding aid is a finished document. Available only in the <eadheader> element.

FRAME

see Tabular Display Attributes

FROM

see Linking Attributes

HREF

see Linking Attributes

ID

see Linking Attributes

IDENTIFIER — A machine-readable unique identifier. Available in <eadid> and <unitid>.

LABEL — A display label for an element can be supplied using this attribute when a meaningful label cannot be derived by the style sheet from the element name or when a heading element <head> is not available. This attribute is available in all <did> subelements.

LANGCODE — The three-lettter code for the language in which an abstract is written <abstract>, for the language of the finding aid and the language of the materials <language>. The codes should be taken from ISO639-2b, as specified in the LANGENCODING attribute in <eadheader>.

LANGENCODING — Language encoding for EAD instances subscribes to ISO 639-2b *Codes for the Representation of Names of Languages*, so the LANGENCODING attribute value in <eadheader> should be "iso639-2b." The codes themselves are specified in the LANGCODE attribute in <abstract> or <language>, as appropriate.

LEVEL — The hierarchical level of the materials being described by the element. This attribute is available in <archdesc>, where the highest level of material represented in the finding aid must be declared (e.g., collection, fonds, record group), and in <c> and <c01-12> (e.g., subgroup, series, file). If none of the values in the semi-closed list are appropriate, the value "otherlevel" may be chosen and the term specified in the OTHERLEVEL attribute. Values are:

- collection
- fonds
- class
- recordgrp
- series
- subfonds
- subgrp
- subseries
- file
- item
- otherlevel

LINKTYPE — see Linking Attributes

General Attributes

MAINAGENCYCODE — A code in <eadid> compliant with ISO/DIS 15511 *Information and Documentation International Standard Identifier for Libraries and Related Organizations* (ISIL). Values should be supplied without the country code, which should be placed instead in the COUNTRYCODE attribute.

MARK — For lists with a TYPE attribute value "marked," the MARK attribute may be used to provide a character(s) or character entity(ies) to mark each list entry. For example, a bulleted list: `<list type="marked" mark="•">`

MOREROWS — see Tabular Display Attributes

NAMEEND — see Tabular Display Attributes

NAMEST — see Tabular Display Attributes

NORMAL — A consistent form, usually from a controlled vocabulary list, of the content of the following elements can be provided to facilitate retrieval: <corpname>, <famname>, <function>, <genreform>, <geogname>, <name>, <occupation>, <persname>, <subject>, and <title>. In <date> and <unitdate>, the NORMAL attribute follows ISO 8601 *Representation of Dates and Times*, as specified in the DATEENCODING attribute in <eadheader>.

NUMERATION — For lists with a TYPE attribute of "ordered," the NUMERATION attribute specifies the type of numeration. Values are:

- arabic
- upperalpha
- loweralpha
- upperroman
- lowerroman

OTHERLEVEL — The hierarchical level of the materials described in <archdesc>, <c>, <c01-12>, and <archdescgrp> can be specified when the semi-closed list in the LEVEL attribute (e.g., collection, fonds, series, etc.) does not contain an appropriate term. Set LEVEL to "otherlevel" and then supply the preferred term in the OTHERLEVEL attribute.

OTHERTYPE — The TYPE attribute in <dsc> has a semi-closed list, of which one of the values is "othertype." If the format of the <dsc> is not one of the types in the semi-closed list, one can be specified in the OTHERTYPE attribute.

PARENT — see Linking Attributes

PGWIDE — see Tabular Display Attributes

PLACEMENT — The location of the information in the <runner> element is displayed in print (foot or head) or as a digital watermark (background). Values are:

- foot
- head
- background

PUBLICID — A formal public identifier (FPI) in <eadid> that includes the owner name and an object name. Defined in ISO/IEC 9070:1991, the FPI is intended to be universally unique, with each owner name being unique, and each object name unique within the name domain controlled by the owner.

RELATEDENCODING — A descriptive encoding system, such as MARC, ISAD(G), or Dublin Core, to which certain EAD elements can be mapped using the ENCODINGANALOG attribute. RELATEDENCODING is available in <ead>, <eadheader>, and <archdesc>; the <eadheader> elements might be mapped to Dublin Core elements while the body of the finding aid (<archdesc>) might instead be mapped to MARC or ISAD(G).

RENDER — The formatting of the content of an element is controlled for display and print purposes. Available in <emph>, <title>, and <titleproper>. See also ALTRENDER. Values are:

- altrender
- bold
- doublequote
- bolddoublequote
- bolditalic
- boldsinglequote
- boldsmcaps
- boldunderline
- italic
- nonproport
- singlequote
- smcaps
- sub
- super
- underline

REPOSITORYCODE	A unique code in <unitid> indicating the repository responsible for intellectual control of the materials being described. The code should be taken from ISO 15511 *Codes for the Representation of Names of Countries and their Subdivisions*, as specified in the <eadheader> REPOSITORYENCODING attribute.
REPOSITORYENCODING	The authoritative source or rules for values supplied in the MAINAGENCYCODE attribute in <eadid> and the REPOSITORYCODE attribute in <unitid>. Available only in <eadheader>, the REPOSITORYENCODING attribute should be set to "iso15511."
ROLE	A contextual role or relationship for the person, family, corporate body, or geographic location within <persname>, <famname>, <corpname>, <geogname>, and <name>, elements. In linking elements such as <ptr>, information that explains to application software the part that a remote resource plays in a link.
ROWSEP	see Tabular Display Attributes
RULES	Name of the descriptive rules or conventions that govern the formulation of the content of the element.
SCRIPTCODE	The three-letter code for the writing script used with a given language. The code should be taken from ISO 15924 *Code for the Representation of Names of Scripts*. Available in <language>.
SCRIPTENCODING	The authoritative source or rules for values supplied in the SCRIPTCODE attribute in <language>. Available only in <eadheader>, the SCRIPTENCODING attribute should be set to "iso15924."
SHOW	see Linking Attributes
SOURCE	The source of the controlled vocabulary term contained in the element. Available in subelements of <controlaccess>, i.e., <corpname>, <famname>, <function>, <genreform>, <geogname>, <name>, <occupation>, <persname>, <physdesc>, <subject>, and <title>.
TARGET	see Linking Attributes

TITLE — see Linking Attributes

TO — see Linking Attributes

TPATTERN — see Tabular Display Attributes

TYPE — The TYPE attribute is available for a number of elements; its characteristics vary depending on the element to which it applies. Some instances of TYPE have closed lists (e.g., <unitdate>), others have semi-closed lists (e.g., <dsc>), and most permit character data (CDATA) (e.g., <accessrestrict> and <physloc>). The semi-closed list in <dsc> contains a value of "othertype," which allows the specification of an appropriate value in the OTHERTYPE attribute. See individual element descriptions for specific uses for this attribute.

UNIT — Any unit of measurement may be expressed in <dimensions>, <extent>, and <physfacet>.

URL — An absolute (http://www.loc.gov/ead/ms99999.xml) or relative (ms99999.xml) Uniform Resource Locator. Available only in <eadid>.

URN — A Uniform Resource Name intended to serve as a persistent, location-independent, resource identifier.

VALIGN — see Tabular Display Attributes

XMLNS — XML Namespace declaration for the EAD standard, which should be set to "urn:isbn:1-931666-00-8." Available only in <ead> and <eadgrp>, but must be manually activated.

XPOINTER — see Linking Attributes

Linking Attributes

The following attributes apply to elements used for linking.

ACTUATE

A control that defines whether a link occurs automatically or must be requested by the user. It is used in conjunction with the SHOW attribute to determine link behavior. Values are:

- onload (element is displayed automatically)
- onrequest (element is displayed if user requests)
- actuateother (some other action occurs with respect to the link)
- actuatenone (no action occurs with respect to the link

ARCROLE

URI preference that identifies a resource that describes some property of an arc-type or simple-type linking element.

ENTITYREF

The name of a nonparsed entity declared in the declaration subset of the document that points to a machine-readable version of the cited reference.

FROM

Resource from which traversal may be initiated, that is, a starting resource, in an extended link. Available only in <arc>.

HREF

The locator for a remote resource in a simple or extended link. An HREF takes the form of a Uniform Resource Identifier (URI). If no URI is specified, the locator is assumed to be within the document that contains the linking element.

ID

An identifier used to name the element so that it can be referred to, or referenced from, somewhere else. Each ID within a document must have a unique value. The ID attribute regularizes the naming of the element and thus facilitates building links between it and other resources.

LINKTYPE

A fixed or default value that identifies the element as XLINK-compatible. Types are, simple, extended, locator, or resource.

PARENT — A pointer to another container that holds the container item being described in the current element, e.g., points to the element that describes the box in which a folder is housed. Available in <container> and <physloc>.

ROLE — Information that explains to application software the part that a remote resource plays in a link.

SHOW — A control that defines whether a remote resource that is the target of a link appears at the point of the link, replaces the existing link, or appears in a new window. It is used in conjunction with the ACTUATE attribute to determine link behavior. Values are:

- embed (the target resource displays at the point of the link)
- new (the target resource appears in a new window)
- replace (the target resource replaces the local resource that initiated the link)
- showother (some other action takes place with respect to the target resource)
- shownone (no target resource displays)

TARGET — A pointer to the ID of another element.

TITLE — Information that serves as a viewable caption which explains to users the part that a resource plays in a link.

TO — Specification of a resource that may be traversed to, that is, an ending resource, in an extended link.

XPOINTER — The locator for a remote resource in a simple or locator link. The XPOINTER attribute takes the form of a Uniform Resource Identifier plus a reference, formulated in XPOINTER syntax, to a sub-resource of the remote resource. XPOINTER enables linking to specific sections of a document that are relative, i.e., based on their position in the document or their content, rather than by reference to a specific identifier such as an ID.

Tabular Display Attributes

The following attributes apply to elements that can be used to format tables and other columnar structures.

ALIGN — Horizontal position of the text within a column. Available in <colspec> and <entry>. Values are:

- left (flush left)
- right (flush right)
- center (centered in the column)
- justify (flush both left and right)
- char (alignment on a single character such as a decimal, as positioned by CHAROFF)

CHAR — Used for horizontal alignment of a single character, such as decimal alignment. This attribute names the character on which the text will be aligned, for example a decimal point, an asterisk, or an em-dash. Available in <colspec> and <entry>.

CHAROFF — Character offset, used with horizontal character alignment, such as decimal alignment. When the ALIGN attribute value is "char," this is the percentage of the current column width to the left edge of the alignment character. Value is a number or starts with a number. Available in <colspec> and <entry>.

COLNAME — Name of a column in which an entry appears. Value is one "word" made up of letters and numbers with no spaces inside it. Available in <colspec> and <entry>.

COLNUM — The number of the column, counting from 1 at the left of the table. Value is a number. Available in <colspec>.

COLS — The number of columns in a table. Required in <tgroup>.

COLSEP — If the columns in the table are to be separated by vertical rules, possible COLSEP values are:

- 1 (display a rule to the right of the column)
- 0 (no rule is displayed)

COLWIDTH — Width of the column measured in fixed units or relative proportions. Fixed measure is in the form "number followed by unit," where unit is "pt" for point, "cm" for centimeters, "in" for inches, etc. (i.e., "2in" for 2 inches). Proportional measure is in the form "number followed by asterisk" (i.e., "5*" for five times the proportion). All integers are positive. Use values that are appropriate to the software that governs the display of the resulting table such as a web browser or XSL format objects processor. Available in <colspec>.

FRAME — Are there rules surrounding the table when the table is printed or displayed? The values of the frame attribute indicate the position of the external rules:

- top (a horizontal rule below the title)
- sides (left and right vertical rules)
- topbot (horizontal rules top and bottom)
- bottom (horizontal rule after the last row)
- all (table is printed in a box)
- none (no rules surround the table)

MOREROWS — Number of additional rows in a vertical straddle. Value is a number; default value is "0" to indicate one row only, no vertical span. Available in <entry> only.

NAMEEND — Name of the rightmost column of a span. The value must be a column name, as defined by the COLNAME attribute on a Column Specification <colspec> element. Available in <entry> only.

NAMEST — Name of leftmost column of a span. The value must be a column name, as defined by the COLNAME attribute on a Column Specification <colspec> element. The extent of a horizontal span is determined by naming the first column (namest) and the last column (nameend) in the span. Available in <entry> only.

PGWIDE — Does the table run the width of the page or the width of the text column? Values are:

- 1 (as wide as the page)
- 0 (fills the text column only)

ROWSEP — If the rows in a table are to be separated by horizontal rules, possible rowsep values are:

- 1 (display a rule below the row)
- 0 (no rule is displayed)

Tabular Display Attributes

TPATTERN	Reference to one of a set of standard patterns that define the specifications of particular HTML output tables. Available in <c>, <c01-12>, and <dsc>.
VALIGN	Vertical positioning of the text within a table cell. Values are: • top • middle • bottom

EAD Elements

<abbr> Abbreviation

Description:

A generic element for a shortened form of a word, including an acronym.

The EXPAN attribute can be used to supply the full form of an abbreviated word for indexing or searching purposes.

See also related element Expansion <expan>.

May contain:

#PCDATA

May occur within:

abstract, archref, bibref, container, creation, descrules, dimensions, emph, entry, event, extent, extref, extrefloc, item, label, langmaterial, langusage, materialspec, origination, p, physdesc, physfacet, physloc, ref, refloc, repository, subtitle, titleproper, unitdate, unitid, unittitle

Attributes:

ALTRENDER	#IMPLIED, CDATA
AUDIENCE	#IMPLIED, external, internal
EXPAN	#IMPLIED, CDATA
ID	#IMPLIED, ID

Example:

```
<note>
   <p>
      <abbr expan="Autograph Letter Signed">ALS</abbr>
   </p>
</note>
```

<abstract> Abstract

Description:

A very brief summary of the materials being described, used primarily to encode bits of biographical or historical information about the creator and abridged statements about the scope, content, arrangement, or other descriptive details about the archival unit or one of its components.

Within the <archdesc><did>, the <abstract> is often extracted from the longer descriptions found in <bioghist> and <scopecontent>. Its purpose is to help readers identify quickly those materials they need to explore at greater length. Within the <c><did>, the <abstract> may describe unique characteristics of an individual Component. This information may have aspects of <arrangement>, <bioghist>, <physdesc>, and <scopecontent>, which are not substantive enough to tag individually under those elements.

Use of the TYPE and ENCODINGANALOG attributes on <abstract> may assist in extracting information for such MARC equivalents as summary note (520$a) and biographical or historical data (545$a). The LANGCODE attribute can be used when abstracts are provided in more than one language.

May contain:

#PCDATA, abbr, archref, bibref, emph, expan, extptr, extref, lb, linkgrp, ptr, ref, title

May occur within:

archref, did

Attributes:

ALTRENDER	#IMPLIED, CDATA
AUDIENCE	#IMPLIED, external, internal
ENCODINGANALOG	#IMPLIED, CDATA
ID	#IMPLIED, ID
LABEL	#IMPLIED, CDATA
LANGCODE	#IMPLIED, NMTOKEN
TYPE	#IMPLIED, CDATA

Example:

```
<archdesc level="fonds">
   <did>
      <head>Descriptive Summary</head>
      <unittitle label="Title">Richard Egan manuscript maps of
         Orange County</unittitle>
      <unitdate type="inclusive" normal="1878/1879">Circa 1878-
         1879</unitdate>
      <unitid countrycode="us" repositorycode="cu-i"
         label="Collection number">MS-R72</unitid>
      <origination label="Creator">
         <persname rules="aacr2">Egan, Richard, 1842-
            1923</persname>
      </origination>
      <physdesc label="Extent">
         <extent>1 linear foot (1 box)</extent>
      </physdesc>
      <repository label="Repository">
         <corpname rules="aacr2">University of California,
            Irvine. Library. Special Collections and
            Archives.</corpname>
      </repository>
      <abstract label="Abstract">Four manuscript survey maps and
         one plat map depicting areas of Orange County and
         attributed to the noted surveyor and judge Richard Egan.
         One map is dated 1878 and 1879 by Egan. The other maps
         are undated and unsigned but it is likely that he drew
         them during these years. These maps primarily depict
         subdivisions of non-rancho tracts of land occupying what
         is now Orange County, with the addition of some
         topographical details.</abstract>
   </did>
</archdesc>
```

<accessrestrict> Conditions Governing Access

Description:

Information about conditions that affect the availability of the materials being described. May indicate the need for an appointment or the nature of restrictions imposed by the donor, legal statute, repository, or other agency. May also indicate the lack of restrictions.

Do not confuse with Conditions Governing Use <userestrict>, which designates information about limitations on the use of the described materials after access has been granted.

In EAD Version 1.0 <accessrestrict> was a subelement of Administrative Information <admininfo>, which has been deprecated in EAD 2002 (see Appendix B). The new Description Group <descgrp> element, which can group any of the <did>-level elements (except the Description of Subordinate Components <dsc>), may be used to wrap elements where a group heading is desirable. The <descgrp> element can be used to replace <admininfo> where it has been used as a wrapper when converting finding aids encoded in EAD V1.0 to EAD 2002.

The <accessrestrict> element is comparable to ISAD(G) data element 3.4.1 and MARC field 506.

May contain:

accessrestrict, address, blockquote, chronlist, head, legalstatus, list, note, p, table

May occur within:

accessrestrict, archdesc, archdescgrp, c, c01, c02, c03, c04, c05, c06, c07, c08, c09, c10, c11, c12, descgrp

Attributes:

ALTRENDER	#IMPLIED, CDATA
AUDIENCE	#IMPLIED, external, internal
ENCODINGANALOG	#IMPLIED, CDATA
ID	#IMPLIED, ID
TYPE	#IMPLIED, CDATA

Examples:

1.
```
<accessrestrict>
   <p>There are no access restrictions on this collection.</p>
</accessrestrict>
```

2.
```
<accessrestrict>
   <p>University records are public records and once fully
      processed are generally open to research use. Records that
      contain personally identifiable information will be closed
      to protect individual privacy.  The closure of university
      records is subject to compliance with applicable laws.</p>
</accessrestrict>
```

3.
```
<c02 level="file">
   <did>
      <container type="box" label="Box">104 </container>
      <container type="folder" label="Folder(s)">6578-6579
      </container>
      <unittitle><title render="italic">Technics and
         Civilization</title> (<title render="italic">Form and
         Personality</title> or <title render="italic">Form and
         Civilization</title>)
      </unittitle>
      <unitdate type="inclusive" normal="1931/1933">1931-
         1933</unitdate>
   </did>
   <scopecontent>
      <p>Draft fragments.</p>
   </scopecontent>
   <accessrestrict>
      <p>Only the photocopies (housed in Box 105) of these
         fragile materials may be used.</p>
   </accessrestrict>
</c02>
```

<accruals> Accruals

Description:

Information about anticipated additions to the materials being described. Can indicate quantity and frequency. Can also be used to indicate that no additions are expected.

In EAD Version 1.0 <accruals> was a subelement of Administrative Information <admininfo>, which has been deprecated in EAD 2002 (see Appendix B). The new Description Group <descgrp> element, which can group any of the <did>-level elements (except the Description of Subordinate Components <dsc>), may be used to wrap elements where a group heading is desirable. The <descgrp> element can be used to replace <admininfo> where it has been used as a wrapper when converting finding aids encoded in EAD V1.0 to EAD 2002.

The <accruals> element is comparable to ISAD(G) data element 3.3.3 and MARC field 584.

May contain:

accruals, address, blockquote, chronlist, head, list, note, p, table

May occur within:

accruals, archdesc, archdescgrp, c, c01, c02, c03, c04, c05, c06, c07, c08, c09, c10, c11, c12, descgrp

Attributes:

ALTRENDER	#IMPLIED, CDATA
AUDIENCE	#IMPLIED, external, internal
ENCODINGANALOG	#IMPLIED, CDATA
ID	#IMPLIED, ID

Examples:

1.
```
<accruals>
   <p>No further materials are expected for this collection.</p>
</accruals>
```

2.
```
<accruals>
   <p>Noncurrent additions to this Record Group are transferred
      from the Development Department annually at the end of the
      fiscal year in June.</p>
</accruals>
```

<acqinfo> Acquisition Information

Description:

The immediate source of the materials being described and the circumstances under which they were received. Includes donations, transfers, purchases, and deposits.

After opening a Paragraph <p> within <acqinfo>, optional subelements may be used to tag separately such common acquisition information as the name of the source, e.g., <persname> or <corpname>; the <date> the materials were received; or the accession number <num> assigned to them. The <address> element could be used to document the address of the source, and the AUDIENCE attribute could be set to "internal," if the address information should only be available to authorized staff. Note that the accession number may also serve as the <unitid> and be encoded as such within a <did>.

For detailed information about items acquired and then subsequently alienated from the materials being described, the Separated Material <separatedmaterial> element can be used. It designates items related by provenance that have been physically removed from the materials being described.

The Custodial History <custodhist> element can be used for information about the chain of ownership before the materials reached the immediate source of acquisition.

In EAD Version 1.0 <acqinfo> was a subelement of Administrative Information <admininfo>, which has been deprecated in EAD 2002 (see Appendix B). The new Description Group <descgrp> element, which can group any of the <did>-level elements (except the Description of Subordinate Components <dsc>), may be used to wrap elements where a group heading is desirable. The <descgrp> element can be used to replace <admininfo> where it has been used as a wrapper when converting finding aids encoded in EAD V1.0 to EAD 2002.

The <acqinfo> element is comparable to ISAD(G) data element 3.2.4 and MARC field 541.

May contain:

acqinfo, address, blockquote, chronlist, head, list, note, p, table

May occur within:

acqinfo, archdesc, archdescgrp, c, c01, c02, c03, c04, c05, c06, c07, c08, c09, c10, c11, c12, custodhist, descgrp

<acqinfo>

Attributes:

ALTRENDER	#IMPLIED, CDATA
AUDIENCE	#IMPLIED, external, internal
ENCODINGANALOG	#IMPLIED, CDATA
ID	#IMPLIED, ID

Examples:

1.
```
<acqinfo>
   <p>Transfer from <corpname>National Park Service, </corpname>
      <date type="accession">1945</date>. Accession number
      <num type="accession">45.22</num>.</p>
</acqinfo>
```

2.
```
<acqinfo>
   <p>Source unknown. Originally deposited in University Library,
      transferred to Department of Palaeography, <date
      normal="19580424">24 April 1958</date>.</p>
</acqinfo>
```

<address> Address

Description:

A generic element for information about the place where someone or something is located and may be reached. Examples include a postal address for a repository, or the electronic mail address and phone number of the party granting publication permission.

Consider using an entity reference to store address information that occurs in many finding aids, as it is easier to update the information when located in a single, shared file. The entity reference can contain both the EAD elements and their content. A style sheet can also be used to supply this kind of information.

May contain:

addressline

May occur within:

accessrestrict, accruals, acqinfo, altformavail, appraisal, arrangement, bibliography, bioghist, blockquote, controlaccess, custodhist, daodesc, descgrp, div, dsc, dscgrp, entry, event, extref, extrefloc, fileplan, index, item, note, odd, originalsloc, otherfindaid, p, phystech, prefercite, processinfo, publicationstmt, ref, refloc, relatedmaterial, repository, scopecontent, separatedmaterial, titlepage, userestrict

Attributes:

ALTRENDER	#IMPLIED, CDATA
AUDIENCE	#IMPLIED, external, internal
ID	#IMPLIED, ID

Examples:

```
<publicationstmt>
   <publisher>The Bancroft Library.</publisher>
   <address>
      <addressline>University of California, Berkeley.</addressline>
      <addressline>Berkeley, California 94720-6000</addressline>
      <addressline>Phone: 510/642-6481</addressline>
      <addressline>Fax: 510/642-7589</addressline>
      <addressline>Email: bancref@library.berkeley.edu</addressline>
   </address>
</publicationstmt>
```

<addressline> Address Line

Description:

A generic element for one line of a postal or other address. May be repeated as many times as necessary to enter all available lines of an address.

May contain:

#PCDATA, emph, extptr, lb, ptr

May occur within:

address

Attributes:

ALTRENDER	#IMPLIED, CDATA
AUDIENCE	#IMPLIED, external, internal
ID	#IMPLIED, ID

Example:

```
<publicationstmt>
   <publisher>Special Collections and Archives</publisher>
   <address>
      <addressline>The UCI Libraries</addressline>
      <addressline>P.O. Box 19557</addressline>
      <addressline>University of California</addressline>
      <addressline>Irvine, California 92623-9557</addressline>
      <addressline>Phone: (949) 824-7227</addressline>
      <addressline>Fax: (949) 824-2472</addressline>
      <addressline>Email: spcoll@uci.edu</addressline>
      <addressline>URL:http://www.lib.uci.edu/rrsc/speccoll.html
      </addressline>
   </address>
   <date>&copy; 2000</date>
   <p>The Regents of the University of California. All rights
      reserved.</p>
</publicationstmt>
```

<altformavail> Alternative Form Available

Description:

Information about copies of the materials being described, including the type of alternative form, significant control numbers, location, and source for ordering if applicable. The additional formats are typically microforms, photocopies, or digital reproductions.

Do not confuse with Location of Originals <originalsloc>, which is used to encode information about the existence, location, and availability of originals where the unit described consists of copies.

In EAD Version 1.0 <altformavail> was a subelement of Administrative Information <admininfo>, which has been deprecated in EAD 2002 (see Appendix B). The new Description Group <descgrp> element, which can group any of the <did>-level elements (except the Description of Subordinate Components <dsc>), may be used to wrap elements where a group heading is desirable. The <descgrp> element can be used to replace <admininfo> where it has been used as a wrapper when converting finding aids encoded in EAD V1.0 to EAD 2002.

The <altformavail> element is comparable to ISAD(G) data element 3.5.2 and MARC field 530.

May contain:

address, altformavail, blockquote, chronlist, head, list, note, p, table

May occur within:

altformavail, archdesc, archdescgrp, c, c01, c02, c03, c04, c05, c06, c07, c08, c09, c10, c11, c12, descgrp

Attributes:

ALTRENDER	#IMPLIED, CDATA
AUDIENCE	#IMPLIED, external, internal
ENCODINGANALOG	#IMPLIED, CDATA
ID	#IMPLIED, ID
TYPE	#IMPLIED, CDATA

<altformavail>

Examples:

1.
```
<altformavail>
   <p>This collection has been microfilmed and is available on
      three reels MF1993-034:1 to MF1993-034:3.</p>
   <p>Researchers interested in purchasing microfilm copies
      should contact the repository.</p>
</altformavail>
```

2.
```
<altformavail>
   <head>Alternate Form of Material</head>
   <p>Microfilm copy available (<num type="microfilm reel">
      M-5030/1</num>).</p>
</altformavail>
```

3.
```
<c02 level="file">
   <did>
      <container type="reel" label="Film Storage">1</container>
      <unittitle><title render="italic">The Man Who Hated
         Children</title>
      </unittitle>
      <unitdate normal="1972">1972</unitdate>
      <physdesc>16 mm. film</physdesc>
   </did>
   <altformavail>
      <p>A VHS Videocassette version is available for viewing.
         Video tape is located in Video Storage.</p>
   </altformavail>
</c02>
```

<appraisal> Appraisal Information

Description:

Information about the process of determining the archival value and thus the disposition of records based upon their current administrative, legal, and fiscal use; their evidential, intrinsic, and informational value; their arrangement and condition; and their relationship to other records.

In EAD Version 1.0 <appraisal> was a subelement of Administrative Information <admininfo>, which has been deprecated in EAD 2002 (see Appendix B). The new Description Group <descgrp> element, which can group any of the <did>-level elements (except the Description of Subordinate Components <dsc>), may be used to wrap elements where a group heading is desirable. The <descgrp> element can be used to replace <admininfo> where it has been used as a wrapper when converting finding aids encoded in EAD V1.0 to EAD 2002.

The <appraisal> element is comparable to ISAD(G) data element 3.3.2 and MARC field 583.

May contain:

address, appraisal, blockquote, chronlist, head, list, note, p, table

May occur within:

appraisal, archdesc, archdescgrp, c, c01, c02, c03, c04, c05, c06, c07, c08, c09, c10, c11, c12, descgrp

Attributes:

ALTRENDER	#IMPLIED, CDATA
AUDIENCE	#IMPLIED, external, internal
ENCODINGANALOG	#IMPLIED, CDATA
ID	#IMPLIED, ID

<appraisal>

Example:

```
<appraisal>
   <p>The records of the Mid-Ocean Dynamics Experiment came to the
      Institute Archives in two accessions in 1980 and 1982. During
      processing the collection was reduced from fifteen cubic feet
      to four by discarding duplicate materials, financial records,
      and publications not authored by MODE participants. Forty
      charts and six inches of raw data presented the primary
      appraisal issues. The raw data consisted of bulletins and
      reports referring to float positions, moorings, isotherms,
      geostrophic velocity calculations, ships' summaries, and work
      proposed and work carried out during the MODE-I experiment. As
      this raw data was recapitulated in weekly <title
      render="underline">MODE Hot Line Bulletins</title>, only a
      sampling was retained in the collection. Also discarded were
      ten charts for which there were no descriptions of indicated
      data points, nor were dates or test site locations
      provided.</p>
   <p>Six inches of materials pertaining to the POLYMODE project,
      1973-1980, were added to the Institute Archives POLYMODE
      collection.</p>
   <p>The appraisal of this collection was carried out in
      consultation with Robert Heinmiller, a research associate at
      Woods Hole Oceanographic Institution during MODE.</p>
</appraisal>
```

<arc> Arc

Description:

Specifies the rules for traversal among the participating resources in an extended link. Arc uses the attributes TO and FROM to define the traversal between named pairs of resources.

While XML Linking Language (XLink) Version 1.0, which is the basis for EAD linking elements, is a stable document, examples of EAD usage are hypothetical and have not been tested in real XLink-based applications. Those wishing to use XLink are encouraged to consult the specification available online at <http://www.w3.org/TR/xlink/>.

May contain:

EMPTY

May occur within:

daogrp, linkgrp

Attributes:

ACTUATE	#IMPLIED, onload, onrequest, actuateother, actuatenone
ALTRENDER	#IMPLIED, CDATA
ARCROLE	#IMPLIED, CDATA
AUDIENCE	#IMPLIED, external, internal
FROM	#IMPLIED, NMTOKEN
ID	#IMPLIED, ID
LINKTYPE	#FIXED, arc, arc
SHOW	#IMPLIED, new, replace, embed, showother, shownone
TITLE	#IMPLIED, CDATA
TO	#IMPLIED, NMTOKEN

<arc>

Example:

```
<c02 level="file">
   <did>
      <unittitle>Photographs of John Smith and family
         members</unittitle>
      <unitdate type="inclusive" normal="1895/1928">1895-
         1928</unitdate>
      <daogrp linktype="extended">
         <daodesc>
            <p>Sample digitized image from this file: John Smith
               graduation portrait, <date normal="18950528">28
               May 1895</date>.</p>
         </daodesc>
         <resource linktype="resource" label="start"/>
         <daoloc entityref="f0042_1tmb" linktype="locator"
            label="thumb"/>
         <daoloc entityref="f0042_1ref" linktype="locator"
            label="reference"/>
         <arc linktype="arc" show="embed" actuate="onload"
            from="start" to="thumb"/>
         <arc linktype="arc" show="new" actuate="onrequest"
            from="thumb" to="reference"/>
      </daogrp>
   </did>
</c02>
```

<archdesc> Archival Description

Description:

A wrapper element for the bulk of an EAD document instance, which describes the content, context, and extent of a body of archival materials, including administrative and supplemental information that facilitates use of the materials. Information is organized in unfolding, hierarchical levels that allow for a descriptive overview of the whole to be followed by more detailed views of the parts, designated by the element Description of Subordinate Components <dsc>. Data elements available at the <archdesc> level are repeated at the various component levels within <dsc>, and information is inherited from one hierarchical level to the next.

The Descriptive Identification <did> element is required to appear in <archdesc> before presenting more detailed descriptions in <bioghist>, <scopecontent>, and <dsc>, in order to provide first a basic description of the archival materials.

The <archdesc> element has several specialized attributes. The required LEVEL attribute identifies the character of the whole unit, for example, "class," "collection," "fonds," "recordgrp," "series," "subfonds," "subgrp," "subseries," or "otherlevel." This attribute is comparable to ISAD(G) data element 3.1.4 and MARC field 351 subfield c.

The TYPE attribute can be used to categorize the finding aid as an inventory, register, or other format.

May contain:

accessrestrict, accruals, acqinfo, altformavail, appraisal, arrangement, bibliography, bioghist, controlaccess, custodhist, dao, daogrp, descgrp, did, dsc, fileplan, index, note, odd, originalsloc, otherfindaid, phystech, prefercite, processinfo, relatedmaterial, runner, scopecontent, separatedmaterial, userestrict

May occur within:

ead

<archdesc>

Attributes:

ALTRENDER	#IMPLIED, CDATA
AUDIENCE	#IMPLIED, external, internal
ENCODINGANALOG	#IMPLIED, CDATA
ID	#IMPLIED, ID
LEVEL	#REQUIRED, class, collection, file, fonds, item, otherlevel, recordgrp, series, subfonds, subgrp, subseries
OTHERLEVEL	#IMPLIED, NMTOKEN
RELATEDENCODING	#IMPLIED, CDATA
TYPE	#IMPLIED, NMTOKEN

Example:

See fully encoded examples in Appendix C.

<archdescgrp> Archival Description Group

Description:

A wrapper element used only within <eadgrp> in the EAD Group Document Type Definition. The <archdescgrp> summarizes the content, context, and extent of the archival materials described in separate EAD documents bundled within the <dscgrp> subelement. The <archdescgrp> may contain all data elements available in <archdesc>, except for <dsc>; the <dscgrp> subelement fills the role of <dsc>. As with <archdesc>, a Descriptive Identification <did> element is required to appear in <archdescgrp> before presenting more detailed descriptions in such elements as <bioghist>.

See also the <eadgrp> element.

May contain:

accessrestrict, accruals, acqinfo, altformavail, appraisal, arrangement, bibliography, bioghist, controlaccess, custodhist, dao, daogrp, descgrp, did, dscgrp, fileplan, index, note, odd, originalsloc, otherfindaid, phystech, prefercite, processinfo, relatedmaterial, runner, scopecontent, separatedmaterial, userestrict

May occur within:

eadgrp

Attributes:

ALTRENDER	#IMPLIED, CDATA
AUDIENCE	#IMPLIED, external, internal
ENCODINGANALOG	#IMPLIED, CDATA
ID	#IMPLIED, ID
LEVEL	#REQUIRED, class, collection, file, fonds, item, otherlevel, recordgrp, series, subfonds, subgrp, subseries
OTHERLEVEL	#IMPLIED, NMTOKEN
RELATEDENCODING	#IMPLIED, CDATA
TYPE	#IMPLIED, NMTOKEN

<archref> Archival Reference

Description:

A reference element that provides a citation and/or an electronic link to separately described archival materials of special interest. Examples of such materials include a record group and one of its large series (which might have separate EAD-encoded finding aids) and a general reference to a collection with similar content.

The <archref> element can be helpful in several situations. It can be used, with the HREF or ENTITYREF attribute, for linking to another EAD instance. The <archref> element can also be used to cite archival materials within a <bibliography>, <relatedmaterial>, or <separatedmaterial> element. The <archref> may contain just text or some of the content-specific elements such as <origination>, <repository>, and <unittitle> to identify the different kinds of information in a citation.

Do not confuse <archref> with the Bibliographic Reference <bibref> element, which is used to cite works that are published entities or individual items that are not usefully designated as archival materials.

While XML Linking Language (XLink) Version 1.0, which is the basis for EAD linking elements, is a stable document, examples of EAD usage are hypothetical and have not been tested in real XLink-based applications. Those wishing to use XLink are encouraged to consult the specification available online at <http://www.w3.org/TR/xlink/>.

May contain:

#PCDATA, abbr, abstract, bibref, container, dao, daogrp, emph, expan, extptr, extref, langmaterial, lb, materialspec, note, origination, physdesc, physloc, ptr, ref, repository, title, unitdate, unitid, unittitle

May occur within:

abstract, bibliography, bibref, container, creation, descrules, dimensions, emph, entry, event, extent, extref, item, label, langmaterial, langusage, materialspec, origination, otherfindaid, p, physdesc, physfacet, physloc, ref, relatedmaterial, repository, separatedmaterial, unitdate, unitid, unittitle

Attributes:

ACTUATE	#IMPLIED, onload, onrequest, actuateother, actuatenone
ALTRENDER	#IMPLIED, CDATA
ARCROLE	#IMPLIED, CDATA
AUDIENCE	#IMPLIED, external, internal
ENTITYREF	#IMPLIED, ENTITY
HREF	#IMPLIED, CDATA
ID	#IMPLIED, ID
LINKTYPE	#FIXED, simple, simple
ROLE	#IMPLIED, CDATA
SHOW	#IMPLIED, new replace, embed, showother, shownone
TITLE	#IMPLIED, CDATA
XPOINTER	#IMPLIED, CDATA

Example:

```
<relatedmaterial>
   <head>Related Collections</head>
   <archref>
      <unitid>BANC PIC 19xx.055--ffALB</unitid>,
      <unittitle><title>Photographs Taken During the U.S. Geological
         Surveys West of the 100th Meridian, 1871-1873</title>, by
         Timothy H. O'Sullivan and William Bell</unittitle>
   </archref>
   <archref>
      <unitid>BANC PIC 19xx.089--STER</unitid>,
      <unittitle><title>Stereoviews of the U.S. Geographical Survey
         Expedition West of the 100th Meridian of 1871</title>, by
         Timothy H. O'Sullivan</unittitle>
   </archref>
   <archref>
      <unitid>BANC PIC 19xx.273--PIC</unitid>,
      <unittitle>Geographical Surveys West of the 100th Meridian
         (U.S.). <title>New Mexico Photographs from the 1873
         Geographical Survey West of the 100th
         Meridian</title></unittitle>
   </archref>
   <archref>
      <unitid>BANC PIC 1905.17116-.17119--STER</unitid>,
      <unittitle><title>Western Survey Expeditions of 1871, 1872,
         1873, and 1874</title>, by Timothy H. O'Sullivan and
         William Bell</unittitle>
   </archref>
</relatedmaterial>
```

<arrangement> Arrangement

Description:

Information on how the described materials have been subdivided into smaller units, e.g., record groups into series, identifying the logical or physical groupings within a hierarchical structure. Can also be used to express the filing sequence of the described materials, such as the principle characteristics of the internal structure, or the physical or logical ordering of materials, including alphabetical, chronological, geographical, office of origin, and other schemes. Identifying logical groupings and the arrangement pattern may enhance retrieval by researchers.

The <arrangement> element may occur within <archdesc> and <c> or as a subelement of <scopecontent>.

The <arrangement> element is comparable to ISAD(G) data element 3.3.4 and MARC field 351. The ENCODINGANALOG attribute may be used to differentiate between the 351 subfield a (organization) and subfield b (arrangement).

May contain:

address, arrangement, blockquote, chronlist, head, list, note, p, table

May occur within:

archdesc, archdescgrp, arrangement, c, c01, c02, c03, c04, c05, c06, c07, c08, c09, c10, c11, c12, descgrp, scopecontent

Attributes:

ALTRENDER	#IMPLIED, CDATA
AUDIENCE	#IMPLIED, external, internal
ENCODINGANALOG	#IMPLIED, CDATA
ID	#IMPLIED, ID

Examples:

```
1. <arrangement>
      <head>Arrangement of the Collection</head>
      <p>The filing system for the Braman Collection has been kept
         substantially in its original form.  That is, original folders
         and their titles have been retained.  The processor devised
         the basic organization scheme for the collection and, where
         necessary, reorganized the papers within the various component
         groups.</p>
   </arrangement>
```

2.
```
<c01 level="series">
   <did>
      <unittitle>Research files</unittitle>
      <unitdate type="inclusive" normal="1887/1995">1887-
         1995</unitdate>
      <physdesc><extent>3.5 linear feet (4 boxes)</extent>
      </physdesc>
   </did>
   <scopecontent>
      <p>This series consists of newspaper clippings and research
         notes of Fred Reed, pertaining to the Champlain
         Transportation Company, its vessels, and the vessels' crew
         members. Several of the folders of chronological clippings
         include subjects, such as the move of the Ticonderoga
         (1954-1955) and the sale of the Champlain Transportation
         Company (1966). A number of clippings under "Persons" are
         obituaries. Two folders under the subseries "Notes" contain
         handwritten notes by Fred Reed broadly pertaining to the
         history of the Champlain Transportation Company, including
         a chronology, a list of crew members, and information about
         the Company's vessels.</p>
      <arrangement>
         <p>Organized into three subseries:
            <list type="simple">
               <item>Clippings--chronological</item>
               <item>Clippings--persons</item>
               <item>Notes</item>
            </list>
         </p>
         <p>"Clippings-persons" is arranged alphabetically by
            surname, and "Notes" alphabetically by subject.</p>
      </arrangement>
   </scopecontent>
</c01>
```

3.
```
<c03 level="file">
   <did>
      <unittitle id="bruce.A.2.3">Letters from various
         correspondents to Craufurd Bruce</unittitle>
      <unitdate normal="1807/1819">1807-19</unitdate>
      <unitid>MS. Eng. c. 5746</unitid>
      <physdesc><extent>126 leaves</extent></physdesc>
   </did>
   <arrangement>
      <p>Alphabetical, Grey - Peterkin</p>
   </arrangement>
   <scopecontent>
      <p>Mainly relating to Michael Bruce, with drafts of a few
         letters from Craufurd Bruce.</p>
   </scopecontent>
</c03>
```

<author> Author

Description:

Name(s) of institution(s) or individual(s) responsible for compiling the intellectual content of the finding aid. May include a brief statement indicating the nature of the responsibility, for example, archivist, collections processor, or records manager. Because acknowledgment of such individuals or institutions often appears on the title page of a finding aid, the <author> element is available in both the required <titlestmt> portion of the <eadheader> and the optional <titlepage> element in <frontmatter>.

Use the <creation> element found under <profiledesc> to designate the encoder of the finding aid. Use the <persname> or <corpname> element with the ROLE attribute to designate the author in a Bibliographic Reference <bibref> citation. Use the <origination> element to designate the compiler, collector, or creator of the materials being described.

May contain:

#PCDATA, emph, extptr, lb, ptr

May occur within:

titlepage, titlestmt

Attributes:

ALTRENDER	#IMPLIED, CDATA
AUDIENCE	#IMPLIED, external, internal
ENCODINGANALOG	#IMPLIED, CDATA
ID	#IMPLIED, ID

Examples:

1.
```
<filedesc>
   <titlestmt>
      <titleproper>Register of the Rhea Higbee Wakeling
         Collection</titleproper>
      <author>The print and machine readable finding aids for
      this collection were created by the Special Collections
      staff, Gerald R. Sherratt Library.</author>
   </titlestmt>
</filedesc>
```

2.
```
<frontmatter>
   <titlepage>
      <titleproper>Indians Overseas</titleproper>
      <subtitle>A guide to source materials in the India Office
         Records for the study of Indian emigration, 1830-
         1950</subtitle>
      <author>Timothy N. Thomas</author>
      <publisher>THE BRITISH LIBRARY<extptr entityref="plachold">
      </publisher>
      <date>1985</date>
   </titlepage>
</frontmatter>
```

<bibliography> Bibliography

Description:

Citations to works that are based on, about, or of special value when using the materials being described, or works in which a citation to or brief description of the materials is available. The works could be books, articles, television programs, unpublished reports, web sites, or other forms of information. The <bibliography> may be a simple <list>, a list of both Bibliographic References <bibref> and Archival References <archref>, or a series of Paragraphs <p>.

The <bibref> element may be used to designate single citations within Paragraphs <p> without opening the <bibliography> element.

In EAD Version 1.0 <bibliography> was a subelement of Adjunct Descriptive Data <add>, which has been deprecated in EAD 2002 (see Appendix B). The new Description Group <descgrp> element, which can group any of the <did>-level elements (except the Description of Subordinate Components <dsc>), may be used to wrap elements where a group heading is desirable. The <descgrp> element can be used to replace <add> when converting finding aids encoded in EAD V1.0 to EAD 2002.

The <bibliography> element is comparable to ISAD(G) data element 3.5.4 and MARC fields 510 and 581.

May contain:

address, archref, bibliography, bibref, blockquote, chronlist, extref, head, linkgrp, list, note, p, ref, table, title

May occur within:

archdesc, archdescgrp, bibliography, c, c01, c02, c03, c04, c05, c06, c07, c08, c09, c10, c11, c12, descgrp

Attributes:

ALTRENDER	#IMPLIED, CDATA
AUDIENCE	#IMPLIED, external, internal
ENCODINGANALOG	#IMPLIED, CDATA
ID	#IMPLIED, ID

Example:

```
<bibliography>
   <head>Bibliography</head>
   <p>Sources consulted by John Kobler.</p>
   <bibliography>
      <head>Monographs</head>
      <bibref><title render="italic">Affiches
         americaines</title>. San Domingo: Imprimerie royale du
         Cap, 1782. Nos. 30, 35.</bibref>
      <bibref>Ardouin, Charles Nicholas Celigny. <title
         render="italic">Essais sur l'histoire d'Haiti</title>.
         Port-au-Prince, 1865.</bibref>
      <bibref>Bastien, Remy. <title render="italic">Anthologie du
         folklore haitien</title>, <title
         render="doublequote">Proverbes</title>. Mexico, 1946.
         pp.83-91.</bibref>
      <bibref>Bellegarde, Dantes. <title render="italic">
         Dessalines a parle</title>. Port-au-Prince, 1948. Chap.
         IV: pp. 47-54.</bibref>
   </bibliography>
   <bibliography>
      <head>Serial publications</head> . . .
   </bibliography>
</bibliography>
```

<bibref> Bibliographic Reference

Description:

A reference element that provides a citation and/or electronic link for a published work such as a book, article, dissertation, motion picture, or sound recording. The <bibref> may contain just text or some of the content-specific elements such as <title>, <imprint>, or <edition>, although the latter two elements are unlikely to be used for unpublished works.

A list of <bibref>s may be gathered into a <bibliography>. A single <bibref> may be part of a Paragraph <p>. Use the HREF or ENTITYREF attribute to point to an electronic bibliographic work.

Use the more specific <archref> element to cite or link to separately described archival materials.

Do not confuse with the Reference <ref> element, which is an internal link from one place in a finding aid to another place in the same finding aid.

While XML Linking Language (XLink) Version 1.0, which is the basis for EAD linking elements, is a stable document, examples of EAD usage are hypothetical and have not been tested in real XLink-based applications. Those wishing to use XLink are encouraged to consult the specification available online at <http://www.w3.org/TR/xlink/>.

May contain:

#PCDATA, abbr, archref, bibseries, corpname, edition, emph, expan, extptr, extref, famname, imprint, lb, name, num, persname, ptr, ref, title

May occur within:

abstract, archref, bibliography, container, creation, descrules, dimensions, emph, entry, event, extent, extref, item, label, langmaterial, langusage, materialspec, origination, otherfindaid, p, physdesc, physfacet, physloc, ref, relatedmaterial, repository, separatedmaterial, unitdate, unitid, unittitle

Attributes:

ACTUATE	#IMPLIED, onload, onrequest, actuateother, actuatenone
ALTRENDER	#IMPLIED, CDATA
ARCROLE	#IMPLIED, CDATA
AUDIENCE	#IMPLIED, external, internal
ENCODINGANALOG	#IMPLIED, CDATA
ENTITYREF	#IMPLIED, ENTITY
HREF	#IMPLIED, CDATA
ID	#IMPLIED, ID
LINKTYPE	#FIXED, simple, simple
ROLE	#IMPLIED, CDATA
SHOW	#IMPLIED, new, replace, embed, showother, shownone
TITLE	#IMPLIED, CDATA
XPOINTER	#IMPLIED, CDATA

Examples:

1.
```
<p>The Archibald MacLeish Papers are described in
   <bibref>
      <title render="italic">Library of Congress Acquisitions:
         Manuscript Division, 1982,</title> p. 29.
   </bibref>
</p>
```

2.
```
<bibliography>
   <head>Bibliography</head>
   <p>Sources consulted by John Kobler.</p>
   <bibref><title render="italic">Affiches americaines</title>.
      San Domingo: Imprimerie royale du Cap, 1782. Nos. 30,
      35.</bibref>
   <bibref>Ardouin, Charles Nicholas Celigny. <title
      render="italic">Essais sur l'histoire d'Haiti</title>.
      Port-au-Prince, 1865.</bibref>
   <bibref>Bastien, Remy. <title render="italic">Anthologie du
      folklore haitien</title>, <title render="doublequote">
      Proverbes</title>. Mexico, 1946. pp.83-91.</bibref>
   <bibref>Bellegarde, Dantes. <title render="italic">Dessalines
      a parle</title>. Port-au-Prince, 1948. Chap. IV: pp. 47-
      54.</bibref> . . .
</bibliography>
```

<bibseries> Bibliographic Series

Description:

Information about the published series in which a book, encoded finding aid, or other published work has appeared. Refers to monographic series only. Not to be used for archival series.

May contain:

#PCDATA, emph, extptr, lb, num, ptr, title

May occur within:

bibref, titlepage, unittitle

Attributes:

ALTRENDER	#IMPLIED, CDATA
AUDIENCE	#IMPLIED, external, internal
ENCODINGANALOG	#IMPLIED, CDATA
ID	#IMPLIED, ID

Examples:

1.
```
<frontmatter>
   <titlepage>
      <bibseries>Guides to Special Collections in the Music
         Division of the Library of Congress</bibseries>
      <titleproper>Irving Fine Collection</titleproper>
   </titlepage>
</frontmatter>
```

2.
```
<bibliography>
   <head>Selected Bibliography of History of the Harvard
      University Department of Physics</head>
   <bibref><persname>Morton, Charles</persname>.
      <title>Compendium Physicae</title>.
         <imprint>[<geogname>Boston </geogname>:
         <publisher>Colonial Society of Massachusetts, </publisher>
         <date normal="1940">1940</date>].</imprint>
      <bibseries>Colonial Society of Massachusetts. Publications ;
         <num>v. 33</num>.</bibseries>
   </bibref>
</bibliography>
```

<bioghist> Biography or History

Description:

A concise essay or chronology that places the archival materials in context by providing information about their creator(s). Includes significant information about the life of an individual or family, or the administrative history of a corporate body. The <bioghist> may contain just text in a series of Paragraphs <p>, and/or a Chronology List <chronlist> that matches dates and date ranges with associated events. Additional <bioghist> elements may be nested inside one another when a complex body of materials, such as a collection of family papers, is being described, and separately headed sections are desired. The <bioghist> element may also be nested to designate a portion of the essay or chronology that might be extracted as a MARC 545 subfield.

Many elements, such as <bioghist> are recursive (i.e., the elements are available within themselves) to facilitate the use of multiple headings with subdivided descriptions for complex collections, and to enable EAD markup to be used for a variety of output. In Example 1 below, <bioghist> is repeated within itself to enable the extraction of a brief biographical note for a MARC record.

The <bioghist> element is comparable to ISAD(G) data element 3.2.2 and MARC field 545.

May contain:

address, bioghist, blockquote, chronlist, dao, daogrp, head, list, note, p, table

May occur within:

archdesc, archdescgrp, bioghist, c, c01, c02, c03, c04, c05, c06, c07, c08, c09, c10, c11, c12, descgrp

Attributes:

ALTRENDER	#IMPLIED, CDATA
AUDIENCE	#IMPLIED, external, internal
ENCODINGANALOG	#IMPLIED, CDATA
ID	#IMPLIED, ID

<bioghist>

Examples:

1.

```
<bioghist>
   <head>Administrative History</head>
   <bioghist encodinganalog="545$a">
      <p id="PRO123">In October 1964 the incoming Labour
         government created new office of Secretary of State for
         Economic Affairs (combined with First Secretary of
         State) and set up the Department of Economic Affairs
         under the Ministers of the Crown Act 1964 to carry
         primary responsibility for long term economic
         planning.</p>
   </bioghist>
   <p>Under the Act the posts of Economic Secretary to the
      Treasury and Secretary of State for Industry, Trade and
      Regional Development were abolished.</p>
   <p>George Brown was appointed as First Secretary of State and
      Secretary of State for Economic Affairs, and as chairman of
      the National Economic Development Council (NEDC).</p>
   <p>Composition of DEA: most of Treasury's National Economy
      Group (excluding the short term forecasting team); economic
      planning staff from the National Economic Development
      Office (NEDO); the regional policy divisions from the Board
      of Trade; a team of industrial experts.</p>
   <p>DEA charged with duty of formulating, with both sides of
      industry, a National Plan (published in September 1965),
      co-ordinating the work of other departments in implementing
      policies of economic growth, particularly in the fields of
      industry, the regions, and prices and incomes.</p> . . .
</bioghist>
```

2.

```
<bioghist>
   <head>Chronology</head>
   <chronlist>
      <chronitem>
         <date normal="18401012">1840</date>
         <event>Born Helena Opid in Krakow, Poland on October
            12th.</event>
      </chronitem>
      <chronitem>
         <date normal="1861">1861</date>
         <event>Made stage debut as Helena Modrzejewska in
            charity fair production of <title>The White
            Camellia</title>, in Bochnia, Poland.</event>
      </chronitem> . . .
      <chronitem>
         <date normal="19090409">1909</date>
         <event>Died April 8th at her home on Bay Island. Funeral
            services held at St. Vibiana's Cathedral in Los
            Angeles, and Modjeska was later buried in her native
            Krakow.</event>
      </chronitem>
   </chronlist>
</bioghist>
```

<blockquote> Block Quote

Description:

A formatting element that designates an extended quotation. The quotation is set off from the text by spacing or other typographic distinction.

Use the Emphasis <emph> element, not <blockquote>, to tag words that are set off with quotations for emphasis or as a small quoted phrase that occurs, "as these words do," in the line of text.

May contain:

address, chronlist, list, note, p, table

May occur within:

accessrestrict, accruals, acqinfo, altformavail, appraisal, arrangement, bibliography, bioghist, controlaccess, custodhist, daodesc, descgrp, div, dsc, dscgrp, event, extref, extrefloc, fileplan, index, item, note, odd, originalsloc, otherfindaid, p, phystech, prefercite, processinfo, ref, refloc, relatedmaterial, scopecontent, separatedmaterial, titlepage, userestrict

Attributes:

ALTRENDER	#IMPLIED, CDATA
AUDIENCE	#IMPLIED, external, internal
ID	#IMPLIED, ID

<blockquote>

Example:

```
<bioghist>
   <head>Administrative History</head>
   <p>The Brewster presidential administration's primary
      objective was to raise academic standards comprehensively
      throughout Yale University. This required the substantial
      revision of certain existing policies and disciplines, as
      well as the development of new programs, schools, and
      departments.</p>
   <p>President Brewster began this process in the 1960s by
      significantly increasing the size of the faculty and by
      actively recruiting renowned non-Yale scholars to fill the
      positions. According to Brewster, previous Yale
      administrations tended to overlook high caliber
      academicians who graduated and specialized outside the
      university. . . .</p>
   <p>As the size of the Yale faculty increased, Brewster's new
      admissions policies caused the make up of the undergraduate
      body to shift. By the early 1960s, most undergraduates had
      prepared at private schools, and many were sons of Yale
      alumni. As with the faculty, Brewster felt that Yale was
      consistently overlooking some of the best intellectual
      student talent necessary to maintain the highest levels of
      academic excellence. In a 1965 speech to alumni, Brewster
      summarized his administration's revised recruitment policy
      by stating that Yale would only seek students
      <blockquote>
         <p>whose capacity for intellectual achievement is
            outstanding and who also have the motivation to put
            their intellectual capacities to creatively
            influential use, in thought, in art, in science, or
            in the exercise of public or private or professional
            responsibility.</p>
      </blockquote>
   </p> . . .
</bioghist>
```

<c> Component (Unnumbered)

Description:

A wrapper element that designates a subordinate part of the materials being described. A Component <c> provides information about the content, context, and extent of a subordinate body of materials. It is always nested within a Description of Subordinate Components <dsc> and often within another <c> element. Each <c> element identifies an intellectually logical section of the described materials. The physical filing separations between components do not always coincide with the intellectual separations. For example, a <c> that designates dramatic works might end in the same box in which the next <c> begins with short stories. Also, not every <c> directly corresponds to a folder or other physical entity. Some <c> elements simply represent a stage within a hierarchical description.

Components may be subdivided into smaller and smaller components and may eventually reach the level of a single item. For example, the components of a collection may be series, components of series may be subseries, components of subseries may be files, and components of files may be items. A component may be either an unnumbered <c> or a numbered <c01>, <c02>, etc. The numbered components <c01> to <c12> assist a finding aid encoder in nesting up to twelve component levels accurately.

Use the LEVEL attribute to identify the descriptive character of the component, for example, "series," "subseries," "subfonds," "subgrp," "file," or "item." Assigning a LEVEL attribute for the highest <c> is recommended; thereafter the attribute may be used when the repository deems it useful.

May contain:

accessrestrict, accruals, acqinfo, altformavail, appraisal, arrangement, bibliography, bioghist, c, controlaccess, custodhist, dao, daogrp, descgrp, did, dsc, fileplan, head, index, note, odd, originalsloc, otherfindaid, phystech, prefercite, processinfo, relatedmaterial, scopecontent, separatedmaterial, thead, userestrict

May occur within:

c, dsc

<c>

Attributes:

ALTRENDER	#IMPLIED, CDATA
AUDIENCE	#IMPLIED, external, internal
ENCODINGANALOG	#IMPLIED, CDATA
ID	#IMPLIED, ID
LEVEL	#IMPLIED, class, collection, file, fonds, item, otherlevel, recordgrp, series, subfonds, subgrp, subseries
OTHERLEVEL	#IMPLIED, NMTOKEN
TPATTERN	#IMPLIED, NMTOKEN

Example:

```
<dsc type="combined">
   <c level="series">
      <did>
         <unitid>Series 1</unitid>
         <unittitle>Correspondence</unittitle>
      </did>
      <scopecontent>[...]</scopecontent>
      <c level="subseries">
         <did>
            <unitid>Subseries 1.1</unitid>
            <unittitle>Outgoing Correspondence</unittitle>
         </did>
         <c level="file">
            <did>
               <unittitle>Abbinger-Aldrich</unittitle>
            </did>
         </c> . . .
      </c>
      <c level="subseries">
         <did>
            <unitid>Subseries 1.2</unitid>
            <unittitle>Incoming Correspondence</unittitle>
         </did>
         <c level="file">
            <did>
               <unittitle>Adams-Ayers</unittitle>
            </did>
         </c> . . .
      </c>
   </c>
</dsc>
```

<c01> Component (First Level)

Description:

A wrapper element that designates the top or first-level subordinate part of the materials being described. Components may be either unnumbered <c> or numbered <c01>, <c02>, etc. The numbered components <c01> to <c12> assist a finding aid encoder in nesting up to twelve component levels accurately.

The LEVEL attribute is used to identify which level of description the <c01> covers, e.g., "series," "subseries," "file," or "item." Do not expect that all elements at the same numbered component designation represent the same level of description. The <c01> element can start at different levels of description in different finding aids, and, the quantity of hierarchical components can vary between, for example, a "series" and a "file." For example, a <c03> element could represent a "file" in one part of a finding aid, and in another part of the finding aid, a file might be a <c05> element because additional hierarchical groupings were needed to categorize the materials being described.

See the description under Component <c> for additional information.

May contain:

accessrestrict, accruals, acqinfo, altformavail, appraisal, arrangement, bibliography, bioghist, c02, controlaccess, custodhist, dao, daogrp, descgrp, did, dsc, fileplan, head, index, note, odd, originalsloc, otherfindaid, phystech, prefercite, processinfo, relatedmaterial, scopecontent, separatedmaterial, thead, userestrict

May occur within:

dsc

Attributes:

ALTRENDER	#IMPLIED, CDATA
AUDIENCE	#IMPLIED, external, internal
ENCODINGANALOG	#IMPLIED, CDATA
ID	#IMPLIED, ID
LEVEL	#IMPLIED, class, collection, file, fonds, item, otherlevel, recordgrp, series, subfonds, subgrp, subseries
OTHERLEVEL	#IMPLIED, NMTOKEN
TPATTERN	#IMPLIED, NMTOKEN

<c01>

Example:

```
<dsc type="combined">
   <c01 level="series">
      <did>
         <unittitle>Topical Files</unittitle>
         <unitdate normal="1918/1945">1918-1945</unitdate>
      </did>
      <scopecontent>[...]</scopecontent>
      <c02 level="file">
         <did>
            <unittitle>California Dining Club</unittitle>
         </did>
         <c03 level="file">
            <did>
               <unittitle>Annual financial statements</unittitle>
               <unitdate type="inclusive"
                  normal="1923/1929">1923-1929</unitdate>
            </did>
         </c03>
         <c03 level="file">
            <did>
               <unittitle>Membership rosters</unittitle>
               <unitdate type="inclusive"
                  normal="1918/1932">1918-1932</unitdate>
            </did>
         </c03>
         <c03 level="file">
            <did>
               <unittitle>Minutes</unittitle>
               <unitdate type="inclusive"
                  normal="1925/1930">1925-1930</unitdate>
            </did>
         </c03>
         <c03 level="file">
            <did>
               <unittitle>Newsletters</unittitle>
               <unitdate type="inclusive"
                  normal="1919/1932">1919-1932</unitdate>
            </did>
         </c03>
      </c02> . . .
   </c01>
</dsc>
```

<c02> Component (Second Level)

Description:

A wrapper element that designates a second-level subordinate part of the materials being described. Components may be either unnumbered <c> or numbered <c01>, <c02>, etc. The numbered components <c01> to <c12> assist a finding aid encoder in nesting up to twelve component levels accurately.

See the description under Component (Unnumbered) <c> and Component (First Level) <c01> for additional information.

May contain:

accessrestrict, accruals, acqinfo, altformavail, appraisal, arrangement, bibliography, bioghist, c03, controlaccess, custodhist, dao, daogrp, descgrp, did, dsc, fileplan, head, index, note, odd, originalsloc, otherfindaid, phystech, prefercite, processinfo, relatedmaterial, scopecontent, separatedmaterial, thead, userestrict

May occur within:

c01

Attributes:

ALTRENDER	#IMPLIED, CDATA
AUDIENCE	#IMPLIED, external, internal
ENCODINGANALOG	#IMPLIED, CDATA
ID	#IMPLIED, ID
LEVEL	#IMPLIED, class, collection, file, fonds, item, otherlevel, recordgrp, series, subfonds, subgrp, subseries
OTHERLEVEL	#IMPLIED, NMTOKEN
TPATTERN	#IMPLIED, NMTOKEN

Examples:

See examples under <c01> Component (First Level) and in fully encoded examples in Appendix C.

<c03> Component (Third Level)

Description:

A wrapper element that designates a third-level subordinate part of the materials being described. Components may be either unnumbered <c> or numbered <c01>, <c02>, etc. The numbered components <c01> to <c12> assist a finding aid encoder in nesting up to twelve component levels accurately.

See the description under Component (Unnumbered) <c> and Component (First Level) <c01> for additional information.

May contain:

accessrestrict, accruals, acqinfo, altformavail, appraisal, arrangement, bibliography, bioghist, c04, controlaccess, custodhist, dao, daogrp, descgrp, did, dsc, fileplan, head, index, note, odd, originalsloc, otherfindaid, phystech, prefercite, processinfo, relatedmaterial, scopecontent, separatedmaterial, thead, userestrict

May occur within:

c02

Attributes:

ALTRENDER	#IMPLIED, CDATA
AUDIENCE	#IMPLIED, external, internal
ENCODINGANALOG	#IMPLIED, CDATA
ID	#IMPLIED, ID
LEVEL	#IMPLIED, class, collection, file, fonds, item, otherlevel, recordgrp, series, subfonds, subgrp, subseries
OTHERLEVEL	#IMPLIED, NMTOKEN
TPATTERN	#IMPLIED, NMTOKEN

Examples:

See examples under <c01> Component (First Level) and in fully encoded examples in Appendix C.

<c04> Component (Fourth Level)

Description:

A wrapper element that designates a fourth-level subordinate part of the materials being described. Components may be either unnumbered <c> or numbered <c01>, <c02>, etc. The numbered components <c01> to <c12> assist a finding aid encoder in nesting up to twelve component levels accurately.

See the description under Component (Unnumbered) <c> and Component (First Level) <c01> for additional information.

May contain:

accessrestrict, accruals, acqinfo, altformavail, appraisal, arrangement, bibliography, bioghist, c05, controlaccess, custodhist, dao, daogrp, descgrp, did, dsc, fileplan, head, index, note, odd, originalsloc, otherfindaid, phystech, prefercite, processinfo, relatedmaterial, scopecontent, separatedmaterial, thead, userestrict

May occur within:

c03

Attributes:

ALTRENDER	#IMPLIED, CDATA
AUDIENCE	#IMPLIED, external, internal
ENCODINGANALOG	#IMPLIED, CDATA
ID	#IMPLIED, ID
LEVEL	#IMPLIED, class, collection, file, fonds, item, otherlevel, recordgrp, series, subfonds, subgrp, subseries
OTHERLEVEL	#IMPLIED, NMTOKEN
TPATTERN	#IMPLIED, NMTOKEN

Examples:

See examples under <c01> Component (First Level) and in fully encoded examples in Appendix C.

<c05> Component (Fifth Level)

Description:

A wrapper element that designates a fifth-level subordinate part of the materials being described. Components may be either unnumbered <c> or numbered <c01>, <c02>, etc. The numbered components <c01> to <c12> assist a finding aid encoder in nesting up to twelve component levels accurately.

See the description under Component (Unnumbered) <c> and Component (First Level) <c01> for additional information.

May contain:

accessrestrict, accruals, acqinfo, altformavail, appraisal, arrangement, bibliography, bioghist, c06, controlaccess, custodhist, dao, daogrp, descgrp, did, dsc, fileplan, head, index, note, odd, originalsloc, otherfindaid, phystech, prefercite, processinfo, relatedmaterial, scopecontent, separatedmaterial, thead, userestrict

May occur within:

c04

Attributes:

ALTRENDER	#IMPLIED, CDATA
AUDIENCE	#IMPLIED, external, internal
ENCODINGANALOG	#IMPLIED, CDATA
ID	#IMPLIED, ID
LEVEL	#IMPLIED, class, collection, file, fonds, item, otherlevel, recordgrp, series, subfonds, subgrp, subseries
OTHERLEVEL	#IMPLIED, NMTOKEN
TPATTERN	#IMPLIED, NMTOKEN

Examples:

See examples under <c01> Component (First Level) and in fully encoded examples in Appendix C.

<c06> Component (Sixth Level)

Description:

A wrapper element that designates a sixth-level subordinate part of the materials being described. Components may be either unnumbered <c> or numbered <c01>, <c02>, etc. The numbered components <c01> to <c12> assist a finding aid encoder in nesting up to twelve component levels accurately.

See the description under Component (Unnumbered) <c> and Component (First Level) <c01> for additional information.

May contain:

accessrestrict, accruals, acqinfo, altformavail, appraisal, arrangement, bibliography, bioghist, c07, controlaccess, custodhist, dao, daogrp, descgrp, did, dsc, fileplan, head, index, note, odd, originalsloc, otherfindaid, phystech, prefercite, processinfo, relatedmaterial, scopecontent, separatedmaterial, thead, userestrict

May occur within:

c05

Attributes:

ALTRENDER	#IMPLIED, CDATA
AUDIENCE	#IMPLIED, external, internal
ENCODINGANALOG	#IMPLIED, CDATA
ID	#IMPLIED, ID
LEVEL	#IMPLIED, class, collection, file, fonds, item, otherlevel, recordgrp, series, subfonds, subgrp, subseries
OTHERLEVEL	#IMPLIED, NMTOKEN
TPATTERN	#IMPLIED, NMTOKEN

Examples:

See examples under <c01> Component (First Level) and in fully encoded examples in Appendix C.

<c07> Component (Seventh Level)

Description:

A wrapper element that designates a seventh-level subordinate part of the materials being described. Components may be either unnumbered <c> or numbered <c01>, <c02>, etc. The numbered components <c01> to <c12> assist a finding aid encoder in nesting up to twelve component levels accurately.

See the description under Component (Unnumbered) <c> and Component (First Level) <c01> for additional information.

May contain:

accessrestrict, accruals, acqinfo, altformavail, appraisal, arrangement, bibliography, bioghist, c08, controlaccess, custodhist, dao, daogrp, descgrp, did, dsc, fileplan, head, index, note, odd, originalsloc, otherfindaid, phystech, prefercite, processinfo, relatedmaterial, scopecontent, separatedmaterial, thead, userestrict

May occur within:

c06

Attributes:

ALTRENDER	#IMPLIED, CDATA
AUDIENCE	#IMPLIED, external, internal
ENCODINGANALOG	#IMPLIED, CDATA
ID	#IMPLIED, ID
LEVEL	#IMPLIED, class, collection, file, fonds, item, otherlevel, recordgrp, series, subfonds, subgrp, subseries
OTHERLEVEL	#IMPLIED, NMTOKEN
TPATTERN	#IMPLIED, NMTOKEN

Examples:

See examples under <c01> Component (First Level) and in fully encoded examples in Appendix C.

<c08> Component (Eighth Level)

Description:

A wrapper element that designates a eighth-level subordinate part of the materials being described. Components may be either unnumbered <c> or numbered <c01>, <c02>, etc. The numbered components <c01> to <c12> assist a finding aid encoder in nesting up to twelve component levels accurately.

See the description under Component (Unnumbered) <c> and Component (First Level) <c01> for additional information.

May contain:

accessrestrict, accruals, acqinfo, altformavail, appraisal, arrangement, bibliography, bioghist, c09, controlaccess, custodhist, dao, daogrp, descgrp, did, dsc, fileplan, head, index, note, odd, originalsloc, otherfindaid, phystech, prefercite, processinfo, relatedmaterial, scopecontent, separatedmaterial, thead, userestrict

May occur within:

c07

Attributes:

ALTRENDER	#IMPLIED, CDATA
AUDIENCE	#IMPLIED, external, internal
ENCODINGANALOG	#IMPLIED, CDATA
ID	#IMPLIED, ID
LEVEL	#IMPLIED, class, collection, file, fonds, item, otherlevel, recordgrp, series, subfonds, subgrp, subseries
OTHERLEVEL	#IMPLIED, NMTOKEN
TPATTERN	#IMPLIED, NMTOKEN

Examples:

See examples under <c01> Component (First Level) and in fully encoded examples in Appendix C.

<c09> Component (Ninth Level)

Description:

A wrapper element that designates a ninth-level subordinate part of the materials being described. Components may be either unnumbered <c> or numbered <c01>, <c02>, etc. The numbered components <c01> to <c12> assist a finding aid encoder in nesting up to twelve component levels accurately.

See the description under Component (Unnumbered) <c> and Component (First Level) <c01> for additional information.

May contain:

accessrestrict, accruals, acqinfo, altformavail, appraisal, arrangement, bibliography, bioghist, c10, controlaccess, custodhist, dao, daogrp, descgrp, did, dsc, fileplan, head, index, note, odd, originalsloc, otherfindaid, phystech, prefercite, processinfo, relatedmaterial, scopecontent, separatedmaterial, thead, userestrict

May occur within:

c08

Attributes:

ALTRENDER	#IMPLIED, CDATA
AUDIENCE	#IMPLIED, external, internal
ENCODINGANALOG	#IMPLIED, CDATA
ID	#IMPLIED, ID
LEVEL	#IMPLIED, class, collection, file, fonds, item, otherlevel, recordgrp, series, subfonds, subgrp, subseries
OTHERLEVEL	#IMPLIED, NMTOKEN
TPATTERN	#IMPLIED, NMTOKEN

Examples:

See examples under <c01> Component (First Level) and in fully encoded examples in Appendix C.

<c10> Component (Tenth Level)

Description:

A wrapper element that designates a tenth-level subordinate part of the materials being described. Components may be either unnumbered <c> or numbered <c01>, <c02>, etc. The numbered components <c01> to <c12> assist a finding aid encoder in nesting up to twelve component levels accurately.

See the description under Component (Unnumbered) <c> and Component (First Level) <c01> for additional information.

May contain:

accessrestrict, accruals, acqinfo, altformavail, appraisal, arrangement, bibliography, bioghist, c11, controlaccess, custodhist, dao, daogrp, descgrp, did, dsc, fileplan, head, index, note, odd, originalsloc, otherfindaid, phystech, prefercite, processinfo, relatedmaterial, scopecontent, separatedmaterial, thead, userestrict

May occur within:

c09

Attributes:

ALTRENDER	#IMPLIED, CDATA
AUDIENCE	#IMPLIED, external, internal
ENCODINGANALOG	#IMPLIED, CDATA
ID	#IMPLIED, ID
LEVEL	#IMPLIED, class, collection, file, fonds, item, otherlevel, recordgrp, series, subfonds, subgrp, subseries
OTHERLEVEL	#IMPLIED, NMTOKEN
TPATTERN	#IMPLIED, NMTOKEN

Examples:

See examples under <c01> Component (First Level) and in fully encoded examples in Appendix C.

<c11> Component (Eleventh Level)

Description:

A wrapper element that designates a eleventh-level subordinate part of the materials being described. Components may be either unnumbered <c> or numbered <c01>, <c02>, etc. The numbered components <c01> to <c12> assist a finding aid encoder in nesting up to twelve component levels accurately.

See the description under Component (Unnumbered) <c> and Component (First Level) <c01> for additional information.

May contain:

accessrestrict, accruals, acqinfo, altformavail, appraisal, arrangement, bibliography, bioghist, c12, controlaccess, custodhist, dao, daogrp, descgrp, did, dsc, fileplan, head, index, note, odd, originalsloc, otherfindaid, phystech, prefercite, processinfo, relatedmaterial, scopecontent, separatedmaterial, thead, userestrict

May occur within:

c10

Attributes:

ALTRENDER	#IMPLIED, CDATA
AUDIENCE	#IMPLIED, external, internal
ENCODINGANALOG	#IMPLIED, CDATA
ID	#IMPLIED, ID
LEVEL	#IMPLIED, class, collection, file, fonds, item, otherlevel, recordgrp, series, subfonds, subgrp, subseries
OTHERLEVEL	#IMPLIED, NMTOKEN
TPATTERN	#IMPLIED, NMTOKEN

Examples:

See examples under <c01> Component (First Level) and in fully encoded examples in Appendix C.

<c12> Component (Twelfth Level)

Description:

A wrapper element that designates a twelfth-level subordinate part of the materials being described. Components may be either unnumbered <c> or numbered <c01>, <c02>, etc. The numbered components <c01> to <c12> assist a finding aid encoder in nesting up to twelve component levels accurately.

See the description under Component (Unnumbered) <c> and Component (First Level) <c01> for additional information.

May contain:

accessrestrict, accruals, acqinfo, altformavail, appraisal, arrangement, bibliography, bioghist, controlaccess, custodhist, dao, daogrp, descgrp, did, dsc, fileplan, head, index, note, odd, originalsloc, otherfindaid, phystech, prefercite, processinfo, relatedmaterial, scopecontent, separatedmaterial, userestrict

May occur within:

c11

Attributes:

ALTRENDER	#IMPLIED, CDATA
AUDIENCE	#IMPLIED, external, internal
ENCODINGANALOG	#IMPLIED, CDATA
ID	#IMPLIED, ID
LEVEL	#IMPLIED, class, collection, file, fonds, item, otherlevel, recordgrp, series, subfonds, subgrp, subseries
OTHERLEVEL	#IMPLIED, NMTOKEN
TPATTERN	#IMPLIED, NMTOKEN

Examples:

See examples under <c01> Component (First Level) and in fully encoded examples in Appendix C.

<change> Change

Description:

An optional subelement in the <revisiondesc> portion of <eadheader> used for a brief description of an update made to an EAD document. Additions to a finding aid or significant recoding should be noted, but not correction of a few typographical errors. The <change> element is modeled on a header element in the Text Encoding Initiative (TEI) DTD. The TEI recommends that revisions be entered and numbered in reverse chronological order, with the most recent <change> first.

The <edition> element can be used to designate a finding aid that has been so substantively changed that it constitutes a new version and supersedes earlier versions of the finding aid.

May contain:

date, item

May occur within:

revisiondesc

Attributes:

ALTRENDER	#IMPLIED, CDATA
AUDIENCE	#IMPLIED, external, internal
ENCODINGANALOG	#IMPLIED, CDATA
ID	#IMPLIED, ID

Example:

```
<eadheader langencoding="iso639-2b"> . . .
   <revisiondesc>
      <change>
         <date normal="19970505">May 5, 1997</date>
         <item>This electronic finding aid was updated to current
            markup standards by Sarah Taylor using a perl script.
            Updates included: eadheader, eadid, and arrangement
            of did elements and their labels.</item>
      </change>
   </revisiondesc>
</eadheader>
```

<chronitem> Chronology List Item

Description:

A formatting element that keeps a date paired with an associated event or group of events within a Chronology List <chronlist>. Each <chronitem> contains a <date> (either a single date or date range) coupled with an <event> or description of what occurred during that time. When multiple <event>s are associated with a single <date>, the <event>s are bundled in an <eventgrp> tag, which is then easily paired with the appropriate <date>.

May contain:

date, event, eventgrp

May occur within:

chronlist

Attributes:

ALTRENDER	#IMPLIED, CDATA
AUDIENCE	#IMPLIED, external, internal
ID	#IMPLIED, ID

Example:

```
<bioghist>
   <head>Chronology</head>
   <chronlist>
      <chronitem>
         <date normal="18401012">1840</date>
         <event>Born Helena Opid in Krakow, Poland on October
            12th.</event>
      </chronitem>
      <chronitem>
         <date normal="1861">1861</date>
         <event>Made stage debut as Helena Modrzejewska in
            charity fair production of <title>The White
            Camellia</title>, in Bochnia, Poland.</event>
      </chronitem> . . .
      <chronitem>
         <date normal="19090409">1909</date>
         <event>Died April 8th at her home on Bay Island. Funeral
            services held at St. Vibiana's Cathedral in Los
            Angeles, and Modjeska was later buried in her native
            Krakow.</event>
      </chronitem>
   </chronlist>
</bioghist>
```

<chronlist> Chronology List

Description:

A formatting element that designates information about the sequence in which significant past events, associated with the described materials, occurred. The <chronlist> also provides a structured display to list these dates and events. Each <chronlist> contains Chronology Items <chronitem>s that pair a <date> or date range with a brief description of an associated <event> or events <eventgrp>.

A <chronlist> most often appears in finding aids as part of the Biography or History <bioghist> element, but <chronlist> is also available for use in other elements that might need to present historical dates and events in a multicolumn list.

May contain:

chronitem, head, listhead

May occur within:

accessrestrict, accruals, acqinfo, altformavail, appraisal, arrangement, bibliography, bioghist, blockquote, controlaccess, custodhist, daodesc, descgrp, div, dsc, dscgrp, event, extref, extrefloc, fileplan, index, item, note, odd, originalsloc, otherfindaid, p, phystech, prefercite, processinfo, ref, refloc, relatedmaterial, scopecontent, separatedmaterial, titlepage, userestrict

Attributes:

ALTRENDER	#IMPLIED, CDATA
AUDIENCE	#IMPLIED, external, internal
ENCODINGANALOG	#IMPLIED, CDATA
ID	#IMPLIED, ID

Example:

```
<bioghist>
   <head>Biographical Note</head>
   <chronlist>
      <chronitem>
         <date>1820, Dec. 20</date>
         <event>Born eighth of ten children of Taylor and Dicey
            (Jones) Duke; Little River, Orange Co., N.C.</event>
      </chronitem>
      <chronitem>
         <date>1842</date>
         <event>Married Mary Caroline Clinton</event>
      </chronitem>
      <chronitem>
         <date>1844</date>
         <event>Sidney Taylor Duke born</event>
      </chronitem> . . .
   </chronlist>
</bioghist>
```

<colspec> Table Column Specification

Description:

An empty formatting element that designates the position and size of a single column in a Table <table>. Attributes specify the unique name of the column, its unique number within the table, its width and rules, and the horizontal alignment of text within the column. The quantity of columns in a <table> is determined by the COLS attribute of the <tgroup> element, not by the number of <colspec>s defined. The values set for <colspec> override any values implied from <tgroup> or <thead> elements.

See also related elements <table> and <tgroup>.

May contain:

EMPTY

May occur within:

tgroup

Attributes:

ALIGN	#IMPLIED, left, right, center, justify, char
CHAR	#IMPLIED, CDATA
CHAROFF	#IMPLIED, NMTOKEN
COLNAME	#IMPLIED, NMTOKEN
COLNUM	#IMPLIED, NMTOKEN
COLSEP	#IMPLIED, NMTOKEN
COLWIDTH	#IMPLIED, CDATA
ROWSEP	#IMPLIED, NMTOKEN

Example:

```
<table frame="none">
   <tgroup cols="3">
      <colspec colnum="1" colname="1" align="left" colwidth="50pt"/>
      <colspec colnum="2" colname="2" align="left" colwidth="50pt"/>
      <colspec colnum="3" colname="3" align="left" colwidth="50pt"/>
      <thead>
         <row>
            <entry colname="1">Major Family Members</entry>
            <entry colname="2">Spouses</entry>
            <entry colname="3">Children</entry>
         </row>
      </thead>
      <tbody>
         <row>
            <entry colname="1">John Albemarle (1760-1806)</entry>
            <entry colname="2">Mary Frances Delaney (1769-
               1835)</entry>
            <entry colname="3">John Delaney Albemarle (1787-
               1848)</entry>
         </row> . . .
      </tbody>
   </tgroup>
</table>
```

<container> Container

Description:

A <did> subelement for information that contributes to locating the described materials by indicating the kinds of devices that hold the materials and identifying any sequential numbers assigned to those devices. The <container> element is used most frequently at the component level, i.e., once a Description of Subordinate Components <dsc> has been opened. This storage information can help researchers understand how extensive the material is, especially in the absence of a specific physical <extent> statement at the component level.

Use of the TYPE attribute is strongly recommended to clarify the nature of the storage device. Use any useful designations, such as "box," "folder," and "reel."

The Physical Location <physloc> element can be used to designate the shelves, stacks, rooms, buildings, or other places where the containers are stored.

Use the ID of the Unit <unitid> element to designate control numbers not associated with a physical container, for example, accession numbers. Most repositories use either <container> or <unitid> as the call numbers for fetching material for researchers. If both elements are used, consider setting the LABEL attribute to specify which element is the call number.

The PARENT attribute can be used to point to the <container> element that describes the box in which a folder is housed.

May contain:

#PCDATA, abbr, archref, bibref, emph, expan, extptr, extref, lb, linkgrp, ptr, ref, title

May occur within:

archref, did

Attributes:

ALTRENDER	#IMPLIED, CDATA
AUDIENCE	#IMPLIED, external, internal
ENCODINGANALOG	#IMPLIED, CDATA
ID	#IMPLIED, ID
LABEL	#IMPLIED, CDATA
PARENT	#IMPLIED, IDREFS
TYPE	#IMPLIED, NMTOKEN

Examples:

1.
```
<dsc type="combined">
   <c level="series">
      <did>
         <unittitle>Correspondence, </unittitle>
         <unitdate normal="1942/1987">1942-1987 </unitdate>
      </did>
      <scopecontent>[...]</scopecontent>
      <c level="file">
         <did>
            <container id="mss1993-043.1.1" type="box">1</container>
            <container parent="mss1993-043.1.1"
               type="folder">1</container>
            <unittitle><unitdate normal="1942/1943">1942-
               1943</unitdate></unittitle>
         </did>
      </c>
      <c level="file">
         <did>
            <container parent="mss1993-043.1.1"
               type="folder">2</container>
            <unittitle><unitdate normal="194401/194408">January-
               August 1944</unitdate></unittitle>
         </did>
      </c>
      <c level="file">
         <did>
            <container parent="mss1993-043.1.1"
               type="folder">3</container>
            <unittitle><unitdate normal="194409/194503">August
               1944-March 1945</unitdate></unittitle>
         </did>
      </c> . . .
   </c> . . .
</dsc>
```

2.
```
<c01 level="series">
   <did>[...]</did>
   <c02 level="file">
      <did>
         <container type="box">3</container>
         <container type="folder">18</container>
         <unittitle>Parent-Teacher Association of Fondsville
         </unittitle>
         <unitdate type="inclusive" normal="1959/1972">1959-
            1972</unitdate>
      </did>
   </c02>
   <c02 level="file">
      <did>
         <container type="box">3</container>
         <container type="folder">19</container>
         <unittitle>Pasta and Politics Club</unittitle>
         <unitdate type="inclusive" normal="1967/1975">1967-
            1975</unitdate>
      </did>
   </c02> . . .
</c01>
```

<controlaccess> Controlled Access Headings

Description:

A wrapper element that designates key access points for the described materials and enables authority-controlled searching across finding aids on a computer network. Hundreds of names and subjects can appear in a finding aid. Prominence can be given to the major ones by bundling them together in a single place within the <archdesc> or within a large Component <c> and tagging them with <controlaccess>.

The <controlaccess> element designates terms comparable to those found in the 1xx, 6xx, and 7xx fields of MARC catalog records. Finding aid searches limited to the <controlaccess> element and its subelements will improve the likelihood of locating strong sources of information on a desired subject, because access terms will have been entered in a consistent form across finding aids, and also because only the most significant terms are likely to have been selected for encoding.

Although names and terms from locally controlled vocabularies are permissible, the <controlaccess> subelements (<corpname>, <famname>, <function>, <genreform>, <geogname>, <occupation>, <persname>, <subject>, and <title>) should come from national or international vocabularies whenever they are available to enable searches in information systems that include multiple finding aids, or finding aids and bibliographic records from many institutions.

These subelements have SOURCE attributes to specify the vocabulary tool from which the heading is taken and RULES attributes to specify the descriptive rules by which it has been formulated. The attribute AUTHFILENUMBER can be used to identify an authority file record that provides additional information about a heading and includes cross references. The ROLE attribute can be used to specify such factors as whether a heading is for the creator of the materials, the subject of the materials, or both.

May contain:

address, blockquote, chronlist, controlaccess, corpname, famname, function, genreform, geogname, head, list, name, note, occupation, p, persname, subject, table, title

May occur within:

archdesc, archdescgrp, c, c01, c02, c03, c04, c05, c06, c07, c08, c09, c10, c11, c12, controlaccess, descgrp

<controlaccess>

Attributes:

ALTRENDER	#IMPLIED, CDATA
AUDIENCE	#IMPLIED, external, internal
ENCODINGANALOG	#IMPLIED, CDATA
ID	#IMPLIED, ID

Example:

```
<archdesc level="collection">
   <did>[...]</did>
   <scopecontent>[...]</scopecontent>
   <controlaccess>
      <head>Index Terms</head>
      <p>These records are indexed under the following headings
         in the catalog of the Minnesota Historical Society.
         Researchers wishing to find related materials should
         search the catalog under these index terms.</p>
      <controlaccess>
         <head>Organizations:</head>
         <corpname encodinganalog="610" source="lcnaf">Board of
            Game and Fish Commissioners of Minnesota.</corpname>
      </controlaccess>
      <controlaccess>
         <head>Topics:</head>
         <subject encodinganalog="650" source="lcsh">Fishery law
            and legislation--Minnesota.</subject>
         <subject encodinganalog="650" source="lcsh">Game-law--
            Minnesota.</subject>
         <subject encodinganalog="650" source="lcsh">Law
            enforcement--Minnesota.</subject>
      </controlaccess>
      <controlaccess>
         <head>Government Functions:</head>
         <function encodinganalog="657" source="aat">Law
            enforcing.</function>
         <function encodinganalog="657"
            source="aat">Convicting.</function>
      </controlaccess>
   </controlaccess> . . .
</archdesc>
```

<corpname> Corporate Name

Description:

The proper noun name that identifies an organization or group of people that acts as an entity. Examples include names of associations, institutions, business firms, nonprofit enterprises, governments, government agencies, projects, programs, religious bodies, churches, conferences, athletic contests, exhibitions, expeditions, fairs, and ships.

All names in a finding aid do not have to be tagged. One option is to tag those names for which access other than basic, undifferentiated keyword retrieval is desired. Use of controlled vocabulary forms is recommended to facilitate access to names within and across finding aid systems. The <corpname> element may be used in text elements such as <p>. To indicate a corporate entity with major representation in the described materials, nest <corpname> within the <controlaccess> element.

When a <corpname> is also the name of the institution providing intellectual access to the described material, nest <corpname> within the <repository> element. The <subarea> element may be used to show a secondary or subsidiary level within the <corpname>. When a <corpname> is also the name of the creator or compiler of the described material, nest <corpname> within the <origination> element.

The ROLE attribute can be used to specify other relationship(s) of the name to the described materials, for example, "compiler," "creator," "collector," or "subject." The ENCODINGANALOG attribute can be used to specify corresponding data categories in another coding system such as MARC. The NORMAL attribute can be used to provide the authority form of a name that has been encoded with <corpname> in narrative text, e.g., within a paragraph. Use the SOURCE attribute to specify the vocabulary from which the name has been taken, and/or the RULES attribute to specify the descriptive rules followed when forming the name. The attribute AUTHFILENUMBER can be used to identify a link to an authority file record that has more information about the name or cross references for alternative forms of the name and related names.

The <corpname> element is comparable to MARC fields 110, 111, 610, 611, 710, and 711.

See also the related elements <controlaccess>, <persname>, <famname>, <name>, and <subarea>.

<corpname>

May contain:

#PCDATA, emph, extptr, lb, ptr, subarea

May occur within:

bibref, controlaccess, entry, event, extref, extrefloc, indexentry, item, label, namegrp, origination, p, physdesc, physfacet, ref, refloc, repository, unittitle

Attributes:

ALTRENDER	#IMPLIED, CDATA
AUDIENCE	#IMPLIED, external, internal
AUTHFILENUMBER	#IMPLIED, CDATA
ENCODINGANALOG	#IMPLIED, CDATA
ID	#IMPLIED, ID
NORMAL	#IMPLIED, CDATA
ROLE	#IMPLIED, CDATA
RULES	#IMPLIED, NMTOKEN
SOURCE	#IMPLIED, NMTOKEN

Examples:

1.

```
<archdesc level="collection">
   <did>
      <head>Collection Summary</head>
      <origination label="Creator">
         <corpname encodinganalog="110" source="lcnaf">National
            Association for the Advancement of Colored
            People</corpname>
      </origination> . . .
   </did> . . .
</archdesc>
```

2.

```
<controlaccess>
   <head>Index Terms</head>
   <p>These records are indexed under the following headings in
      the catalog of the Minnesota Historical Society.
      Researchers wishing to find related materials should search
      the catalog under these index terms.</p>
   <controlaccess>
      <head>Organizations:</head>
      <corpname encodinganalog="610" source="lcnaf">Board of Game
         and Fish Commissioners of Minnesota.</corpname>
   </controlaccess> . . .
</controlaccess>
```

<creation> Creation

Description:

A subelement of the <profiledesc> portion of <eadheader> used for information about the encoding of the finding aid, including the person(s) or agency(ies) responsible for the encoding, the date, and the circumstances under which the encoding was done.

This element is modeled on a Text Encoding Initiative (TEI) DTD header element.

May contain:

#PCDATA, abbr, archref, bibref, date, emph, expan, extptr, extref, lb, linkgrp, ptr, ref, title

May occur within:

profiledesc

Attributes:

ALTRENDER	#IMPLIED, CDATA
AUDIENCE	#IMPLIED, external, internal
ENCODINGANALOG	#IMPLIED, CDATA
ID	#IMPLIED, ID

Example:

```
<eadheader langencoding="iso639-2b"> . . .
   <profiledesc>
      <creation>Machine-readable finding aid and skeletal markup
         derived via a macro from WordPerfect file; markup
         checked and completed by Sarah Taylor. <date
         normal="19950423">April 23, 1995.</date>
      </creation>
   </profiledesc> . . .
</eadheader>
```

<custodhist> Custodial History

Description:

Information about the chain of ownership of the materials being described, before they reached the immediate source of acquisition. Both physical possession and intellectual ownership can be described, providing details of changes of ownership and/or custody that may be significant in terms of authority, integrity, and interpretation.

Although the history of custody is sometimes synonymous with provenance, a description of archival provenance may be more appropriate for the <origination>, <bioghist>, or <scopecontent> elements.

Use Acquisition Information <acqinfo> for text about the immediate source of the described materials and the circumstances under which they were received by the repository.

In EAD Version 1.0 <custodhist> was a subelement of Administrative Information <admininfo>, which has been deprecated in EAD 2002 (see Appendix B). The new Description Group <descgrp> element, which can group any of the <did>-level elements (except the Description of Subordinate Components <dsc>), may be used to wrap elements where a group heading is desirable. The <descgrp> element can be used to replace <admininfo> where it has been used as a wrapper when converting finding aids encoded in EAD V1.0 to EAD 2002.

The <custodhist> element is comparable to ISAD(G) data element 3.2.3 and MARC field 561.

May contain:

acqinfo, address, blockquote, chronlist, head, list, note, p, table

May occur within:

archdesc, archdescgrp, c, c01, c02, c03, c04, c05, c06, c07, c08, c09, c10, c11, c12, descgrp

Attributes:

ALTRENDER	#IMPLIED, CDATA
AUDIENCE	#IMPLIED, external, internal
ENCODINGANALOG	#IMPLIED, CDATA
ID	#IMPLIED, ID

Example:

```
<custodhist>
   <p>The George Franklin Papers were maintained by the staff of
      the Mayor's Office, City of Irvine, California, in the
      records storage facility at City Hall from the time of
      Franklin's death in 1972 until they were transferred, at
      his family's request, to Special Collections and Archives,
      The UC Irvine Libraries, in 1988.</p>
</custodhist>
```

<dao> Digital Archival Object

Description:

A linking element that uses the attributes ENTITYREF or HREF to connect the finding aid information to electronic representations of the described materials. The <dao> and <daogrp> elements allow the content of an archival collection or record group to be incorporated in the finding aid. These digital representations include graphic images, audio or video clips, images of text pages, and electronic transcriptions of text. The objects can be selected examples, or digital surrogates all the materials in an archival fonds or series.

Use the Extended Pointer <extptr> element to link the finding aid to electronic objects that are not part of the described materials.

Use the ACTUATE attribute to designate whether the object is displayed automatically ("onload") or only if the user requests it ("onrequest"). Use the SHOW attribute to define whether a remote resource appears at the point of the link, in a new window, or replaces the link.

See also related elements <daodesc>, <daogrp>, and <daoloc>.

While XML Linking Language (XLink) Version 1.0, which is the basis for EAD linking elements, is a stable document, examples of EAD usage are hypothetical and have not been tested in real XLink-based applications. Those wishing to use XLink are encouraged to consult the specification available online at <http://www.w3.org/TR/xlink/>.

May contain:

daodesc

May occur within:

archdesc, archdescgrp, archref, bioghist, c, c01, c02, c03, c04, c05, c06, c07, c08, c09, c10, c11, c12, did, odd, scopecontent

Attributes:

ACTUATE	#IMPLIED, onload, onrequest, actuateother, actuatenone
ALTRENDER	#IMPLIED, CDATA
ARCROLE	#IMPLIED, CDATA
AUDIENCE	#IMPLIED, external, internal
ENTITYREF	#IMPLIED, ENTITY
HREF	#IMPLIED, CDATA
ID	#IMPLIED, ID
LINKTYPE	#FIXED, simple, simple
ROLE	#IMPLIED, CDATA
SHOW	#IMPLIED, new, replace, embed, showother, shownone
TITLE	#IMPLIED, CDATA
XPOINTER	#IMPLIED, CDATA

Example:

```
<c02 level="file">
   <did>
      <unittitle>Photographs</unittitle>
      <unitdate type="inclusive" normal="1895/1928">1895-
         1928</unitdate>
   </did>
   <c03 level="item">
      <did>
         <unittitle>John Smith graduation portrait</unittitle>
         <unitdate type="single" normal="18950528">May 28,
            1895</unitdate>
         <dao linktype="simple"
            href="http://imgs.ud.edu/archives/image/f12001_1.jpg"
            actuate="onrequest" show="new"/>
      </did>
   </c03>
   <c03 level="item">
      <did>
         <unittitle>Photographs of John Smith and family
            members</unittitle>
         <unitdate type="inclusive" normal="1907-1928">1907-
            1928</unitdate>
         <physdesc><extent>12 photographic
            prints</extent></physdesc>
      </did>
   </c03>
</c02>
```

<daodesc> Digital Archival Object Description

Description:

Information about the contents, usage, or source of a Digital Archival Object <dao> or Digital Archival Object Group <daogrp>. When the <unittitle> or other descriptive information in a Component <c> is sufficient to identify one or more digital objects, the <daodesc> caption is not necessary.

See also related elements <dao>, <daogrp>, and <daoloc>.

May contain:

address, blockquote, chronlist, head, list, note, p, table

May occur within:

dao, daogrp, daoloc

Attributes:

ALTRENDER	#IMPLIED, CDATA
AUDIENCE	#IMPLIED, external, internal
ID	#IMPLIED, ID

Example:

```
<c02 level="file">
   <did>
      <unittitle>Photographs of John Smith and family
         members</unittitle>
      <unitdate type="inclusive" normal="1895/1928">1895-
         1928</unitdate>
      <daogrp linktype="extended">
         <daodesc>
            <p>Sample digitized image from this file: John Smith
               graduation portrait, <date normal="18950528">28
               May 1895</date>.</p>
         </daodesc>
         <resource linktype="resource" label="start"/>
         <daoloc entityref="f0042_1tmb" linktype="locator"
            label="thumb"/>
         <daoloc entityref="f0042_1ref" linktype="locator"
            label="reference"/>
         <arc linktype="arc" show="embed" actuate="onload"
            from="start" to="thumb"/>
         <arc linktype="arc" show="new" actuate="onrequest"
            from="thumb" to="reference"/>
      </daogrp>
   </did>
</c02>
```

<daogrp> Digital Archival Object Group

Description:

A wrapper element that contains two or more related Digital Archival Object Locations <daoloc> that should be thought of as a group and may share a single common Digital Archival Object Description <daodesc>. They may also form an extended link group to enable a set of multidirectional links. The <dao>, <daogrp>, and <daoloc> elements allow the content of the described materials to be incorporated in the finding aid.

See also related elements <dao>, <daodesc>, <daoloc> and <linkgrp>.

While XML Linking Language (XLink) Version 1.0, which is the basis for EAD linking elements, is a stable document, examples of EAD usage are hypothetical and have not been tested in real XLink-based applications. Those wishing to use XLink are encouraged to consult the specification available online at <http://www.w3.org/TR/xlink/>.

May contain:

arc, daodesc, daoloc, extptrloc, extrefloc, ptrloc, refloc, resource

May occur within:

archdesc, archdescgrp, archref, bioghist, c, c01, c02, c03, c04, c05, c06, c07, c08, c09, c10, c11, c12, did, odd, scopecontent

Attributes:

ALTRENDER	#IMPLIED, CDATA
AUDIENCE	#IMPLIED, external, internal
ID	#IMPLIED, ID
LINKTYPE	#FIXED, extended, extended
ROLE	#IMPLIED, CDATA
TITLE	#IMPLIED, CDATA

<daogrp>

Example:

```
<c02 level="file">
   <did>
      <unittitle>Photographs of John Smith and family
         members</unittitle>
      <unitdate type="inclusive" normal="1895/1928">1895-
         1928</unitdate>
      <daogrp linktype="extended">
         <daodesc>
            <p>Sample digitized image from this file: John Smith
               graduation portrait, <date normal="18950528">28
               May 1895</date>.</p>
         </daodesc>
         <resource linktype="resource" label="start"/>
         <daoloc entityref="f0042_1tmb" linktype="locator"
            label="thumb"/>
         <daoloc entityref="f0042_1ref" linktype="locator"
            label="reference"/>
         <arc linktype="arc" show="embed" actuate="onload"
            from="start" to="thumb"/>
         <arc linktype="arc" show="new" actuate="onrequest"
            from="thumb" to="reference"/>
      </daogrp>
   </did>
</c02>
```

<daoloc> Digital Archival Object Location

Description:

The location of a Digital Archival Object <dao> that is a resource in an extended link. Within a Digital Archival Object Group <daogrp>, a <daoloc> element is used instead of a <dao> element to indicate that an extended, possibly multidirectional link is being tagged. See also related elements <dao>, <daogrp>, and <daodesc>.

While XML Linking Language (XLink) Version 1.0, which is the basis for EAD linking elements, is a stable document, examples of EAD usage are hypothetical and have not been tested in real XLink-based applications. Those wishing to use XLink are encouraged to consult the specification available online at <http://www.w3.org/TR/xlink/>.

May contain:

daodesc

May occur within:

daogrp

Attributes:

ALTRENDER	#IMPLIED, CDATA
AUDIENCE	#IMPLIED, external, internal
ENTITYREF	#IMPLIED, ENTITY
HREF	#IMPLIED, CDATA
ID	#IMPLIED, ID
LABEL	#IMPLIED, NMTOKEN
LINKTYPE	#FIXED, locator, locator
ROLE	#IMPLIED, CDATA
TITLE	#IMPLIED, CDATA
XPOINTER	#IMPLIED, CDATA

<daoloc>

Example:

```
<c02 level="file">
   <did>
      <unittitle>Photographs of John Smith and family
         members</unittitle>
      <unitdate type="inclusive" normal="1895/1928">1895-
         1928</unitdate>
      <daogrp linktype="extended">
         <daodesc>
            <p>Sample digitized image from this file: John Smith
               graduation portrait, <date normal="18950528">28
               May 1895</date>.</p>
         </daodesc>
         <resource linktype="resource" label="start"/>
         <daoloc entityref="f0042_1tmb" linktype="locator"
            label="thumb"/>
         <daoloc entityref="f0042_1ref" linktype="locator"
            label="reference"/>
         <arc linktype="arc" show="embed" actuate="onload"
            from="start" to="thumb"/>
         <arc linktype="arc" show="new" actuate="onrequest"
            from="thumb" to="reference"/>
      </daogrp>
   </did>
</c02>
```

<date> Date

Description:

A generic element that contains a month, day, or year in any format. Use <date> to identify any dates that merit encoding, except for the creation and other relevant dates of the described materials, which are instead tagged with the <unitdate> element. Examples of dates that might merit encoding are a person's birth date, the date the materials were acquired, or the date of an event in a chronology. These dates may be entered in the form of text or numbers, and may consist of a single date or range of dates.

A standard numeric form of the date (YYYYMMDD, etc.) can be specified with the NORMAL attribute to facilitate machine comparison of dates for searching, for example, 19480101/19980401 (YYYYMMDD/YYYYMMDD), or 1948/1998 (YYYY/YYYY). The TYPE attribute can be used to supply a more specific designation, for example, "life," "flourish," "depiction," "publication," or "acquisition." The CERTAINTY attribute may be used to indicate the degree of precision in the dating, for example, "circa," "approximately," or "after." The CALENDAR attribute, which has a default value of "gregorian," specifies the calendar from which the date stems. The value "ce" (common or Christian era) is the default for the ERA attribute.

May contain:

#PCDATA, emph, extptr, lb, ptr

May occur within:

change, chronitem, creation, entry, event, extref, extrefloc, imprint, item, label, legalstatus, p, physdesc, physfacet, publicationstmt, ref, refloc, subtitle, title, titlepage, titleproper, unittitle

Attributes:

ALTRENDER	#IMPLIED, CDATA
AUDIENCE	#IMPLIED, external, internal
CALENDAR	gregorian, NMTOKEN
CERTAINTY	#IMPLIED, CDATA
ENCODINGANALOG	#IMPLIED, CDATA
ERA	ce, NMTOKEN
ID	#IMPLIED, ID
NORMAL	#IMPLIED, CDATA
TYPE	#IMPLIED, CDATA

<date>

Examples:

1.
```
<bibref>
   <persname role="author">Kinder, Dolores.</persname>
   <title render="italic>Once Upon a Lullaby.</title>
   <imprint><geogname>New York: </geogname>
      <publisher>Wells &amp; Sons, </publisher>
      <date type="publication">1931</date>
   </imprint>
</bibref>
```

2.
```
<acqinfo>
   <p>This collection, number
      <num type="donor">1988-015,</num> was donated by Mrs.
      Dolores Franklin on <date type="acquisition"
      normal="19880423">April 23, 1988.</date>
   </p>
</acqinfo>
```

<defitem> Definition List Item

Description:

A formatting element in a special type of list that keeps an entry in a list (called a <label>) paired with its definition, description, or explanation (called an <item>). The <defitem> can be thought of as an entry with two cells: <label> followed by <item>. Lists with <defitem>s are often displayed in two columns.

See also related element <list>.

May contain:

item, label

May occur within:

list

Attributes:

ALTRENDER	#IMPLIED, CDATA
AUDIENCE	#IMPLIED, external, internal
ID	#IMPLIED, ID

Example:

```
<list type="deflist">
   <listhead>
      <head01>Abbreviation</head01>
      <head02>Expansion</head02>
   </listhead>
   <defitem>
      <label>ALS</label>
      <item>Autograph Letter Signed</item>
   </defitem>
   <defitem>
      <label>TLS</label>
      <item>Typewritten Letter Signed</item>
   </defitem>
</list>
```

<descgrp> Description Group

Description:

An element that can be used to bring together any group of elements that are children of the Archival Description <archdesc> element except for the <did> and <dsc> elements. Description Group might be used, for example, to cluster elements into groups that correspond to the areas specified by the General International Standard Archival Description (ISAD(G)).

Description Group can be used in place of wrapper elements from EAD Version 1.0 such as Administrative Information <admininfo> and Adjunct Descriptive Data <add>.

Use the TYPE attribute to characterize the nature of the groupings.

May contain:

accessrestrict, accruals, acqinfo, address, altformavail, appraisal, arrangement, bibliography, bioghist, blockquote, chronlist, controlaccess, custodhist, descgrp, fileplan, head, index, list, note, odd, originalsloc, otherfindaid, p, phystech, prefercite, processinfo, relatedmaterial, scopecontent, separatedmaterial, table, userestrict

May occur within:

archdesc, archdescgrp, c, c01, c02, c03, c04, c05, c06, c07, c08, c09, c10, c11, c12, descgrp

Attributes:

ALTRENDER	#IMPLIED, CDATA
AUDIENCE	#IMPLIED, external, internal
ENCODINGANALOG	#IMPLIED, CDATA
ID	#IMPLIED, ID
TYPE	#IMPLIED, CDATA

Examples:

1.
```
<descgrp>
   <head>Related and Associated Materials</head>
   <separatedmaterial>
      <p>Photographs and sound recordings have been transferred
         to the appropriate custodial divisions of the Library
         where they are identified as part of these papers. Among
         the sound recordings are the following broadcasts:</p>
      <list>[...]</list>
   </separatedmaterial>
   <separatedmaterial>
      <p>Other papers of Earl Warren, which relate chiefly to his
         early years and public service in California, are held
         by the California State Archives in Sacramento.</p>
   </separatedmaterial>
   <relatedmaterial>
      <p>Records relating to the Warren Commission are held in
         the National Archives and Records Administration.</p>
   </relatedmaterial>
</descgrp>
```

2.
```
<descgrp>
   <head>Important Information for Users of the Collection</head>
   <accessrestrict>
      <head>Access</head>
      <p>Collection is open for research. Scrapbooks are
         extremely fragile and require close supervision by
         Special Collections staff during use.</p>
   </accessrestrict>
   <userestrict>
      <head>Publication Rights</head>
      <p>Property rights reside with the University of
         California. Literary rights are retained by the creators
         of the records and their heirs. For permissions to
         reproduce or to publish, please contact the Head of
         Special Collections and Archives.</p>
   </userestrict>
   <prefercite>
      <head>Preferred Citation</head>
      <p>Eugene Loring Papers. MS-P02. Special Collections and
         Archives, The UCI Libraries, Irvine, California.</p>
   </prefercite>
   <acqinfo>
      <head>Acquisition Information</head>
      <p>Gift of Eugene Loring, 1975 and 1980.</p>
   </acqinfo>
   <processinfo>
      <head>Processing History</head>
      <p>Preliminary processing by Roger Berry in 1975 and 1980.
         Processing completed by Emma Kheradyar in 1996-1997.
         Guide edited by Laura Clark Brown in 1998 and completed
         by William Landis in 2000.</p>
   </processinfo>
</descgrp>
```

<descrules> Descriptive Rules

Description:

A subelement of Profile Description <profiledesc> for the enumeration of the rules, standards, conventions, and protocols used in preparing the description.

Do not confuse this element with the RULES attribute in the <controlaccess> subelements, e.g., <persname>, <geogname>, and <title>, which are used to specify the descriptive rules, such as AACR2R, used in formulating individual access points.

The <descrules> element is comparable to ISAD(G) data element 3.7.2.

May contain:

#PCDATA, abbr, archref, bibref, emph, expan, extptr, extref, lb, linkgrp, ptr, ref, title

May occur within:

profiledesc

Attributes:

ALTRENDER	#IMPLIED, CDATA
AUDIENCE	#IMPLIED, external, internal
ENCODINGANALOG	#IMPLIED, CDATA
ID	#IMPLIED, ID

Example:

```
<descrules>Finding aid prepared using
   <title render="italic">Rules for Archival Description</title>
</descrules>
```

<did> Descriptive Identification

Description:

A required wrapper element that bundles other elements identifying core information about the described materials in either Archival Description <archdesc> or a Component <c>. The various <did> subelements are intended for brief, clearly designated statements of information and, except for <note>, do not require Paragraphs <p> to enter text.

The <did> groups elements that constitute a good basic description of an archival unit. This grouping ensures that the same data elements and structure are available at every level of description within the EAD hierarchy. It facilitates the retrieval or other output of a cohesive body of elements for resource discovery and recognition.

The <did> in <archdesc> is sometimes called the high level <did>, because it describes the collection as a whole. Consider using the following elements for this high level <did>: <head>, <origination>, <unittitle>, <physdesc>, <repository>, and <abstract>. The <unitid> and <physloc> elements are suggested if applicable to a repository's practice. A <did> within a Component <c> can be less complete, and might have only a <container> or <unitid> and a <unittitle>.

May contain:

abstract, container, dao, daogrp, head, langmaterial, materialspec, note, origination, physdesc, physloc, repository, unitdate, unitid, unittitle

May occur within:

archdesc, archdescgrp, c, c01, c02, c03, c04, c05, c06, c07, c08, c09, c10, c11, c12

Attributes:

ALTRENDER	#IMPLIED, CDATA
AUDIENCE	#IMPLIED, external, internal
ENCODINGANALOG	#IMPLIED, CDATA
ID	#IMPLIED, ID

<did>

Examples:

1.
```
<archdesc type="inventory" level="subgrp">
   <did>
      <head>Overview of the Records</head>
      <repository label="Repository:">
         <corpname>Minnesota Historical Society</corpname>
      </repository>
      <origination label="Creator:">Minnesota. Game and Fish
         Department</origination>
      <unittitle label="Title:">Game laws violation records,
      </unittitle>
      <unitdate label="Dates:">1908-1928</unitdate>
      <abstract label="Abstract:">Records of prosecutions for and
         seizures of property resulting from violation of the
         state's hunting and fishing laws.</abstract>
      <physdesc label="Quantity:">2.25 cu. ft. (7 v. and 1 folder
         in 3 boxes)</physdesc>
      <physloc label="Location:">See Detailed Description section
         for box location</physloc>
   </did> . . .
</archdesc>
```

2.
```
<archdesc level="collection">
   <did>
      <unittitle>Early Durham Cartularies</unittitle>
      <unitid>GB-0033-DCD</unitid>
      <unitdate label="Date range:" normal="1220/1230">compiled
         between 1220 and 1230, with later additions</unitdate>
      <physdesc label="Extent:">1 cartulary (175ff. and inserts),
         1 fragment and 1 [photostat of] fragment.</physdesc>
      <repository label="Repository:">Durham University Library,
         Archives and Special Collections</repository>
      <origination label="Origination:">early cartularies
         produced by the Durham monastic administration.
      </origination>
   </did>
</archdesc>
```

3.
```
<dsc type="combined">
   <c01 level="series">
      <did>
         <unittitle>Series 1: Correspondence,</unittitle>
         <unitdate type="inclusive">1943-1978</unitdate>
         <physdesc><extent>2.5 linear ft. </extent>(5 document
            boxes)</physdesc>
      </did>
      <scopecontent>[...]</scopecontent>
      <c02 level="subseries">
         <did>
            <unittitle>Subseries 1.1: Outgoing Correspondence,
               </unittitle>
            <unitdate type="inclusive">1943-1969</unitdate>
            <physdesc><extent>0.75 linear ft.</extent></physdesc>
         </did>
         <c03 level="file">
            <did>
               <physloc audience="internal">B:14:D</physloc>
               <container type="box">1</container>
               <container type="folder">1</container>
               <unittitle>Abbinger-Aldrich</unittitle>
               <physdesc><extent>14 letters</extent></physdesc>
            </did>
         </c03>
      </c02>
   </c01>
</dsc>
```

<dimensions> Dimensions

Description:

A subelement of <physdesc> for information about the size of the materials being described; usually includes numerical data. Measurements may be expressed in any convenient unit. Attributes may be used when the unit of measurement or type of dimension is not clear in the finding aid text. The UNIT attribute specifies the kind of measurement, for example, "inches" or "meters." The TYPE attribute specifies the kind of dimensions being measured, for example, "height" or "circumference." Multiple dimensions, for example, height-by-width, can be tagged in a single <dimensions> element or in separate <dimensions> with distinctive attribute values.

Do not confuse with the <extent> element, which is used to tag the quantity of described materials.

May contain:

#PCDATA, abbr, archref, bibref, dimensions, emph, expan, extptr, extref, lb, linkgrp, ptr, ref, title

May occur within:

dimensions, physdesc

Attributes:

ALTRENDER	#IMPLIED, CDATA
AUDIENCE	#IMPLIED, external, internal
ENCODINGANALOG	#IMPLIED, CDATA
ID	#IMPLIED, ID
LABEL	#IMPLIED, CDATA
TYPE	#IMPLIED, CDATA
UNIT	#IMPLIED, CDATA

Example:

```
<dsc type="in-depth">
   <head>Handlist</head>
   <c01>
      <did>
         <unittitle>Cartuarium vetus</unittitle>
         <physdesc>3 paper leaves; 1 parchment on paper leaf; 175
            leaves, 4 inserts, 2 schedules, parchment; 4 paper
            leaves <dimensions>approximately 230 mm x 163
            mm.</dimensions>
         </physdesc>
      </did>
   </c01> . . .
</dsc>
```

<div> Text Division

Description:

A generic element that designates a major section of text within <frontmatter>. Examples of these text divisions include a title page, preface, acknowledgments, or instructions for using a finding aid. Use the <head> element to identify the <div>'s purpose.

May contain:

address, blockquote, chronlist, div, head, list, note, p, table

May occur within:

div, frontmatter

Attributes:

ALTRENDER	#IMPLIED, CDATA
AUDIENCE	#IMPLIED, external, internal
ID	#IMPLIED, ID

Examples:

1.
```
<frontmatter>
   <titlepage>[...]</titlepage>
   <div>
      <head>Acknowledgements</head>
      <p>The University of California, Irvine Libraries wishes to
         acknowledge the generosity of the family of Edgar Holden
         for an endowment in support of the processing and
         maintenance of this collection and the University of
         California Office of the President for grant funding in
         support of the encoding of this and other finding aids
         using the Encoded Archival Description standard.</p>
   </div> . . .
</frontmatter>
```

<div>

2.

```
<frontmatter>
   <titlepage>
      <titleproper>Inventory of the Rietta Hines Herbert Papers,
         1940-1969</titleproper>
      <author>Processed by: Debra Carter</author>
      <publisher>Schomburg Center for Research in Black
         Culture<lb/>
      The New York Public Library</publisher>
      <date>August, 1977</date>
      &schtp;
      <p> &copy; <date>1999 </date> The New York Public Library,
         Astor, Lenox and Tilden Foundations.  All rights
         reserved.</p>
   </titlepage>
   <div>
      <head>Preface</head>
      <p>This inventory is one of several prepared as a part of
         the archival preservation program at the Schomburg
         Center for Research in Black Culture, a research
         division of The New York Public Library.</p>
      <p>The Schomburg archival preservation program involves the
         organization and preservation of primary source material
         held by the Center and of significance to the study of
         the Black Experience. It furthermore includes the
         preparation of detailed inventories of these records,
         making the information contained therein accessible as
         well as available to scholars.</p>
      <p>The necessary staff and supplies for this program were
         made available through a combination of Library,
         National Endowment for the Humanities grant, and State
         of New York grant funds.</p>
   </div>
</frontmatter>
```

<dsc> Description of Subordinate Components

Description:

A wrapper element that bundles information about the hierarchical groupings of the materials being described. The subordinate components can be presented in several different forms or levels of descriptive detail, which are identified by the element's required TYPE attribute. For example, "analyticover" identifies an overview description of series and subseries, which might be followed by a second <dsc> with the TYPE attribute set to "in-depth" that provides a more detailed listing of the content of the materials, including information about the container numbers associated with those materials. The TYPE attribute value "combined" is used when the description of a series is followed immediately by a listing of the contents of that series. The TYPE attribute "othertype" is for models that do not follow any of the above-mentioned formats, in which case the OTHERTYPE attribute can then be used to specify a particular presentation model.

See also related elements <c> and <c01> through <c12>.

May contain:

address, blockquote, c, c01, chronlist, dsc, head, list, note, p, table, thead

May occur within:

archdesc, c, c01, c02, c03, c04, c05, c06, c07, c08, c09, c10, c11, c12, dsc

Attributes:

ALTRENDER	#IMPLIED, CDATA
AUDIENCE	#IMPLIED, external, internal
ENCODINGANALOG	#IMPLIED, CDATA
ID	#IMPLIED, ID
OTHERTYPE	#IMPLIED, NMTOKEN
TPATTERN	#IMPLIED, NMTOKEN
TYPE	#REQUIRED, analyticover, combined, in-depth, othertype

<dsc>

Examples:

1.

```
<dsc type="combined">
  <c01 level="series">
    <did>
      <unittitle>Activities, </unittitle>
      <unitdate type="inclusive">1965-1971</unitdate>
      <physdesc><extent>0.3 linear ft.</extent></physdesc>
    </did>
    <scopecontent>
      <p>The Activities series gives examples of the types of
        activities offered at the camp.  The folders contain
        <genreform>reports,</genreform>
        <genreform>schedules,</genreform> and
        <genreform>inventories</genreform> from each activity
        area of the camp.  These records are predominantly
        from the late 1960s and early 1970s and replicate
        some of the information found in the staff
        manuals.</p>
    </scopecontent>
    <c02 level="file">
      <did>
        <container label="Box" type="box">1</container>
        <unittitle>General, </unittitle>
        <unitdate type="inclusive">1970-1971</unitdate>
      </did>
    </c02>
    <c02 level="file">
      <did>
        <container type="box">1</container>
        <unittitle>Camp Crafts, </unittitle>
        <unitdate>1967</unitdate>
      </did>
    </c02>
    <c02 level="file">
      <did>
        <container type="box">1</container>
        <unittitle>Education Program, </unittitle>
        <unitdate>1967</unitdate>
      </did>
    </c02>
    <c02 level="file">
      <did>
        <container type="box">1</container>
        <unittitle>Expressive Arts, </unittitle>
        <unitdate>1970</unitdate>
      </did>
    </c02> . . .
  </c01> . . .
</dsc>
```

2.

```
<dsc type="analyticover">
   <c01 level="series">
      <did>
         <unitid>1-429-1</unitid>
         <unittitle>Forest Stand Maps by Township and Basemap
            </unittitle>
         <unitdate type="inclusive">1958-1979</unitdate>
         <physdesc><extent>36 ft. (approx. 1700 sheets)</extent>
            of <genreform>cartographic records.</genreform>
         </physdesc>
         <materialspec>Scale: predominantly 4 inches to 1 mile
            (1:15,840)</materialspec>
      </did>
      <scopecontent><p>Series consists of forest stand maps.  A
         map sheet was created for each township of the surveyed
         section of the province and for each basemap area in
         unsurveyed areas.</p> . . .
      </scopecontent>
   </c01>
   <c01 level="series">
      <did>
         <unitid>RG 1-429-2</unitid>
         <unittitle>Forest Stand Map Composites</unittitle>
         <unitdate type="inclusive">1958-1971</unitdate>
         <physdesc><extent>ca.70</extent><genreform>maps
            </genreform></physdesc>
         <materialspec>Scale: 1 inch to 1 mile</materialspec>
      </did>
      <scopecontent><p>Series consists of composite maps  of the
         forest resource inventory data from all the townships
         within a Forestry Management Unit.  The composites offer
         a broader view of an area than the township/basemaps,
         however the forest stand statistics are quite small and
         difficult to read.</p> . . .
      </scopecontent>
   </c01> . . .
</dsc>
```

<dsc>

3.

```
<dsc type="in-depth">
   <c01 level="series">
      <did>
         <unittitle>Series 1: Administrative Records, </unittitle>
         <unitdate type="inclusive">1912-1956.</unitdate>
      </did>
      <c02>
         <did>
            <container id="mss92-894c-bx1" type="box">Box
               1</container>
            <container parent="mss92-894c-bx1" label="Folder"
               type="folder">7-8 </container>
            <unittitle>Annual reports, </unittitle>
            <unitdate type="inclusive">1912-16, 1922</unitdate>
         </did>
      </c02>
      <c02>
         <did>
            <container parent="mss92-894c-bx1" label="Folder"
               type="folder">9 </container>
            <unittitle>Board of Directors&mdash;Minutes and
               correspondence, </unittitle>
            <unitdate type="inclusive">1947-1949</unitdate>
         </did>
      </c02>
      <c02>
         <did>
            <container parent="mss92-894c-bx1" label="Folder"
               type="folder">10 </container>
            <unittitle>Contracts and specifications for
               construction of nurses' quarters, </unittitle>
            <unitdate>ca. 1947</unitdate>
         </did>
      </c02>
      <c02>
         <did>
            <container parent="mss92-894c-bx1" label="Folder"
               type="folder">11 </container>
            <unittitle>Marin County Reports, </unittitle>
            <unitdate type="inclusive">1955-1956</unitdate>
         </did>
      </c02>
   </c01>
   <c01 level="series">
      <did>
         <unittitle>Series 3: Philip King Brown, </unittitle>
         <unitdate type="inclusive">1910-1931, n.d.</unitdate>
      </did>
      <c02>
         <did>
            <container parent="mss92-894c-bx1" label="Folder"
               type="folder">21 </container>
            <unittitle>Correspondence, </unittitle>
            <unitdate type="inclusive">1910-1931</unitdate>
         </did>
      </c02>
```

```
      <c02>
         <did>
            <container parent="mss92-894c-bx1" label="Folder"
               type="folder">22 </container>
            <unittitle>Writings, </unittitle>
            <unitdate>n.d.</unitdate>
         </did>
      </c02> . . .
   </c01>
</dsc>
```

<dscgrp> Description of Subordinate Components Group

Description:

A wrapper element used only within the <archdescgrp> subelement of <eadgrp> in the EAD Group Document Type Definition. The <dscgrp> contains two or more <ead> encoded finding aids, one after the other.

See also the <eadgrp> element.

May contain:

address, blockquote, chronlist, ead, head, list, note, p, table

May occur within:

archdescgrp

Attributes:

ALTRENDER	#IMPLIED, CDATA
AUDIENCE	#IMPLIED, external, internal
ENCODINGANALOG	#IMPLIED, CDATA
ID	#IMPLIED, ID

<ead> Encoded Archival Description

Description:

The outermost wrapper element for an information access tool known generically as a finding aid. A finding aid establishes physical and intellectual control over many types of archival materials and helps researchers understand and access the materials being described. The <ead> element defines a particular instance of a document encoded with the EAD Document Type Definition. It contains a required <eadheader>, optional <frontmatter>, and a required <archdesc> element, in that order.

The AUDIENCE attribute value may be set to "external" to display data in all subelements, unless the value is changed for a specific element. To facilitate use of EAD as XML Schema, an XMLNS attribute may be switched on in the default DTD by making the following change:

<!ENTITY % namespace 'IGNORE' >	to	<!ENTITY % namespace 'INCLUDE' >

A separate Document Type Definition called EAD Group can be used to bundle <ead> finding aids that describe different parts of a collection that have been dispersed among various institutions or custodial units. See the <eadgrp> element description for additional information.

May contain:

archdesc, eadheader, frontmatter

May occur within:

dscgrp

Attributes:

ALTRENDER	#IMPLIED, CDATA
AUDIENCE	#IMPLIED, external, internal
ID	#IMPLIED, ID
RELATEDENCODING	#IMPLIED, CDATA

Example:

The following elements constitute the minimum set of elements for an EAD instance (i.e., those required by the DTD). Although the Description of Subordinate Components <dsc> is not itself required, if it is used its TYPE attribute must be set. See Appendix C for fully encoded examples.

```
<ead>
   <eadheader>
      <eadid>[...]</eadid>
      <filedesc>
         <titlestmt>
            <titleproper>[...]</titleproper>
         </titlestmt>
      </filedesc>
   </eadheader>
   <archdesc level="fonds">
      <did>[...]</did>
      <dsc type="combined">[...]</dsc>
   </archdesc>
</ead>
```

<eadgrp> EAD Group

Description:

A wrapper element in the EAD Group Document Type Definition (DTD), which allows several archival finding aids encoded with the EAD DTD to be combined into a single document. The EAD Group DTD was designed as a "super wrapper" for multiple finding aids describing materials dispersed among various administrative bodies, i.e., among multiple repositories or among different custodial divisions within a single repository. The EAD Group approach makes it possible to summarize the dispersed materials in <archdescgrp> and to connect closely finding aids that should be viewed together to understand the dispersed materials. Examples of an <eadgrp> might be a set of finding aids to Mark Twain papers held in several repositories, or finding aids for moving image material and manuscript material from a single collection that was separated according to formats among custodial departments.

The <eadgrp> begins with a required <eadheader>, followed by an optional <frontmatter>, then a required <archdescgrp>. The <archdescgrp> contains not only typical <archdesc> subelements such as <did> and <bioghist>, but a special <dscgrp> to bundle the <ead> instances as subordinate components.

The EAD Group DTD should not be used for assembling documentation about multiple accessions of a single collection or fonds held by a single administrative unit; such accessions should be described in a single <ead> instance.

Use the <ead><archref> element to link between a finding aid for a large body of records and the finding aids for its subordinate series. One example of this situation is a government agency record group with series so large that each series has a separate finding aid.

To facilitate use of EAD Group as XML Schema, an XMLNS attribute may be switched on in the default DTD by making the following change:

<!ENTITY % namespace 'IGNORE' >	to	<!ENTITY % namespace 'INCLUDE' >

May contain:

archdescgrp, eadheader, frontmatter

May occur within:

Not applicable; highest-level element in EAD Group DTD.

<eadgrp>

Attributes:

ALTRENDER	#IMPLIED, CDATA
AUDIENCE	#IMPLIED, external, internal
ID	#IMPLIED, ID
RELATEDENCODING	#IMPLIED, CDATA

<eadheader> EAD Header

Description:

A wrapper element for bibliographic and descriptive information about the finding aid document rather than the archival materials being described. The <eadheader> is modeled on the Text Encoding Initiative (TEI) header element to encourage uniformity in the provision of metadata across document types.

The <eadheader> is required, because information that was often unrecorded for a local paper finding aid is essential in a machine-readable environment. Four subelements are available, which must occur in the following order: <eadid> (required), <filedesc> (required), <profiledesc> (optional), and <revisiondesc> (optional). These elements and their subelements provide: a unique identification code for the finding aid; bibliographic information, such as the author and title of the finding aid; information about the encoding of the finding aid; and statements about significant revisions.

The FINDAIDSTATUS attribute can be used to indicate how complete or polished the information in the finding aid is. The COUNTRYENCODING, DATEENCODING, LANGENCODING, REPOSITORYENCODING, and SCRIPTENCODING attributes are used to specify the ISO standards from which code values for other attributes, such as COUNTRYCODE in <eadid> and <unitid>, are taken.

Some or all of the <eadheader> subelements can be used to display title page information. Alternatively, the <eadheader> can be blocked from display by setting the AUDIENCE attribute to "internal" and using the <frontmatter> <titlepage> elements to create a title page.

May contain:

eadid, filedesc, profiledesc, revisiondesc

May occur within:

ead, eadgrp

<eadheader>

Attributes:

ALTRENDER	#IMPLIED, CDATA
AUDIENCE	#IMPLIED, external, internal
COUNTRYENCODING	iso3166-1, NMTOKEN
DATEENCODING	iso8601, NMTOKEN
ENCODINGANALOG	#IMPLIED, CDATA
FINDAIDSTATUS	#IMPLIED, NMTOKEN
ID	#IMPLIED, ID
LANGENCODING	iso639-2b, NMTOKEN
RELATEDENCODING	#IMPLIED, CDATA
REPOSITORYENCODING	iso15511, NMTOKEN
SCRIPTENCODING	iso15924, NMTOKEN

Example:

Following are the required <eadheader> elements. See fully encoded examples in Appendix C for more detail.

```
<eadheader>
   <eadid>[...]</eadid>
   <filedesc>
      <titlestmt>
         <titleproper>[...]</titleproper>
      </titlestmt>
   </filedesc>
</eadheader>
```

<eadid> EAD Identifier

Description:

A required subelement of <eadheader> that designates a unique code for a particular EAD finding aid document.

Two of the attributes, COUNTRYCODE and MAINAGENCYCODE, are required to make the <eadid> compliant with ISAD(G) element 3.1.1. MAINAGENCYCODE provides the ISO 15511 code for the institution that maintains the finding aid (which may not be the same as the institution that is the custodian of the materials described). COUNTRYCODE supplies the ISO 3166-1 code for the country of the maintenance agency. In addition to these two attributes, it is recommended that repositories also use at least one of the following attributes: URL, PUBLICID, or IDENTIFIER to make the <eadid> globally unique. PUBLICID should be a Formal Public Identifier, URL an absolute or relative address, and IDENTIFIER a machine-readable unique identifier for the finding aid file. (The proper syntax for PUBLICID is defined in ISO/IEC 9070:1991 Information technology – SGML support facilities – Registration procedures for public text owner identifiers.)

May contain:

#PCDATA

May occur within:

eadheader

Attributes:

COUNTRYCODE	#IMPLIED, NMTOKEN
ENCODINGANALOG	#IMPLIED, CDATA
IDENTIFIER	#IMPLIED, CDATA
MAINAGENCYCODE	#IMPLIED, NMTOKEN
PUBLICID	#IMPLIED, CDATA
URL	#IMPLIED, CDATA
URN	#IMPLIED, CDATA

Examples:

```
<eadid countrycode="us" mainagencycode="txu-hu"
   publicid="-//us::txu-hu//TEXT us::txu-hu::hrc.00001//EN"
   url="www.lib.utexas.edu/taro/hrc/00001.xml">hrc.00001
</eadid>
```

<edition> Edition

Description:

A version of the finding aid or other bibliographic entity. When used in the <editionstmt> subelement of the <eadheader> or in the <titlepage> subelement of <frontmatter>, the <edition> refers to the version of the finding aid. A new edition of a finding aid represents substantial additions or changes and should supersede previous online versions. When used in a Bibliographic Reference <bibref>, the <edition> element specifies the version of a published work.

May contain:

#PCDATA, emph, extptr, lb, ptr

May occur within:

bibref, editionstmt, titlepage, unittitle

Attributes:

ALTRENDER	#IMPLIED, CDATA
AUDIENCE	#IMPLIED, external, internal
ENCODINGANALOG	#IMPLIED, CDATA
ID	#IMPLIED, ID

Examples:

```
<eadheader audience="internal" langencoding="iso639-2b">
   <eadid>[...]</eadid>
   <filedesc>
      <titlestmt>[...]</titlestmt>
      <editionstmt>
         <edition>2nd ed.</edition>
         <p>This edition reflects substantial additions to the
            collection in 1994.</p>
      </editionstmt>
   </filedesc> . . .
</eadheader>
```

<editionstmt> Edition Statement

Description:

An optional subelement within the <filedesc> portion of the <eadheader> element that groups information about a finding aid edition by providing an <edition> element as well as a Paragraph <p> element for narrative statements.

May contain:

edition, p

May occur within:

filedesc

Attributes:

ALTRENDER	#IMPLIED, CDATA
AUDIENCE	#IMPLIED, external, internal
ENCODINGANALOG	#IMPLIED, CDATA
ID	#IMPLIED, ID

Examples:

1.
```
<eadheader audience="internal" langencoding="iso639-2b">
   <eadid>[...]</eadid>
   <filedesc>
      <titlestmt>[...]</titlestmt>
      <editionstmt>
         <edition>2nd ed.</edition>
         <p>This edition reflects substantial additions to the
            collection in 1994.</p>
      </editionstmt>
   </filedesc> . . .
</eadheader>
```

<editionstmt>

2.
```
<filedesc>
   <titlestmt>
      <titleproper>Etat sommaire des fonds d'archives
         priv&eacute;es du Centre historique des Archives
         nationales</titleproper>
      <subtitle> S&eacute;ries AP et AB XIX</subtitle>
      <author>Instrument de recherche r&eacute;dig&eacute; par
         Claire Sibille, avec la collaboration de George-
         Andr&eacute;e Banguio et de Violaine Le N&eacute;naon,
         sous la direction de Christine Nougaret</author>
   </titlestmt>
   <editionstmt>
      <edition> Premi&egrave;re &Eacute;dition</edition>
   </editionstmt>
   <publicationstmt>
      <publisher>Centre historique des Archives nationales de
         France (CHAN)</publisher>
      <address>
         <addressline>60 rue des Francs-Bourgeois</addressline>
         <addressline>F-75141 PARIS CEDEX 03</addressline>
      </address>
      <date>mai 2001</date>
   </publicationstmt>
</filedesc>
```

<emph> Emphasis

Description:

A formatting element for marking words or phrases that are stressed or emphasized for linguistic effect. Use the RENDER attribute to specify the kind of emphasis, e.g., bold or italics.

When the content of an entire element should always be rendered in italics or some other display feature, use the style sheet functions instead of the <emph> element.

May contain:

#PCDATA, abbr, archref, bibref, emph, expan, extptr, extref, lb, linkgrp, ptr, ref, title

May occur within:

abstract, addressline, archref, author, bibref, bibseries, container, corpname, creation, date, descrules, dimensions, edition, emph, entry, event, extent, extref, extrefloc, famname, function, genreform, geogname, head, head01, head02, imprint, item, label, langmaterial, language, langusage, legalstatus, materialspec, name, num, occupation, origination, p, persname, physdesc, physfacet, physloc, publisher, ref, refloc, repository, resource, runner, sponsor, subarea, subject, subtitle, title, titleproper, unitdate, unitid, unittitle

Attributes:

ALTRENDER	#IMPLIED, CDATA
ID	#IMPLIED, ID
RENDER	#IMPLIED, altrender, bold, bolddoublequote, bolditalic, boldsinglequote, boldsmcaps, boldunderline, doublequote, italic, nonproport, singlequote, smcaps, sub, super, underline

Example:

```
<abstract label="Abstract">Papers document Donald C. Stone's work
   with Ornstein and Swencionis on the <emph
   render="italic">est</emph> Outcome Project, and the
   development of his doctoral research, including his various
   publications on the human potential movement, up to the
   completion of his doctoral dissertation.</abstract>
```

<entry> Table Entry

Description:

A formatting element that designates the contents of a cell in a table. A cell is the intersection of a row and a column. The <entry> attributes control cell spanning, alignment of the contents, and the rules on the cell edges. The attributes can be specified for <entry> or inherited from the nearest of the following table elements: <table>, <tgroup>, <colspec>, <tbody>, or <row>.

Three attributes are used together to force horizontal alignment on a specific character, such as a decimal point. The ALIGN attribute must be set to "char" (align="char"). The CHAR attribute should be set to the specific character on which the text will align (for example the decimal point, char="."). The CHAROFF attribute controls the position of the alignment by naming the percentage of the current column width that is to the left of the alignment character (for example, charoff="30").

The extent of a horizontal span is determined by naming the first column (NAMEST) and the last column (NAMEEND) in the span.

By convention, the specified rule is printed or displayed to the right of the column. External rules are specified using the FRAME attribute of the <table> element, horizontal rules are specified using ROWSEP.

May contain:

#PCDATA, abbr, address, archref, bibref, corpname, date, emph, expan, extptr, extref, famname, function, genreform, geogname, lb, linkgrp, list, name, note, num, occupation, origination, pcrsnamc, ptr, rcf, rcpository, subject, title, unitdate, unittitle

May occur within:

row

Attributes:

ALIGN	#IMPLIED, left, right, center, justify, char
ALTRENDER	#IMPLIED, CDATA
AUDIENCE	#IMPLIED, external, internal
CHAR	#IMPLIED, CDATA
CHAROFF	#IMPLIED, NMTOKEN
COLNAME	#IMPLIED, NMTOKEN
COLSEP	#IMPLIED, NMTOKEN
ID	#IMPLIED, ID
MOREROWS	#IMPLIED, NMTOKEN
NAMEEND	#IMPLIED, NMTOKEN
NAMEST	#IMPLIED, NMTOKEN
ROWSEP	#IMPLIED, NMTOKEN
VALIGN	#IMPLIED, top, middle, bottom

Example:

```
<table frame="none">
   <tgroup cols="3">
      <colspec colnum="1" colname="1" align="left" colwidth="50pt"/>
      <colspec colnum="2" colname="2" align="left" colwidth="50pt"/>
      <colspec colnum="3" colname="3" align="left" colwidth="50pt"/>
      <thead>
         <row>
            <entry colname="1">Major Family Members</entry>
            <entry colname="2">Spouses</entry>
            <entry colname="3">Children</entry>
         </row>
      </thead>
      <tbody>
         <row>
            <entry colname="1">John Albemarle (1760-1806)</entry>
            <entry colname="2">Mary Frances Delaney (1769-
               1835)</entry>
            <entry colname="3">John Delaney Albemarle (1787-
               1848)</entry>
         </row> . . .
      </tbody>
   </tgroup>
</table>
```

<event> Event

Description:

That part of a Chronology List Item <chronitem> which describes or names something that happened. The <event> is paired with a <date> (a single date or date range) and can be grouped with other events in <eventgrp>, if multiple events need to be associated with the same <date>.

See related element Chronology List <chronlist>.

May contain:

#PCDATA, abbr, address, archref, bibref, blockquote, chronlist, corpname, date, emph, expan, extptr, extref, famname, function, genreform, geogname, lb, linkgrp, list, name, note, num, occupation, origination, persname, ptr, ref, repository, subject, table, title, unitdate, unittitle

May occur within:

chronitem, eventgrp

Attributes:

ALTRENDER	#IMPLIED, CDATA
AUDIENCE	#IMPLIED, external, internal
ID	#IMPLIED, ID

Example:

```
<bioghist>
   <head>Biographical Note</head>
   <chronlist>
      <chronitem>
         <date>1892, May 7</date>
         <event>Born, <geogname>Glencoe, Ill.</geogname></event>
      </chronitem>
      <chronitem>
         <date>1915</date>
         <event>A.B., <corpname>Yale University, </corpname>New
            Haven, Conn.</event>
      </chronitem>
      <chronitem>
         <date>1916</date>
         <event>Married <persname>Ada Hitchcock</persname>
         </event>
      </chronitem>
      <chronitem>
         <date>1917-1919</date>
         <event>Served in <corpname>United States
            Army</corpname></event>
      </chronitem>
   </chronlist>
</bioghist>
```

<eventgrp> Event Group

Description:

An element within a Chronology List Item <chronitem> that bundles multiple <event>s associated with the same <date>.

See related element Chronology List <chronlist>.

May contain:

event

May occur within:

chronitem

Attributes:

ALTRENDER	#IMPLIED, CDATA
AUDIENCE	#IMPLIED, external, internal
ID	#IMPLIED, ID

Example:

```
<bioghist>
   <head>Biographical Note</head>
   <chronlist>
      <chronitem>
         <date normal="19010718">1901 July 18</date>
         <event>Born, Holsterhausen, Westphalia, Germany </event>
      </chronitem>
      <chronitem>
         <date normal="1918">1918</date>
         <event>Member and active participant of Sokoly, Polish
            insurrection against the Germans</event>
      </chronitem>
      <chronitem>
         <date normal="1920">1920</date>
         <eventgrp>
            <event>Private, Polish Army, Polish-Russo War</event>
            <event>Graduated from Agricultural High School,
               People's University</event>
         </eventgrp>
      </chronitem> . . .
   </chronlist>
</bioghist>
```

<expan> Expansion

Description:

A generic element to designate the full form of a word that often appears as an abbreviation or acronym. Use the ABBR attribute to supply the abbreviated form for indexing or searching purposes.

See also related element Abbreviation <abbr>.

May contain:

#PCDATA

May occur within:

abstract, archref, bibref, container, creation, descrules, dimensions, emph, entry, event, extent, extref, extrefloc, item, label, langmaterial, langusage, materialspec, origination, p, physdesc, physfacet, physloc, ref, refloc, repository, subtitle, titleproper, unitdate, unitid, unittitle

Attributes:

ABBR	#IMPLIED, CDATA
ALTRENDER	#IMPLIED, CDATA
AUDIENCE	#IMPLIED, external, internal
ID	#IMPLIED, ID

Example:

```
<note>
   <p>
      <expan abbr="ALS">Autograph Letter Signed</expan>
   </p>
</note>
```

<extent> Extent

Description:

A <physdesc> subelement for information about the quantity of the materials being described or an expression of the physical space they occupy. Includes such traditional archival measurements as cubic and linear feet and meters; also includes counts of microfilm reels, photographs, or other special formats, the number of logical records in a database, or the volume of a data file in bytes.

Repeat the element when more than one type or unit of extent is provided, such as, when both linear feet and quantity of containers are given. Use the UNIT attribute to indicate the measurement unit, e.g., "bytes" or "cubic meter."

Use the <dimension> element when it is necessary to specify the size of the archival materials being described, for example, height and width.

May contain:

#PCDATA, abbr, archref, bibref, emph, expan, extptr, extref, lb, linkgrp, ptr, ref, title

May occur within:

physdesc

Attributes:

ALTRENDER	#IMPLIED, CDATA
AUDIENCE	#IMPLIED, external, internal
ENCODINGANALOG	#IMPLIED, CDATA
ID	#IMPLIED, ID
LABEL	#IMPLIED, CDATA
TYPE	#IMPLIED, CDATA
UNIT	#IMPLIED, CDATA

<extent>

Examples:

1.
```
<archdesc level="collection">
   <did>
      <origination>
         <persname encodinganalog="100" label="Creator:"
            source="lcnaf">Franklin, George A. (George
            Albert).</persname>
      </origination>
      <unittitle>The George Franklin Papers, </unittitle>
      <unitdate type="inclusive">1928-1972</unitdate>
      <physdesc>
         <extent>100 boxes; </extent>
         <extent>50 linear feet</extent>
      </physdesc>
   </did>
</archdesc>
```

2.
```
<c level="file">
   <did>
      <physloc audience="internal">B:14:D</physloc>
      <container type="box">1</container>
      <container type="folder">1</container>
      <unittitle>Abbinger-Aldrich</unittitle>
      <physdesc><extent>14 letters</extent></physdesc>
   </did>
</c>
```

<extptr> Extended Pointer

Description:

An empty linking element that uses attributes to connect the EAD document to an external electronic object, which is not part of the materials being described. Examples include graphic representations of a repository's seal or logo, and pointers to an institution's web page.

Use the ENTITYREF or HREF attribute to identify the external object.

Do not confuse with the Pointer <ptr> element, which is an internal link for movement from one place in a finding aid to another place in the same finding aid.

While XML Linking Language (XLink) Version 1.0, which is the basis for EAD linking elements, is a stable document, examples of EAD usage are hypothetical and have not been tested in real XLink-based applications. Those wishing to use XLink are encouraged to consult the specification available online at <http://www.w3.org/TR/xlink/>.

May contain:

EMPTY

May occur within:

abstract, addressline, archref, author, bibref, bibseries, container, corpname, creation, date, descrules, dimensions, edition, emph, entry, event, extent, extref, extrefloc, famname, function, genreform, geogname, head, head01, head02, imprint, item, label, langmaterial, language, langusage, legalstatus, materialspec, name, num, occupation, origination, p, persname, physdesc, physfacet, physloc, publisher, ref, refloc, repository, runner, sponsor, subarea, subject, subtitle, title, titleproper, unitdate, unitid, unittitle

Attributes:

ACTUATE	#IMPLIED, onload, onrequest, actuateother, actuatenone
ALTRENDER	#IMPLIED, CDATA
ARCROLE	#IMPLIED, CDATA
AUDIENCE	#IMPLIED, external, internal
ENTITYREF	#IMPLIED, ENTITY
HREF	#IMPLIED, CDATA
ID	#IMPLIED, ID
LINKTYPE	#FIXED, simple, simple
ROLE	#IMPLIED, CDATA
SHOW	#IMPLIED, new, replace, embed, showother, shownone
TITLE	#IMPLIED, CDATA
XPOINTER	#IMPLIED, CDATA

<extptr>

Example:

```
<frontmatter>
   <titlepage>
      <titleproper>Inventory of the Rietta Hines Herbert Papers,
         1940-1969</titleproper>
      <author>Processed by: Debra Carter</author>
      <publisher>Schomburg Center for Research in Black
         Culture<lb/>
      <extptr linktype="simple" entityref="phyllis" title="Image
         of Phyllis Wheatley" actuate="onload" show="embed"><lb/>
      The New York Public Library</publisher>
      <date>August, 1977</date>
      &schtp;
      <p> &copy; <date>1999 </date> The New York Public Library,
         Astor, Lenox and Tilden Foundations.  All rights
         reserved.</p>
   </titlepage>
</frontmatter>
```

<extptrloc> Extended Pointer Location

Description:

The location of an Extended Pointer <extptr> that is a resource in an extended link.

While XML Linking Language (XLink) Version 1.0, which is the basis for EAD linking elements, is a stable document, examples of EAD usage are hypothetical and have not been tested in real XLink-based applications. Those wishing to use XLink are encouraged to consult the specification available online at <http://www.w3.org/TR/xlink/>.

May contain:

EMPTY

May occur within:

daogrp, linkgrp

Attributes:

ALTRENDER	#IMPLIED, CDATA
AUDIENCE	#IMPLIED, external, internal
ENTITYREF	#IMPLIED, ENTITY
HREF	#IMPLIED, CDATA
ID	#IMPLIED, ID
LABEL	#IMPLIED, NMTOKEN
LINKTYPE	#FIXED, locator, locator
ROLE	#IMPLIED, CDATA
TITLE	#IMPLIED, CDATA
XPOINTER	#IMPLIED, CDATA

<extref> Extended Reference

Description:

A linking element that can include text and subelements as part of its reference to an electronic object that is external to the EAD document.

Use the ENTITYREF or HREF attribute to identify the external object.

Use the <ref> element to point to another location within the EAD document.

While XML Linking Language (XLink) Version 1.0, which is the basis for EAD linking elements, is a stable document, examples of EAD usage are hypothetical and have not been tested in real XLink-based applications. Those wishing to use XLink are encouraged to consult the specification available online at <http://www.w3.org/TR/xlink/>.

May contain:

#PCDATA, abbr, address, archref, bibref, blockquote, chronlist, corpname, date, emph, expan, extptr, famname, function, genreform, geogname, lb, list, name, note, num, occupation, origination, persname, ptr, ref, repository, subject, table, title, unitdate, unittitle

May occur within:

abstract, archref, bibliography, bibref, container, creation, descrules, dimensions, emph, entry, event, extent, item, label, langmaterial, langusage, materialspec, origination, otherfindaid, p, physdesc, physfacet, physloc, ref, relatedmaterial, repository, separatedmaterial, unitdate, unitid, unittitle

Attributes:

ACTUATE	#IMPLIED, onload, onrequest, actuateother, actuatenone
ALTRENDER	#IMPLIED, CDATA
ARCROLE	#IMPLIED, CDATA
AUDIENCE	#IMPLIED, external, internal
ENTITYREF	#IMPLIED, ENTITY
HREF	#IMPLIED, CDATA
ID	#IMPLIED, ID
LINKTYPE	#FIXED, simple, simple
ROLE	#IMPLIED, CDATA
SHOW	#IMPLIED, new, replace, embed, showother, shownone
TITLE	#IMPLIED, CDATA
XPOINTER	#IMPLIED, CDATA

Example:

```
<bioghist>
   <head>Chronology</head>
   <chronlist> . . .
      <chronitem>
         <date normal="199510">October 1995</date>
         <event>
            <extref linktype="simple" entityref="nobelsite"
               title="Nobel Prize eMuseum" actuate="onrequest"
               show="new">Awarded Nobel Prize in Physics by the
               Royal Swedish Academy of Sciences.</extref>
         </event>
      </chronitem> . . .
   </chronlist>
</bioghist>
```

<extrefloc> Extended Reference Location

Description:

The location of an Extended Reference <extref> that is a resource in an extended link.

While XML Linking Language (XLink) Version 1.0, which is the basis for EAD linking elements, is a stable document, examples of EAD usage are hypothetical and have not been tested in real XLink-based applications. Those wishing to use XLink are encouraged to consult the specification available online at <http://www.w3.org/TR/xlink/>.

May contain:

#PCDATA, abbr, address, blockquote, chronlist, corpname, date, emph, expan, extptr, famname, function, genreform, geogname, lb, list, name, note, num, occupation, origination, persname, ptr, repository, subject, table, unitdate, unittitle

May occur within:

daogrp, linkgrp

Attributes:

ALTRENDER	#IMPLIED, CDATA
AUDIENCE	#IMPLIED, external, internal
ENTITYREF	#IMPLIED, ENTITY
HREF	#IMPLIED, CDATA
ID	#IMPLIED, ID
LABEL	#IMPLIED, NMTOKEN
LINKTYPE	#FIXED, locator, locator
ROLE	#IMPLIED, CDATA
TITLE	#IMPLIED, CDATA
XPOINTER	#IMPLIED, CDATA

Example:

```
<relatedmaterial>
   <p>The Society also has records of other conservation
      organizations in Minnesota.</p>
   <p>
      <linkgrp linktype="extended">
         <extrefloc
            href="http://www.someserver.edu/findaids/3270.xml">
            <archref>Issak Walton League of Minnesota</archref>
         </extrefloc>
         <extrefloc
            href="http://www.someserver.edu/findaids/9248.xml">
            <archref>Minnesota Audubon Council</archref>
         </extrefloc>
         <extrefloc entityref="FBWW">
            <archref>Friends of the Boundary Waters
               Wilderness</archref>
         </extrefloc>
         <extrefloc
            href="http://www.someserver.edu/findaids/23145.sgm">
            <archref>Minnesota Emergency Conservation
               Committee</archref>
         </extrefloc>
      </linkgrp>
   </p>
</relatedmaterial>
```

<famname> Family Name

Description:

The proper noun designation for a group of persons closely related by blood or persons who form a household. Includes single families and family groups, e.g., Patience Parker Family and Parker Family.

All names in a finding aid do not have to be tagged. One option is to tag those names for which access other than basic, undifferentiated keyword retrieval is desired. Use of authorized forms is recommended to facilitate access to the names within and across finding aid systems. The <famname> element may be used in text elements such as <p>. To indicate a family name with major representation in the materials being described, nest <famname> within the <controlaccess> element.

The ROLE attribute can be used to specify the relationship(s) of the name to the materials being described, for example, "compiler," "creator," "collector," or "subject." The NORMAL attribute can be used to provide the authority form of a name that has been encoded with <famname> in narrative text, e.g., within a paragraph. The AUTHFILENUMBER attribute can be used to identify a link to an authority file record that has more information about the name or cross references for alternative forms of the name and related names. Use the SOURCE attribute to specify the vocabulary from which the name has been taken and/or the RULES attribute to specify the descriptive rules followed when forming the name.

See also the related elements <controlaccess>, <corpname>, <persname>, and <name>.

The <famname> element is comparable to MARC fields 100, 600, 700.

May contain:

#PCDATA, emph, extptr, lb, ptr

May occur within:

bibref, controlaccess, entry, event, extref, extrefloc, indexentry, item, label, namegrp, origination, p, physdesc, physfacet, ref, refloc, unittitle

Attributes:

ALTRENDER	#IMPLIED, CDATA
AUDIENCE	#IMPLIED, external, internal
AUTHFILENUMBER	#IMPLIED, CDATA
ENCODINGANALOG	#IMPLIED, CDATA
ID	#IMPLIED, ID
NORMAL	#IMPLIED, CDATA
ROLE	#IMPLIED, CDATA
RULES	#IMPLIED, NMTOKEN
SOURCE	#IMPLIED, NMTOKEN

Examples:

1.
```
<indexentry>
   <famname>Hely-Hutchinson family</famname>
   <indexentry>
      <genreform> Pedigree, 20th cent.</genreform>
      <ref linktype="simple" role="internal" target="EngC5769-
         f74" show="replace" actuate="onrequest">MS. Eng. c.
         5769, fol. 74</ref>
   </indexentry>
</indexentry>
```

2.
```
<archdesc level="collection">
   <did>[...]</did> . . .
   <controlaccess>
      <head>Controlled Vocabulary Indexing Terms:</head>
      <controlaccess>
         <head>Subjects:</head>
         <famname encodinganalog="600" source="lcnaf">Ferry
            family.</famname>
         <geogname encodinganalog="651" source="lcsh">Ferry Field
            (University of Michigan)</geogname>
      </controlaccess>
   </controlaccess>
</archdesc>
```

<filedesc> File Description

Description:

A required subelement of the <eadheader> that bundles much of the bibliographic information about the finding aid, including its author, title, subtitle, and sponsor (all in the <titlestmt>), as well as the edition, publisher, publishing series, and related notes (encoded separately).

This element has been modeled on a Text Encoding Initiative (TEI) DTD element and includes the following subelements, in this order: a required <titlestmt>, an optional <editionstmt>, an optional <publicationstmt>, an optional <seriesstmt>, and an optional <notestmt>. The <filedesc> provides information that is helpful for citing a finding aid in a bibliography or footnote. Institutions that catalog finding aids separately from the archival materials being described might use the <filedesc> elements to build a basic bibliographic record for the finding aid.

Do not confuse with the <profiledesc> element, which describes the encoding of the finding aid. Do not confuse with <archdesc> elements, which refer to the materials being described rather than the finding aid itself.

May contain:

editionstmt, notestmt, publicationstmt, seriesstmt, titlestmt

May occur within:

eadheader

Attributes:

ALTRENDER	#IMPLIED, CDATA
AUDIENCE	#IMPLIED, external, internal
ENCODINGANALOG	#IMPLIED, CDATA
ID	#IMPLIED, ID

Examples:

1.
```
<eadheader>
   <eadid>[. . .]</eadid>
   <filedesc>
      <titlestmt>
         <titleproper>Guide to the Bank of Willows Records,
            <date>1880-1905</date>
         </titleproper>
      </titlestmt>
      <publicationstmt>
         &hdr-cst-spcoll;
         <date>&copy; 1999</date>
         <p>The Board of Trustees of Stanford University. All
         rights reserved.</p>
      </publicationstmt>
   </filedesc>
   <profiledesc>[. . .]</profiledesc>
</eadheader>
```

2.
```
<filedesc>
   <titlestmt>
      <titleproper>Inventory of the Otis Turner Papers, 1978-
         1990</titleproper>
      <author>Processed by Hanna Bailey</author>
   </titlestmt>
   <publicationstmt>
      &hdrscm;
      <p>&copy;
      <date>2000</date>
      The New York Public Library. Astor, Lenox and Tilden
         Foundations. All rights reserved.</p>
   </publicationstmt>
</filedesc>
```

<fileplan> File Plan

Description:

Information about any classification scheme used for arranging, storing, and retrieving the described materials by the parties originally responsible for creating or compiling them. A filing plan is usually identified by the type of system used, e.g., alphabetical, numerical, alpha-numerical, decimal, color-coded, etc. It is often hierarchical and may include the filing guidelines of the originating organization. Additional types include a drawing of a room layout or a scientific scheme.

Do not confuse with Other Finding Aid <otherfindaid> which contains references to additional descriptions of the material rather than descriptions of classification schemes by which the materials might still be arranged.

In EAD Version 1.0 <fileplan> was a subelement of Adjunct Descriptive Data <add>, which has been deprecated in EAD 2002 (see Appendix B). The new Description Group <descgrp> element, which can group any of the <did>-level elements (except the Description of Subordinate Components <dsc>), may be used to wrap elements where a group heading is desirable. The <descgrp> element can be used to replace <add> when converting finding aids encoded in EAD V1.0 to EAD 2002.

May contain:

address, blockquote, chronlist, fileplan, head, list, note, p, table

May occur within:

archdesc, archdescgrp, c, c01, c02, c03, c04, c05, c06, c07, c08, c09, c10, c11, c12, descgrp, fileplan

Attributes:

ALTRENDER	#IMPLIED, CDATA
AUDIENCE	#IMPLIED, external, internal
ENCODINGANALOG	#IMPLIED, CDATA
ID	#IMPLIED, ID

Example:

```
<fileplan>
   <head>File List</head>
   <note><p>The list below outlines the classification system
      used for the central files of Vice President Mondale's
      office. This structure assigned alpha-numeric codes to
      primary subjects and to secondary and tertiary subdivisions
      thereunder.</p>
   </note>
   <fileplan>
      <head>AGRICULTURE (AG)</head>
      <list type="ordered">
         <defitem>
            <label>1</label>
            <item>Home Economics</item>
         </defitem>
         <defitem>
            <label>2</label>
            <item>Horticulture</item>
         </defitem>
         <defitem>
            <label>3</label>
            <item>Marketing</item>
         </defitem>
         <defitem>
            <label>4</label>
            <item>Price Support</item>
         </defitem>
      </list>
   </fileplan>
   <fileplan>
      <head>ARTS (AR)</head>
      <list type="ordered">
         <defitem>
            <label>1</label>
            <item>Languages</item>
         </defitem>
         <defitem>
            <label>2</label>
            <item>Museums</item>
         </defitem>
         <defitem>
            <label>3</label>
            <item>Music</item>
         </defitem>
         <defitem>
            <label>4</label>
            <item>Painting/Drawing</item>
         </defitem>
      </list>
   </fileplan>
</fileplan>
```

<frontmatter> Front Matter

Description:

A wrapper element that bundles prefatory text found before the start of the Archival Description <archdesc>. It focuses on the creation, publication, or use of the finding aid rather than information about the materials being described. Examples include a title page, preface, dedication, and instructions for using a finding aid. The optional <titlepage> element within <frontmatter> can be used to repeat selected information from the <eadheader> to generate a title page that follows local preferences for sequencing information. The other <frontmatter> structures, such as a dedication, are encoded as Text Divisions <div>s, with a <head> element containing word(s) that identify the nature of the text.

May contain:

div, titlepage

May occur within:

ead, eadgrp

Attributes:

ALTRENDER	#IMPLIED, CDATA
AUDIENCE	#IMPLIED, external, internal
ID	#IMPLIED, ID

Example:

```
<frontmatter>
   <titlepage>
      <titleproper>Register of the Gibbons (Stuart C.) Papers,
         <date>1955-1964</date>
      </titleproper>
      <num>Collection number: Ms28</num>
      <publisher>San Joaquin County Historical Society and Museum
         <lb/>
         <extptr actuate="onload" show="embed
         entityref="sjmlogo">
         <lb/>
      Lodi, California</publisher>
      &tp-cstoh;
      <list type="deflist">
         <defitem>
            <label>Processed by: </label>
            <item>Don Walker</item>
         </defitem>
         <defitem>
            <label>Date Completed: </label>
            <item>1997</item>
         </defitem>
         <defitem>
            <label>Encoded by: </label>
            <item>Don Walker</item>
         </defitem>
      </list>
      <p>&copy; 2000 San Joaquin County Historical Society &amp;
      Museum. All rights reserved.</p>
   </titlepage>
</frontmatter>
```

<function> Function

Description:

Terms for the spheres of activities and processes that generated the described materials. Such terms often provide useful access points to the materials, especially for corporate, government, or institutional records. Examples include: collecting taxes and entertaining.

All functions mentioned in a finding aid do not have to be tagged. One option is to tag those functions for which access other than basic, undifferentiated keyword retrieval is desired. Use of controlled vocabulary forms is recommended to facilitate access to the functions within and across finding aid systems. The <function> element may be used in text elements such as <p>. To indicate a function with major representation in the materials being described, nest <function> within the <controlaccess> element.

Use the SOURCE attribute to specify the vocabulary from which the term has been taken. The AUTHFILENUMBER attribute can be used to identify a link to an authority file record that has more information about the function or cross references for alternative forms of a function term.

Do not confuse with <occupation>, which designates a type of work or business and is often associated with personal papers.

See also the related access elements under <controlaccess>.

The <function> element is comparable to MARC field 657.

May contain:

#PCDATA, emph, extptr, lb, ptr

May occur within:

controlaccess, entry, event, extref, extrefloc, indexentry, item, label, namegrp, p, physdesc, physfacet, ref, refloc, unittitle

Attributes:

ALTRENDER	#IMPLIED, CDATA
AUDIENCE	#IMPLIED, external, internal
AUTHFILENUMBER	#IMPLIED, CDATA
ENCODINGANALOG	#IMPLIED, CDATA
ID	#IMPLIED, ID
NORMAL	#IMPLIED, CDATA
RULES	#IMPLIED, NMTOKEN
SOURCE	#IMPLIED, NMTOKEN

Example:

```
<controlaccess>
   <head>Index Terms</head>
   <p>These records are indexed under the following headings in
      the catalog of the Minnesota Historical Society.
      Researchers wishing to find related materials should search
      the catalog under these index terms.</p>
   <controlaccess>
      <head>Government Functions:</head>
      <function encodinganalog="657" source="aat">Law
         enforcing.</function>
      <function encodinganalog="657"
         source="aat">Convicting.</function>
   </controlaccess>
</controlaccess>
```

<genreform> Genre/Physical Characteristic

Description:

A term that identifies the types of material being described, by naming the style or technique of their intellectual content (genre); order of information or object function (form); and physical characteristics. Examples include: account books, architectural drawings, portraits, short stories, sound recordings, and videotapes.

All genres and forms of material mentioned in a finding aid do not have to be tagged. One option is to tag those <genreform> terms for which access other than basic, undifferentiated keyword retrieval is desired. Use of controlled vocabulary terms is recommended to facilitate access to the information within and across finding aid systems. The <genreform> element may be used in text elements such as <p>. To indicate a function with major representation in the materials being described, nest <genreform> within the <controlaccess> element. To associate a <genreform> term with more detailed physical characteristics, use <genreform> within the <physdesc> or <physfacet> elements.

Use the SOURCE attribute to specify the vocabulary from which the term has been taken. The NORMAL attribute can be used to provide the authority form of a term that has been encoded with <genreform> in narrative text, e.g., within a paragraph. The AUTHFILENUMBER attribute can be used to identify a link to an authority file record that has more information about the term or cross references for alternative forms of a genre term.

See also the related access elements under <controlaccess>.

The <genreform> element is comparable to ISAD(G) data element 3.1.5 and MARC field 655, and, when used in conjunction with <extent>, to MARC field 300.

May contain:

#PCDATA, emph, extptr, lb, ptr

May occur within:

controlaccess, entry, event, extref, extrefloc, indexentry, item, label, namegrp, p, physdesc, physfacet, ref, refloc, unittitle

Attributes:

ALTRENDER	#IMPLIED, CDATA
AUDIENCE	#IMPLIED, external, internal
AUTHFILENUMBER	#IMPLIED, CDATA
ENCODINGANALOG	#IMPLIED, CDATA
ID	#IMPLIED, ID
NORMAL	#IMPLIED, CDATA
RULES	#IMPLIED, NMTOKEN
SOURCE	#IMPLIED, NMTOKEN
TYPE	#IMPLIED, CDATA

Examples:

1.
```
<controlaccess>
   <head>Index Terms</head>
   <controlaccess>
      <head>Physical Characteristics of Materials in the
         Collection:</head>
      <genreform encodinganalog="655$a"
         source="gmgpc">Architectural drawings</genreform>
      <genreform encodinganalog="655$a"
         source="gmgpc">Photographs</genreform>
   </controlaccess>
</controlaccess>
```

2.
```
<scopecontent>
   <head>Scope and Content of the Collection</head>
   <p>Although the bulk of the collection is composed of
      <genreform>letters</genreform>, <genreform>portrait
      photographs </genreform>appear in several series.</p>
</scopecontent>
```

3.
```
<c01 level="series">
   <did>[...]</did>
   <c02 level="file">
      <did>
         <unittitle>Diaries, </unittitle>
         <unitdate type="inclusive">1820-1864</unitdate>
         <physdesc><extent>14 </extent><genreform>diaries
            </genreform>bound in <physfacet type="cover
            material">red leather</physfacet></physdesc>
      </did>
   </c02>
</c01>
```

<geogname> Geographic Name

Description:

The proper noun designation for a place, natural feature, or political jurisdiction. Examples include: Appalachian Mountains; Baltimore, Md.; Chinatown, San Francisco; and Kew Gardens, England.

All names in a finding aid do not have to be tagged. One option is to tag those names for which access other than basic, undifferentiated keyword retrieval is desired. Use of controlled vocabulary names is recommended to facilitate access to the names within and across finding aid systems. The <geogname> element may be used in text elements such as <p>. To indicate a place name with major representation in the materials being described, nest <geogname> within the <controlaccess> element.

The ROLE attribute can be used to specify the relationship(s) of the name to the materials being described, for example, "subject." The NORMAL attribute can be used to provide the authority form of a term that has been encoded with <geogname> in narrative text, e.g., within a paragraph. Use the SOURCE attribute to specify the vocabulary from which the name has been taken and/or the RULES attribute to specify the descriptive rules followed when forming the name. The AUTHFILENUMBER attribute can be used to identify a link to an authority file record that has more information about the name or cross references for alternative forms of the name and related names.

See also the related access elements under <controlaccess>.

The <geogname> element is comparable to MARC fields 651 and 752.

May contain:

#PCDATA, emph, extptr, lb, ptr

May occur within:

controlaccess, entry, event, extref, extrefloc, imprint, indexentry, item, label, namegrp, p, physdesc, physfacet, ref, refloc, unittitle

Attributes:

ALTRENDER	#IMPLIED, CDATA
AUDIENCE	#IMPLIED, external, internal
AUTHFILENUMBER	#IMPLIED, CDATA
ENCODINGANALOG	#IMPLIED, CDATA
ID	#IMPLIED, ID
NORMAL	#IMPLIED, CDATA
ROLE	#IMPLIED, CDATA
RULES	#IMPLIED, NMTOKEN
SOURCE	#IMPLIED, NMTOKEN

Example:

```
<controlaccess>
   <head>Controlled Vocabulary Indexing Terms:</head>
   <controlaccess>
      <head>Subjects:</head>
      <famname encodinganalog="600" source="lcnaf">Ferry
         family.</famname>
      <geogname encodinganalog="651" source="lcsh">Ferry Field
         (University of Michigan)</geogname>
   </controlaccess>
</controlaccess>
```

<head> Heading

Description:

A generic element that designates the title or caption for a section of text, including a list. When a <head> is used, it should be the first subelement, followed by one or more other elements.

Do not confuse with the <listhead> subelements <head01> and <head02>, which designate headings for columns in a list. A <thead> element is used for column heads in a table.

May contain:

#PCDATA, emph, extptr, lb, ptr

May occur within:

accessrestrict, accruals, acqinfo, altformavail, appraisal, arrangement, bibliography, bioghist, c, c01, c02, c03, c04, c05, c06, c07, c08, c09, c10, c11, c12, chronlist, controlaccess, custodhist, daodesc, descgrp, did, div, dsc, dscgrp, fileplan, index, list, odd, originalsloc, otherfindaid, phystech, prefercite, processinfo, relatedmaterial, scopecontent, separatedmaterial, table, userestrict

Attributes:

ALTHEAD	#IMPLIED, CDATA
ALTRENDER	#IMPLIED, CDATA
AUDIENCE	#IMPLIED, external, internal
ID	#IMPLIED, ID

Examples:

1.
```
<chronlist>
   <head>Publications List</head>
   <listhead>
      <head01>Publication Year</head01>
      <head02>Book Title</head02>
   </listhead>
   <chronitem>[...]</chronitem>
</chronlist>
```

2.
```
<bioghist id="PRO123">
   <head>Administrative History</head>
   <p>In October 1964, the incoming Labour government created new
      office of Secretary of State for Economic Affairs (combined
      with First Secretary of State) and set up the Department of
      Economic Affairs under the Ministers of the Crown Act 1964
      to carry primary responsibility for long term economic
      planning.</p>
</bioghist>
```

<head01> First Heading

Description:

A formatting element within <listhead> that designates the heading over the first column in a multicolumn list.

Do not confuse with the generic <head> element, which designates a heading for an entire list or other section of text. Do not confuse with the <thead> element, which is used for column heads in a table.

May contain:

#PCDATA, emph, extptr, lb, ptr

May occur within:

listhead

Attributes:

ALTRENDER	#IMPLIED, CDATA
AUDIENCE	#IMPLIED, external, internal
ID	#IMPLIED, ID

Example:

```
<chronlist>
   <head>Publications List</head>
   <listhead>
      <head01>Publication Year</head01>
      <head02>Book Title</head02>
   </listhead>
   <chronitem>
      <date type="publication">1928</date>
      <event><title render="italic">The Happy Little
         Lamb</title></event>
   </chronitem> . . .
</chronlist>
```

<head02> Second Heading

Description:

A formatting element within <listhead> that designates the heading over the second column in a multicolumn list.

Do not confuse with the generic <head> element, which designates a heading for an entire list or other section of text. Do not confuse with the <thead> element, which is used for column heads in a table.

May contain:

#PCDATA, emph, extptr, lb, ptr

May occur within:

listhead

Attributes:

ALTRENDER	#IMPLIED, CDATA
AUDIENCE	#IMPLIED, external, internal
ID	#IMPLIED, ID

Example:

```
<chronlist>
   <head>Publications List</head>
   <listhead>
      <head01>Publication Year</head01>
      <head02>Book Title</head02>
   </listhead>
   <chronitem>
      <date type="publication">1928</date>
      <event><title render="italic">The Happy Little
         Lamb</title></event>
   </chronitem> . . .
</chronlist>
```

<imprint> Imprint

Description:

Information relating to the publication or distribution of a work cited in a Bibliographic Reference <bibref> or <unittitle>. In both elements the place of publication, name of the publisher, and date of publication can be encoded as either plain text or wrapped in the <imprint> subelements <geogname>, <publisher>, and <date>. It is seldom, if ever, appropriate to use <imprint> in a citation for an unpublished work cited in a <bibref>.

May contain:

#PCDATA, date, emph, extptr, geogname, lb, ptr, publisher

May occur within:

bibref, unittitle

Attributes:

ALTRENDER	#IMPLIED, CDATA
AUDIENCE	#IMPLIED, external, internal
ENCODINGANALOG	#IMPLIED, CDATA
ID	#IMPLIED, ID

Example:

```
<bibref>
   <title render="italic">Action For Outdoor Recreation For
      America.</title>,
   <imprint>
      <geogname>Washington, D.C.</geogname>:
      <publisher>Citizen's Committee For The Outdoor Recreation
         Resources Review Commission Report</publisher>,
      <date type="publication" normal="1964">1964</date>.
   </imprint>
</bibref>
```

<index> Index

Description:

A list of key terms and reference pointers that have been assembled to enhance access to the materials being described. The <index> can also serve as a helpful alphabetical overview of subjects, correspondents, photographers, or other entities represented in the collection. This back-of-the volume <index> may provide hypertext links, or it may note the container numbers useful for locating the position in the finding aid where the indexed material appears.

The <index> is assumed to be text that has to be tagged, not text generated automatically from the encoded finding aid. In some cases, the <index> repeats terms and names found elsewhere in the finding aid. In other cases, such as in some literary manuscript collections, the <index> may be the only place where a name is listed, and the references point to one or more files, which include letters from that person or corporate body, but which are described only in general terms, e.g., "Correspondents T-Z."

The <index> should contain <indexentry> elements, which consist of an access element, such as <name> or <subject>, followed by a Pointer <ptr>, Pointer Group <ptrgrp>, or Reference <ref> element. Plain text cannot be used in an <indexentry>. If the <indexentry> elements are expected to provide access points other than basic keyword retrieval, use authority file terms to facilitate access to the information within and across finding aid systems.

In EAD Version 1.0 <index> was a subelement of Adjunct Descriptive Data <add>, which has been deprecated in EAD 2002 (see Appendix B). The new Description Group <descgrp> element, which can group any of the <did>-level elements (except the Description of Subordinate Components <dsc>), may be used to wrap elements where a group heading is desirable. The <descgrp> element can be used to replace <add> when converting finding aids encoded in EAD V1.0 to EAD 2002.

May contain:

address, blockquote, chronlist, head, index, indexentry, list, listhead, note, p, table

May occur within:

archdesc, archdescgrp, c, c01, c02, c03, c04, c05, c06, c07, c08, c09, c10, c11, c12, descgrp, index

Attributes:

ALTRENDER	#IMPLIED, CDATA
AUDIENCE	#IMPLIED, external, internal
ENCODINGANALOG	#IMPLIED, CDATA
ID	#IMPLIED, ID

Example:

```
<index>
   <head>Photographer Index</head>
   <p>Names of photographers and studios--and the cities and
      states in which they operated--are usually noted as they
      appear on the photographs (usually stamped or written on
      the versos). Corporate names appear in direct order;
      personal names in inverted order (i.e., filed by surname).
      Rectos and versos of photographs were microfilmed to
      capture information exactly as it appears on the
      photographs.  To locate a specific photographer/studio, a
      user should consider all possible forms of entry (corporate
      and personal), browse the index under these forms, identify
      which LOT(s) contain photographs by that
      photographer/studio, then browse the relevant LOT on the
      microfilm to locate specific photographs that bear the
      markings of the specific photographer/studio.</p>
   <indexentry>
      <name>12th Air Force Photo:</name>
      <ref target="LOT13105" actuate="onrequest"
         show="replace">LOT 13105</ref>
   </indexentry>
   <indexentry>
      <name>15th Air Force Command:</name>
      <ref target="LOT13105" actuate="onrequest"
         show="replace">LOT 13105</ref>
   </indexentry>
   <indexentry>
      <name>324th Service Corp.:</name>
      <ref target="LOT13105" actuate="onrequest"
         show="replace">LOT 13105</ref>
   </indexentry>
   <indexentry>
      <name>A.L. Adams Photo Studio--Atlanta, Ga.:</name>
      <ref target="LOT13076" actuate="onrequest"
         show="replace">LOT 13076</ref>
   </indexentry>
   <indexentry>
      <name>AAA Agricultural Adjustment Agency by Cooper:</name>
      <ref target="LOT13121" actuate="onrequest"
         show="replace">LOT 13121</ref>
   </indexentry>
</index>
```

<indexentry> Index Entry

Description:

A formatting element that pairs an index term with one or more linking elements. Each <indexentry> contains an access element, such as <namegrp> or <subject>; an optional <note> that can divide the entry into subcategories, e.g., "during office" and "family life"; followed by optional Pointer <ptr>, Pointer Group <ptrgrp>, or Reference <ref> elements. Plain text cannot be used in an <indexentry>. If the <indexentry> subelements are expected to provide access points other than basic keyword retrieval, use controlled vocabulary terms to facilitate access to information within and across finding aid systems, with the SOURCE attribute to indicate which vocabulary provided the term.

Use the Name Group <namegrp> element to bundle access element entries, e.g., several <famname> and <persname> elements, that share the same <ref>, <ptr>, or <ptrgrp> element.

Use the Pointer Group <ptrgrp> element to bundle several <ref> or <ptr> links to a single access term. Use the <ptr> element when no text is needed with the link. Use the <ref> element when text as well as a link are needed.

May contain:

corpname, famname, function, genreform, geogname, indexentry, name, namegrp, occupation, persname, ptr, ptrgrp, ref, subject, title

May occur within:

index, indexentry

Attributes:

ALTRENDER	#IMPLIED, CDATA
AUDIENCE	#IMPLIED, external, internal
ID	#IMPLIED, ID

Example:

```
<index>
   <indexentry>
      <name>12th Air Force Photo:</name>
      <ref target="LOT13105" actuate="onrequest"
         show="replace">LOT 13105</ref>
   </indexentry>
   <indexentry>
      <name>15th Air Force Command:</name>
      <ref target="LOT13105" actuate="onrequest"
         show="replace">LOT 13105</ref>
   </indexentry>
</index>
```

<item> Item

Description:

A formatting element used in one of three contexts: as an entry in a simple, random, or ordered <list>; as part of a <defitem> inside a definition list; or as an entry within the <change> element. In the first instance, the <item> can be a number, word, or phrase. In a definition list, which is usually displayed as two columns, a <defitem> pairs a <label> with a corresponding <item> containing text that defines, describes, or explains the terms or other text tagged as the <label>. In the <eadheader> <revisiondesc> <change> element, the <item> designates information about a revision to the finding aid and is often paired with a <date>.

Do not confuse with <chronitem>, which designates entries in a Chronology List <chronlist>.

See also related elements <list>, <defitem>, and <change>.

May contain:

#PCDATA, abbr, address, archref, bibref, blockquote, chronlist, corpname, date, emph, expan, extptr, extref, famname, function, genreform, geogname, lb, linkgrp, list, name, note, num, occupation, origination, persname, ptr, ref, repository, subject, table, title, unitdate, unittitle

May occur within:

change, defitem, list

Attributes:

ALTRENDER	#IMPLIED, CDATA
AUDIENCE	#IMPLIED, external, internal
ID	#IMPLIED, ID

<item>

Examples:

1.
```
<eadheader langencoding="iso639-2b">
   <eadid>[...]</eadid> . . .
   <revisiondesc>
      <change>
         <date normal="19970505">May 5, 1997</date>
         <item>This electronic finding aid was updated to current
            markup standards by Sarah Taylor using a perl script.
            Updates included: eadheader, eadid, arrangement of
            did elements and their labels.</item>
      </change>
   </revisiondesc>
</eadheader>
```

2.
```
<list type="deflist">
   <defitem>
      <label>ALS</label>
      <item>Autograph Letter Signed</item>
   </defitem>
   <defitem>
      <label>TLS</label>
      <item>Typewritten Letter Signed</item>
   </defitem>
</list>
```

<label> Label

Description:

A formatting element that identifies the term or concept being described, defined, or explained in a Definition List Item <defitem>. The <defitem> can be thought of as an entry in a <list> that is usually displayed in two columns: <label> followed by <item>. Each list item <defitem> contains a term or concept (called a <label>) and a definition, description, or explanation of that <label> (called an <item>).

Do not confuse with the attribute called LABEL, which identifies the kind of information in an element for public display in the <did> subelements.

See also related elements <list> and <defitem>.

May contain:

#PCDATA, abbr, archref, bibref, corpname, date, emph, expan, extptr, extref, famname, function, genreform, geogname, lb, linkgrp, name, num, occupation, origination, persname, ptr, ref, repository, subject, title, unitdate, unittitle

May occur within:

defitem

Attributes:

ALTRENDER	#IMPLIED, CDATA
AUDIENCE	#IMPLIED, external, internal
ID	#IMPLIED, ID

Example:

```
<list type="deflist">
   <defitem>
      <label>ALS</label>
      <item>Autograph Letter Signed</item>
   </defitem>
   <defitem>
      <label>TLS</label>
      <item>Typewritten Letter Signed</item>
   </defitem>
</list>
```

<langmaterial> Language of the Material

Description:

A prose statement enumerating the language(s) of the archival materials found in the unit being described.

Language of the material may also be recorded in coded form in the LANGCODE attribute in the <language> subelement using the ISO 639-2b three-letter language codes.

Do not confuse with the Language Usage <langusage> element which specifies the language(s) in which the finding aid is written. See also the description for the <language> element.

The <langmaterial> element is comparable to the ISAD(G) data element 3.4.3 and MARC field 546.

May contain:

#PCDATA, abbr, archref, bibref, emph, expan, extptr, extref, language, lb, linkgrp, ptr, ref, title

May occur within:

archref, did

Attributes:

ALTRENDER	#IMPLIED, CDATA
AUDIENCE	#IMPLIED, external, internal
ENCODINGANALOG	#IMPLIED, CDATA
ID	#IMPLIED, ID
LABEL	#IMPLIED, CDATA

Examples:

1.
```
<c01 level="series">
   <did>
      <unittitle>Correspondence, </unittitle>
      <unitdate type="inclusive">1854-1902. </unitdate>
      <physdesc>4 boxes</physdesc>
      <langmaterial>Correspondence in <language>French,
         </language><language>German, </language>and
         <language>English.</language>
      </langmaterial>
   </did>
</c01>
```

2.
```
<eadheader langencoding="iso639-2b">[...]</eadheader>
   <archdesc level="fonds">
      <did> . . .
         <langmaterial>Texte <language
            langcode="ara">arabe</language> et traduction
            <language langcode="fre">fran&ccedil;aise</language>
            par Lacroix fils
         </langmaterial>
      </did> . . .
   </archdesc>
```

3.
```
<did>
   <unitid label="Reference Code">DL 42</unitid>
   <unittitle label="Title">Duchy of Lancaster: Cartularies,
      Enrolments, Surveys and other Miscellaneous
      Books</unittitle>
   <unitdate label="Creation Dates" type="inclusive">13th Century
      -1894</unitdate>
   <langmaterial label="Language(s)">
      <language langcode="eng">English</language>,
      <language langcode="fre">French</language> and
      <language langcode="lat">Latin</language>
   </langmaterial>
</did>
```

<language> Language

Description:

A subelement of <langusage> within the <profiledesc> portion of the <eadheader> that specifies the language or communication system in which the finding aid is written. For bilingual or multilingual finding aids, either identify each language in a separate <language> element, or mention only the predominant language. The LANGCODE attribute can be used to provide the three-letter ISO 639-2b code for the language.

Also a subelement of <langmaterial> within <did>, where it specifies the language of the materials being described. In this instance, the LANGCODE attribute may be used to provide the three-letter ISO 639-2b code which is the equivalent of the MARC 041 field.

The SCRIPTCODE attribute may be used to specify the ISO 15924 code for the script in which the language is written.

May contain:

#PCDATA, emph, extptr, lb, ptr

May occur within:

langmaterial, langusage

Attributes:

ALTRENDER	#IMPLIED, CDATA
AUDIENCE	#IMPLIED, external, internal
ENCODINGANALOG	#IMPLIED, CDATA
ID	#IMPLIED, ID
LANGCODE	#IMPLIED, NMTOKEN
SCRIPTCODE	#IMPLIED, NMTOKEN

Examples:

1.
```
<eadheader langencoding="iso639-2b">
   <eadid>[...]</eadid>
   <filedesc>[...]</filedesc>
   <profiledesc>
      <creation>[...]</creation>
      <langusage>Bilingual finding aid written in
         <language langcode="fre">French</language> and
         <language langcode="eng">English.</language>
      </langusage>
   </profiledesc>
</eadheader>
```

2.
```
<c01 level="series">
   <did>
      <unittitle>Correspondence, </unittitle>
      <unitdate type="inclusive">1854-1902.</unitdate>
      <physdesc>4 boxes</physdesc>
      <langmaterial>Correspondence in <language>French,
         </language><language>German, </language>and
         <language>English.</language>
      </langmaterial>
   </did>
</c01>
```

<langusage> Language Usage

Description:

An optional subelement within the <profiledesc> portion of the <eadheader> that provides a statement about languages, sublanguages, and dialects represented in an encoded finding aid. The language(s) in which the finding aid is written can be further specified using the <language> subelement within <langusage>. For bilingual or multilingual finding aids, either identify each language in a separate <language> element, or mention only the predominant language.

The <langusage> element is modeled on a Text Encoding Initiative (TEI) DTD element.

May contain:

#PCDATA, abbr, archref, bibref, emph, expan, extptr, extref, language, lb, linkgrp, ptr, ref, title

May occur within:

profiledesc

Attributes:

ALTRENDER	#IMPLIED, CDATA
AUDIENCE	#IMPLIED, external, internal
ENCODINGANALOG	#IMPLIED, CDATA
ID	#IMPLIED, ID

Example:

```
<eadheader langencoding="iso639-2b">
   <eadid>[...]</eadid>
   <filedesc>[...]</filedesc>
   <profiledesc>
      <creation>[...]</creation>
      <langusage>Bilingual finding aid written in
         <language langcode="fre">French</language> and
         <language langcode="eng">English.</language>
      </langusage>
   </profiledesc>
</eadheader>
```

<lb> Line Break

Description:

An empty formatting element that forces text to start on a new line at a point chosen by the author rather than a linewrap algorithm or style sheet. Use only when a line break is needed within an element, for example, within a <titlepage>. Use a style sheet to specify line breaks between elements.

May contain:

EMPTY

May occur within:

abstract, addressline, archref, author, bibref, bibseries, container, corpname, creation, date, descrules, dimensions, edition, emph, entry, event, extent, extref, extrefloc, famname, function, genreform, geogname, head, head01, head02, imprint, item, label, langmaterial, language, langusage, legalstatus, materialspec, name, num, occupation, origination, p, persname, physdesc, physfacet, physloc, publisher, ref, refloc, repository, resource, runner, sponsor, subarea, subject, subtitle, title, titleproper, unitdate, unitid, unittitle

Attributes:

None

Example:

```
<publisher>
   San Joaquin County Historical Society and Museum
   <lb/>
   <extptr actuate="onload" show="embed" entityref="sjmlogo">
   <lb/>
   Lodi, California
</publisher>
```

<legalstatus> Legal Status

Description:

The statutorily-defined status of the materials being described in the encoded finding aid, as, for example, defined by the Public Records Act of 1958 in the United Kingdom.

The <legalstatus> element is comparable to the ISAD(G) data element 3.4.1 and MARC field 506.

May contain:

#PCDATA, date, emph, extptr, lb, ptr

May occur within:

accessrestrict

Attributes:

ALTRENDER	#IMPLIED, CDATA
AUDIENCE	#IMPLIED, external, internal
ID	#IMPLIED, ID
TYPE	#IMPLIED, NMTOKEN

Example:

```
<did>
   <unitid label="Reference Code">PREM 8</unitid>
   <unittitle label="Title">Prime Minister's Office:
      Correspondence and Papers</unittitle>
   <unitdate label="Creation Dates" type="inclusive">1935-
      1951</unitdate>
</did>
<accessrestrict>
   <legalstatus>Public Record(s)</legalstatus>
</accessrestrict>
```

<linkgrp> Linking Group

Description:

A wrapper element that contains two or more linking elements which form an extended link group so as to enable a set of multidirectional, out-of-line links.

May contain:

arc, extptrloc, extrefloc, ptrloc, refloc, resource

May occur within:

abstract, bibliography, container, creation, descrules, dimensions, emph, entry, event, extent, item, label, langmaterial, langusage, materialspec, origination, otherfindaid, p, physdesc, physfacet, physloc, relatedmaterial, repository, separatedmaterial, unitdate, unitid, unittitle

Attributes:

ALTRENDER	#IMPLIED, CDATA
AUDIENCE	#IMPLIED, external, internal
ID	#IMPLIED, ID
LINKTYPE	#FIXED, extended, extended
ROLE	#IMPLIED, CDATA
TITLE	#IMPLIED, CDATA

Example:

```
<relatedmaterial>
   <p>The Society also has records of other conservation
      organizations in Minnesota.</p>
   <p>
      <linkgrp linktype="extended">
         <extrefloc
            href="http://www.someserver.edu/findaids/3270.xml">
            <archref>Issak Walton League of Minnesota</archref>
         </extrefloc>
         <extrefloc
            href="http://www.someserver.edu/findaids/9248.xml">
            <archref>Minnesota Audubon Council</archref>
         </extrefloc>
         <extrefloc entityref="FBWW">
            <archref>Friends of the Boundary Waters
               Wilderness</archref>
         </extrefloc>
         <extrefloc
            href="http://www.someserver.edu/findaids/23145.sgm">
            <archref>Minnesota Emergency Conservation
               Committee</archref>
         </extrefloc>
      </linkgrp>
   </p>
</relatedmaterial>
```

<list> List

Description:

A formatting element that contains a series of words or numerals (called <item>s) separated from one another and arranged in a linear, often vertical sequence.

The TYPE attribute is used to identify and format the list. The choices are: "simple," "deflist," "marked," and "ordered." In a "simple" list, <item>s are not numbered or bulleted. In a "deflist" or definition list, each <defitem> pairs a <label> with a corresponding <item> containing the text that defines, describes, or explains the term or other text tagged as the <label>. In a "marked" list, the sequence of the list items is not critical, and a bullet, box, dash, or other character is displayed at the beginning of each <item>. In an "ordered" list, the sequence of the list <item>s is important, and each list <item> is lettered or numbered.

See also the related elements <defitem> and <item>.

May contain:

defitem, head, item, listhead

May occur within:

accessrestrict, accruals, acqinfo, altformavail, appraisal, arrangement, bibliography, bioghist, blockquote, controlaccess, custodhist, daodesc, descgrp, div, dsc, dscgrp, entry, event, extref, extrefloc, fileplan, index, item, note, odd, originalsloc, otherfindaid, p, phystech, prefercite, processinfo, ref, refloc, relatedmaterial, revisiondesc, scopecontent, separatedmaterial, titlepage, userestrict

Attributes:

ALTRENDER	#IMPLIED, CDATA
AUDIENCE	#IMPLIED, external, internal
CONTINUATION	#IMPLIED, continues, starts
ID	#IMPLIED, ID
MARK	#IMPLIED, CDATA
NUMERATION	#IMPLIED, arabic, upperalpha, loweralpha, upperroman, lowerroman
TYPE	#IMPLIED, simple, deflist, marked, ordered

Example:

```
<bibliography>
   <head>Major Works of Archibald MacLeish</head>
   <list type="ordered" numeration="arabic">
      <item>
         <bibref><imprint><date>1924</date></imprint><title
            render="italic">The Happy Marriage, and Other
            Poems</title> (Boston and New York: Houghton Mifflin.
            79 pp.)
         </bibref>
      </item>
      <item>
         <bibref><imprint><date>1925</date></imprint>
         <title render="italic">The Pot of Earth</title> (Boston
         and New York: Houghton Mifflin. 44 pp.)</bibref>
      </item> . . .
   </list>
</bibliography>
```

<listhead> List Heading

Description:

A formatting element that groups headings for columns in a definition, marked, or ordered list, Chronology List <chronlist>, or <index>. The headings are called <head01> and <head02>.

May contain:

head01, head02

May occur within:

chronlist, index, list

Attributes:

ALTRENDER	#IMPLIED, CDATA
AUDIENCE	#IMPLIED, external, internal
ID	#IMPLIED, ID

Example:

```
<chronlist>
   <head>Publications List</head>
   <listhead>
      <head01>Publication Year</head01>
      <head02>Book Title</head02>
   </listhead>
   <chronitem>[...]</chronitem>
</chronlist>
```

<materialspec> Material Specific Details

Description:

Data which are unique to a particular class or form of material and which are not assigned to any other element of description. Examples of material specific details include mathematical data, such as scale for cartographic and architectural records, jurisdictional and denominational data for philatelic records, and physical presentation data for music records.

The <matspec> element is comparable to MARC fields 254, 255, and 256.

May contain:

#PCDATA, abbr, archref, bibref, emph, expan, extptr, extref, lb, linkgrp, materialspec, num, ptr, ref, title

May occur within:

archref, did, materialspec

Attributes:

ALTRENDER	#IMPLIED, CDATA
AUDIENCE	#IMPLIED, external, internal
ENCODINGANALOG	#IMPLIED, CDATA
ID	#IMPLIED, ID
LABEL	#IMPLIED, CDATA
TYPE	#IMPLIED, CDATA

Example:

```
<c03 level="file">
   <did> . . .
      <materialspec label="Mathematical Data">
         <materialspec label="Scale:">1:10000</materialspec>
         <materialspec label="Projection:">Universal transverse
            Mercator projection</materialspec>
      </materialspec>
   </did> . . .
</c03>
```

<name> Name

Description:

The proper noun or noun phrase designation for an entity that is difficult to tag more specifically as a <corpname>, <famname>, <geogname>, <persname>, or <title>. The <name> element may be used in place of the more specific access elements when it is not known what kind of name is being described or when a high degree of precision is unnecessary. For example, the <name> element might be used in an <indexentry> when it is not clear if the name "Bachrach" refers to a person or a photographic corporation.

All names in a finding aid do not have to be tagged. One option is to tag those names for which access other than basic, undifferentiated keyword retrieval is desired. Use of controlled vocabulary names is recommended to facilitate access to the names within and across finding aid systems. The <name> element may be used in text elements such as <p>. To indicate a name with major representation in the materials being described, nest <name> within the <controlaccess> element.

The ROLE attribute can be used to specify the relationship(s) of the name to the materials being described, for example, "subject" or "photographer." The SOURCE attribute can be used to specify the vocabulary from which the name has been taken. The RULES attribute can be used to specify the descriptive rules followed when forming the name, such as AACR2R.

See also the related access elements under <controlaccess>.

The <name> element is comparable to MARC field 720, when it is not from a controlled vocabulary.

May contain:

#PCDATA, emph, extptr, lb, ptr

May occur within:

bibref, controlaccess, entry, event, extref, extrefloc, indexentry, item, label, namegrp, origination, p, physdesc, physfacet, ref, refloc, repository, unittitle

Attributes:

ALTRENDER	#IMPLIED, CDATA
AUDIENCE	#IMPLIED, external, internal
AUTHFILENUMBER	#IMPLIED, CDATA
ENCODINGANALOG	#IMPLIED, CDATA
ID	#IMPLIED, ID
NORMAL	#IMPLIED, CDATA
ROLE	#IMPLIED, CDATA
RULES	#IMPLIED, NMTOKEN
SOURCE	#IMPLIED, NMTOKEN

Example:

```
<c02 level="file">
   <did>
      <unittitle><name>Bartleby </name>barn purchase files,
         </unittitle>
      <unitdate>1799.</unitdate>
      <physdesc><extent>3 items, </extent>heavily
         <physfacet>foxed.</physfacet></physdesc>
      <note><p>Items relate to the purchase by Mr. Wigglethorpe
         from <persname normal="Brookes, Josiah">Jos. Brookes
         </persname>of a building colloquially known as the
         Bartleby barn.</p>
      </note>
   </did>
</c02>
```

<namegrp> Name Group

Description:

A formatting element used in an <indexentry> to group access element entries that share the same <ref>, <ptr>, or <ptrgrp> element. A <note> is available to divide a name or term into subcategories, for example, "during office" and "family life."

May contain:

corpname, famname, function, genreform, geogname, name, note, occupation, persname, subject, title

May occur within:

indexentry

Attributes:

ALTRENDER	#IMPLIED, CDATA
AUDIENCE	#IMPLIED, external, internal
ID	#IMPLIED, ID

Example:

```
<index>
   <head>Index to Correspondents and Recipients</head>
   <indexentry>
      <corpname>Bach &amp; Bros.</corpname>
      <ref linktype="simple" target="NonC:21-2" show="replace"
         actuate="onrequest">(In non correspondence)</ref>
   </indexentry>
   <indexentry>
      <namegrp>
         <corpname>Bacon and Lewis, Ltd.</corpname>
         <persname>Levering, Alexander M.</persname>
         <persname>Windom, Lucious</persname>
      </namegrp>
      <ref linktype="simple" target="Cres:18610408"
         show="replace" actuate="onrequest">(1861 Apr. 8, ALS, to
         W.W., re: inquiry into what to do with unsold
         flour)</ref>
   </indexentry> . . .
</index>
```

<note> Note

Description:

A generic element that provides a short statement explaining the text, indicating the basis for an assertion, or citing the source of a quotation or other information. Used both for general comments and as an annotation for the text in a finding aid. Not used when more specific content designation elements are appropriate, e.g., <abstract>, <altformavail>, <archref>, or <scopecontent>. Do not confuse with Other Descriptive Data <odd> element, which is used within <archdesc> and <c> to designate information that is more than a short comment in a <note>.

The placement of a <note> is dependent on the design of the document and the purpose of the <note>. A <note> may appear at the end of the text as endnotes, at the foot of a section as <footnotes> or embedded within the text. One or more <note> elements may be grouped in a <notestmt> element in the <filedesc> portion of the <eadheader>. The ACTUATE and SHOW attributes can be used to mask a <note> from display until it is requested by a finding aid user.

The <note> element is comparable to ISAD(G) data element 3.6.1 and MARC field 500.

May contain:

address, blockquote, chronlist, list, note, p, table

May occur within:

accessrestrict, accruals, acqinfo, altformavail, appraisal, archdesc, archdescgrp, archref, arrangement, bibliography, bioghist, blockquote, c, c01, c02, c03, c04, c05, c06, c07, c08, c09, c10, c11, c12, controlaccess, custodhist, daodesc, descgrp, did, div, dsc, dscgrp, entry, event, extref, extrefloc, fileplan, index, item, namegrp, note, notestmt, odd, originalsloc, otherfindaid, p, phystech, prefercite, processinfo, ref, refloc, relatedmaterial, scopecontent, separatedmaterial, titlepage, userestrict

Attributes:

ACTUATE	#IMPLIED, onload, onrequest
ALTRENDER	#IMPLIED, CDATA
AUDIENCE	#IMPLIED, external, internal
ENCODINGANALOG	#IMPLIED, CDATA
ID	#IMPLIED, ID
LABEL	#IMPLIED, CDATA
SHOW	#IMPLIED, embed, new
TYPE	#IMPLIED, CDATA

<note>

Example:

```
<archdesc level="collection">
   <did> . . .
      <repository label="repository" encodinganalog="852">
         <corpname>Library of Congress, <subarea>Prints and
            Photographs Division,</subarea></corpname>
            Washington, D.C. 20540
      </repository>
      <note>
         <p>For information about Prints and Photographs Division
            collections and services, see the Prints and
            Photographs Division's Reading Room Home Page:
            <extptr actuate="onrequest"
            href="http://lcweb.loc.gov/rr/print.htm" show="new">
         </p>
      </note>
   </did> . . .
</archdesc>
```

<notestmt> Note Statement

Description:

An optional subelement within the <filedesc> portion of the <eadheader> that groups <note> elements, each of which contains a single piece of descriptive information about the finding aid. These <note>s are similar to the "general notes" in traditional bibliographic descriptions.

The <notestmt> element is modeled on a header element found in the Text Encoding Initiative (TEI).

May contain:

note

May occur within:

filedesc

Attributes:

ALTRENDER	#IMPLIED, CDATA
AUDIENCE	#IMPLIED, external, internal
ENCODINGANALOG	#IMPLIED, CDATA
ID	#IMPLIED, ID

Example:

In the California Digital Library, access points are put in the <eadheader> for system use in the resource directory. These same access points are also provided in <controlaccess> for public use.

```
<notestmt>
   <note>
      <p>
         <subject source="cdl">Arts and Humanities--Performing
            Arts--Dance</subject>
         <subject source="cdl">Arts and Humanities--Performing
            Arts--Theater</subject>
      </p>
   </note>
</notestmt>
```

<num> Number

Description:

A generic element for numeric information in any form. The <num> element is used only when it is necessary to display a number in a special way, or to identify it with a TYPE attribute. For example, an accession number in the <acqinfo> element might be designated as <num type="accession">. A publication number might be designated as <publicationstmt> ... <num>no. 42</num> ...

Do not confuse with <container>, <unitid>, or <eadid>, which may also consist of numeric information.

May contain:

#PCDATA, emph, extptr, lb, ptr

May occur within:

bibref, bibseries, entry, event, extref, extrefloc, item, label, materialspec, p, publicationstmt, ref, refloc, seriesstmt, subtitle, title, titlepage, titleproper, unittitle

Attributes:

ALTRENDER	#IMPLIED, CDATA
AUDIENCE	#IMPLIED, external, internal
ENCODINGANALOG	#IMPLIED, CDATA
ID	#IMPLIED, ID
TYPE	#IMPLIED, CDATA

Examples:

1.
```
<filedesc>
   <titlestmt>[...]</titlestmt>
   <seriesstmt>
      <titleproper encodinganalog="440$a">Archival Inventories
         and Guides of the World; </titleproper>
         <num encodinganalog="440$v">no. 148</num>
   </seriesstmt>
</filedesc>
```

2.
```
<acqinfo>
   <p>The collection (Donor No. <num type="donor">8338</num>) was
      donated by <persname role="donor">Vonda Thomas
      </persname>and <persname role="donor"> Francine Farrow
      </persname>in March 1995.</p>
</acqinfo>
```

<occupation> Occupation

Description:

A term identifying a type of work, profession, trade, business, or avocation significantly reflected in the materials being described.

All occupations in a finding aid do not have to be tagged. One option is to tag those occupations for which access other than basic, undifferentiated keyword retrieval is desired. Use of controlled vocabulary forms is recommended to facilitate access to occupations within and across finding aid systems. The <occupation> element may be used in text elements such as <p>. To indicate an occupation with major representation in the described materials, nest <occupation> within the <controlaccess> element.

Use the SOURCE attribute to specify the vocabulary from which the term has been taken. The NORMAL attribute can be used to provide the authority form of a term that has been encoded with <occupation> in narrative text, e.g., within a paragraph. The AUTHFILENUMBER attribute can be used to identify a link to an authority file record that has more information about the occupation.

Do not confuse with <function>, which designates the spheres of activities and processes that generated the described materials, e.g., collecting taxes or entertaining.

Do not confuse with the ROLE attribute available on the various name elements, e.g., <corpname>, <persname>, <famname>, etc., which may be used to specify the relationship of a name to the described materials, e.g., "compiler," "creator," "collector," or "subject."

See also the related access terms under <controlaccess>.

The <occupation> element is comparable to MARC field 656.

May contain:

#PCDATA, emph, extptr, lb, ptr

May occur within:

controlaccess, entry, event, extref, extrefloc, indexentry, item, label, namegrp, p, physdesc, physfacet, ref, refloc, unittitle

<occupation>

Attributes:

ALTRENDER	#IMPLIED, CDATA
AUDIENCE	#IMPLIED, external, internal
AUTHFILENUMBER	#IMPLIED, CDATA
ENCODINGANALOG	#IMPLIED, CDATA
ID	#IMPLIED, ID
NORMAL	#IMPLIED, CDATA
RULES	#IMPLIED, NMTOKEN
SOURCE	#IMPLIED, NMTOKEN

Example:

```
<controlaccess>
   <head>Selected Search Terms</head>
   <controlaccess>
      <head>Occupations:</head>
      <occupation encodinganalog="656">Dramatists</occupation>
      <occupation encodinganalog="656">Librarians of
         Congress</occupation>
      <occupation encodinganalog="656">Poets</occupation>
      <occupation encodinganalog="656">Public
         officers</occupation>
   </controlaccess>
</controlaccess>
```

<odd> Other Descriptive Data

Description:

An element for information about the described materials that is not easily incorporated into one of the other named elements within <archdesc> and <c>. When converting finding aids to an ideal EAD markup, some shifting of text or addition of data may be necessary to conform to the DTD's sequencing of elements and the consignment of certain elements to specific settings. The <odd> element helps to minimize conversion difficulties by designating, as "other," information that does not fit easily into one of EAD's more distinct categories.

Some situations in which <odd> may be used are when the information does not correspond to another element's definition; when the information is of such mixed content as to make a single classification difficult; and when shifting the information to permit more specific content designation would be too costly or burdensome for the finding aid encoder. The first situation may occur especially when additional narrative description is required beyond what is included in the <bioghist> and <scopecontent> elements, such as when the finding aid is describing a computer file. Applying the TYPE and ENCODINGANALOG attributes may help provide additional content specification in situations where the unspecified <odd> is used.

Despite its wide availability under <archdesc> and <c>, the <odd> element should be used with restraint and only after carefully considering the consequences that unspecified content designation poses for searching, retrieving, and displaying information in a networked environment.

The <odd> element is comparable to ISAD(G) data element 3.6.1 and MARC field 500.

May contain:

address, blockquote, chronlist, dao, daogrp, head, list, note, odd, p, table

May occur within:

archdesc, archdescgrp, c, c01, c02, c03, c04, c05, c06, c07, c08, c09, c10, c11, c12, descgrp, odd

Attributes:

ALTRENDER	#IMPLIED, CDATA
AUDIENCE	#IMPLIED, external, internal
ENCODINGANALOG	#IMPLIED, CDATA
ID	#IMPLIED, ID
TYPE	#IMPLIED, CDATA

<odd>

Example:

Note: The Public Record Office of the United Kingdom uses a 7 level system of intellectual units devised specifically for that repository. In that system "division" is the equivalent of "subfonds" and "class" is the equivalent of "series."

```
<c01 level="otherlevel" otherlevel="division">
   <did>
      <unittitle>Records of the Industrial Division</unittitle>
      <origination>
         <corpname>Department of Economic Affairs, Industrial
            Group; </corpname>
         <corpname>Department of Economic Affairs, Industrial
            Division; </corpname>
         <corpname>Department of Economic Affairs, Industrial
            Policy; Division </corpname>
         <corpname>Department of Economic Affairs, Industrial
            Prices and Incomes Department; </corpname>
      </origination>
      <unitdate>1949-1969</unitdate>
      <physdesc><extent>2 </extent><genreform>classes</genreform>
      </physdesc>
   </did>
   <scopecontent>[...]</scopecontent>
   <bioghist>[...]</bioghist>
   <controlaccess>[...]</controlaccess>
   <odd>
      <list type="simple">
         <item>Department of Economic Affairs: Industrial Policy
            Group: Registered Files (1-IG and 2-IG Series)<ref
            actuate="onrequest" target="ew26" show="new">EW
            26</ref>
         </item>
         <item>Department of Economic Affairs: Industrial
            Division and Industrial Policy Division: Registered
            Files (IA Series)<ref actuate="onrequest"
            target="ew27" show="new">EW 27</ref>
         </item>
      </list>
   </odd>
</c01>
```

<originalsloc> Location of Originals

Description:

Information about the existence, location, availability, and/or the destruction of originals where the unit described consists of copies.

Do not confuse <originalsloc> with Alternative Form Available <altformavail>, which is used to encode information about copies of the material being described.

The <originalsloc> element is comparable to ISAD(G) data element 3.5.1 and MARC field 535.

May contain:

address, blockquote, chronlist, head, list, note, originalsloc, p, table

May occur within:

archdesc, archdescgrp, c, c01, c02, c03, c04, c05, c06, c07, c08, c09, c10, c11, c12, descgrp, originalsloc

Attributes:

ALTRENDER	#IMPLIED, CDATA
AUDIENCE	#IMPLIED, external, internal
ENCODINGANALOG	#IMPLIED, CDATA
ID	#IMPLIED, ID
TYPE	#IMPLIED, CDATA

Examples:

1.
```
<c01 level="file">
   <did>
      <unittitle>Dream diary, </unittitle>
      <unitdate normal="1947/1948>1947-48</unitdate>
   </did>
   <originalsloc>
      <p>File contains photocopies of original still held by the
         donor.</p>
   </originalsloc>
</c01>
```

2.
```
<c01 level="series">
   <did>[...]</did>
   <originalsloc>
      <p>Originals destroyed after microfilming, 1981.</p>
   </originalsloc>
</c01>
```

<originalsloc>

3.
```
<c03 level="file">
   <did>[...]</did>
   <originalsloc>
      <p>Original glass plate negatives are held by the Bailly
         family, Lunenburg, Nova Scotia.</p>
   </originalsloc>
</c03>
```

<origination> Origination

Description:

Information about the individual or organization responsible for the creation, accumulation, or assembly of the described materials before their incorporation into an archival repository. The <origination> element may be used to indicate such agents as correspondents, records creators, collectors, and dealers. Using the LABEL attribute may help identify for a finding aid reader the role of the originator, e.g., "creator," "collector," or "photographer." It is also possible to set the ROLE attribute on the name elements that are available within <origination>, i.e., <corpname>, <famname>, <name>, and <persname>.

The <origination> element is comparable to ISAD(G) data element 3.2.1 and MARC fields 100, 110, 700, and 710.

May contain:

#PCDATA, abbr, archref, bibref, corpname, emph, expan, extptr, extref, famname, lb, linkgrp, name, persname, ptr, ref, title

May occur within:

archref, did, entry, event, extref, extrefloc, item, label, p, ref, refloc

Attributes:

ALTRENDER	#IMPLIED, CDATA
AUDIENCE	#IMPLIED, external, internal
ENCODINGANALOG	#IMPLIED, CDATA
ID	#IMPLIED, ID
LABEL	#IMPLIED, CDATA

Examples:

1.
```
<archdesc level="collection">
   <did>
      <origination label="Creator:"><persname
         encodinganalog="100" normal="Frisell, Toni"
         role="photographer">Toni Frisell</persname>
      </origination>
   </did>
</archdesc>
```

<origination>

2.

```
<archdesc type="inventory" level="subgrp">
   <did>
      <head>Overview of the Records</head>
      <repository label="Repository:"><corpname>Minnesota
         Historical Society</corpname></repository>
      <origination label="Creator:"><corpname>Minnesota. Game and
         Fish Department</corpname></origination>
      <unittitle label="Title:">Game laws violation records,
      </unittitle>
      <unitdate label="Dates:">1908-1928</unitdate>
      <abstract label="Abstract:">Records of prosecutions for and
         seizures of property resulting from violation of the
         state's hunting and fishing laws.</abstract>
      <physdesc label="Quantity:">2.25 cu. ft. (7 v. and 1 folder
         in 3 boxes)</physdesc>
      <physloc label="Location:">See Detailed Description section
         for box location</physloc>
   </did>
</archdesc>
```

<otherfindaid> Other Finding Aid

Description:

Information about additional or alternative guides to the described material, such as card files, dealers' inventories, or lists generated by the creator or compiler of the materials. It is used to indicate the existence of additional finding aids; it is not designed to encode the content of those guides.

Do not confuse with <fileplan>, which designates information about a particular type of access tool, known as a file plan, which explains the classification scheme used by the parties originally responsible for creating or compiling the described materials.

The <archref> element may be used to give a formal citation to the other finding aid or to link to an online version of it.

In EAD Version 1.0 <otherfindaid> was a subelement of Adjunct Descriptive Data <add>, which has been deprecated in EAD 2002 (see Appendix B). The new Description Group <descgrp> element, which can group any of the <did>-level elements (except the Description of Subordinate Components <dsc>), may be used to wrap elements where a group heading is desirable. The <descgrp> element can be used to replace <add> when converting finding aids encoded in EAD V1.0 to EAD 2002.

The <otherfindaid> element is comparable to ISAD(G) data element 3.4.5.

May contain:

address, archref, bibref, blockquote, chronlist, extref, head, linkgrp, list, note, otherfindaid, p, ref, table, title

May occur within:

archdesc, archdescgrp, c, c01, c02, c03, c04, c05, c06, c07, c08, c09, c10, c11, c12, descgrp, otherfindaid

Attributes:

ALTRENDER	#IMPLIED, CDATA
AUDIENCE	#IMPLIED, external, internal
ENCODINGANALOG	#IMPLIED, CDATA
ID	#IMPLIED, ID

<otherfindaid>

Example:

```
<otherfindaid>
   <bibref>The Society has published an expanded guide to this
      collection: <title>Guide to the Records of the American
      Crystal Sugar Company. </title>Compiled by <persname
      role="author">David Carmichael; </persname>assisted by
      <persname role="author">Lydia A. Lucas </persname>and
      <persname role="author">Marion E. Matters. </persname>St.
      Paul. Division of Archives and Manuscripts. Minnesota
      Historical Society. 1985.
   </bibref>
</otherfindaid>
```

<p> Paragraph

Description:

One or more sentences that form a logical prose passage. A paragraph may be a subdivision of a larger composition, or it may exist alone. It is usually typographically distinct: A line space is often left blank before it; the text begins on a new line; and the first letter of the first word is often indented, enlarged, or both. The <p> element is an important textual feature, which may be used inside of more than thirty other elements. The content model of a <p> provides access to thirty-three other elements, including reference and linking elements, formatting elements, controlled access elements, and some of the Descriptive Identification <did> subelements.

May contain:

#PCDATA, abbr, address, archref, bibref, blockquote, chronlist, corpname, date, emph, expan, extptr, extref, famname, function, genreform, geogname, lb, linkgrp, list, name, note, num, occupation, origination, persname, ptr, ref, repository, subject, table, title, unitdate, unittitle

May occur within:

accessrestrict, accruals, acqinfo, altformavail, appraisal, arrangement, bibliography, bioghist, blockquote, controlaccess, custodhist, daodesc, descgrp, div, dsc, dscgrp, editionstmt, fileplan, index, note, odd, originalsloc, otherfindaid, phystech, prefercite, processinfo, publicationstmt, relatedmaterial, scopecontent, separatedmaterial, seriesstmt, titlepage, userestrict

Attributes:

ALTRENDER	#IMPLIED, CDATA
AUDIENCE	#IMPLIED, external, internal
ID	#IMPLIED, ID

<p>

Example:

```
<bioghist>
   <head>Biographical Sketch</head>
   <p>John Ferguson Godfrey was born in Toronto on December 19,
      1942. He received a B.A. (Hons.) from Trinity College,
      University of Toronto, in 1965, a M.Phil. degree from
      Balliol College, Oxford University, England, in 1967, and a
      D.Phil. degree from St. Anthony's College, Oxford
      University, in 1975. He holds the title of Doctor of Sacred
      letters (honoris causa), Trinity College (1987).</p>
   <p>Mr. Godfrey taught in the Department of History of
      Dalhousie University, Halifax, first as Assistant Professor
      (1970-1975), and then as Associate Professor (1980-1987).
      At <corpname>King's College University, Halifax</corpname>
      he held the position of Assistant Professor (1975-1976),
      before becoming President and Vice-Chancellor (1977-
      1987).</p>
</bioghist>
```

<persname> Personal Name

Description:

The proper noun designation for an individual, including any or all of that individual's forenames, surnames, honorific titles, and added names.

All names in a finding aid do not have to be tagged. One option is to tag those names for which access other than basic, undifferentiated keyword retrieval is desired. Use of controlled vocabulary forms is recommended to facilitate access to names within and across finding aid systems. The <persname> element may be used in text elements such as <p>. To indicate a personal name with major representation in the materials being described, nest <persname> within the <controlaccess> element.

The ROLE attribute can be used to specify the relationship(s) of the name to the materials being described, for example, "compiler," "creator," "collector," or "subject." The NORMAL attribute can be used to provide the authority form of a name that has been encoded with <persname> in narrative text, e.g., within a paragraph. Use the SOURCE attribute to specify the vocabulary from which the name has been taken. The AUTHFILENUMBER attribute can be used to identify a link to an authority file record that has more information about the name or cross references for alternative forms of the name and related names. The RULES attribute can be used to specify the descriptive rules followed when forming the name, such as AACR2R.

See also related elements <controlaccess>, <corpname>, <famname>, and <name>.

The <persname> element is comparable to MARC fields 100, 600, and 700.

May contain:

#PCDATA, emph, extptr, lb, ptr

May occur within:

bibref, controlaccess, entry, event, extref, extrefloc, indexentry, item, label, namegrp, origination, p, physdesc, physfacet, ref, refloc, unittitle

<persname>

Attributes:

ALTRENDER	#IMPLIED, CDATA
AUDIENCE	#IMPLIED, external, internal
AUTHFILENUMBER	#IMPLIED, CDATA
ENCODINGANALOG	#IMPLIED, CDATA
ID	#IMPLIED, ID
NORMAL	#IMPLIED, CDATA
ROLE	#IMPLIED, CDATA
RULES	#IMPLIED, NMTOKEN
SOURCE	#IMPLIED, NMTOKEN

Examples:

1.
```
<scopecontent>
   <head>Scope and Content Note</head>
   <p>The papers of university professor and economist Mark
      Perlman span the dates 1952-1994, with most of the papers
      being dated between 1967 and 1989.  The papers consist
      chiefly of professional correspondence to and from Perlman,
      indexes to these letters and a small number of subject
      files, but include none of his personal papers.  The
      collection documents Perlman's career as an economist and
      author at <corpname normal="Cornell
      University">Cornell,</corpname> <corpname normal="Johns
      Hopkins University">Johns Hopkins,</corpname> and the
      <corpname>University of Pittsburgh</corpname> and reflects
      his interest in work arbitration, trade unions, and the
      economics of public health.  Among correspondents are many
      noted economists, including <persname normal="Abramovitz,
      Moses">Moses Abramovitz, </persname><persname
      normal="Shubik, Martin">Martin Shubik, </persname>and
      <persname normal="Bronfenbrenner, Martin">Martin
      Bronfenbrenner. </persname>  While many of the letters are
      personal in nature, others contain considerable information
      about Perlman's work, particularly in the years around the
      publication of his works <title render="italic">Judges in
      Industry: A Study of Labor Arbitration in Australia</title>
      <date type="publication">(1954)</date> and <title
      render="italic">Spatial, Regional, and Population
      Economics: Essays in Honor of Edgar M. Hoover</title> <date
      type="publication">(1972).</date>  Additional
      correspondence relates to the publication of the <title
      render="italic">Journal of Economic Literature.</title></p>
</scopecontent>
```

2.

```
<controlaccess>
   <head>Subjects:</head>
   <persname encodinganalog="600$a" source="lcnaf">Reimann, Lewis
      Charles, 1909-1978.</persname>
   <persname encodinganalog="600$a" source="lcnaf">Evans,
      Thomas.</persname>
   <persname encodinganalog="600$a" source="lcnaf">Trippe,
      Matthew J., 1915-1967.</persname>
   <persname encodinganalog="600$a" source="lcnaf">Elliot,
      Raymond.</persname>
</controlaccess>
```

<physdesc> Physical Description

Description:

A wrapper element for bundling information about the appearance or construction of the described materials, such as their dimensions, a count of their quantity or statement about the space they occupy, and terms describing their genre, form, or function, as well as any other aspects of their appearance, such as color, substance, style, and technique or method of creation. The information may be presented as plain text, or it may be divided into the <dimension>, <extent>, <genreform>, and <physfacet> subelements.

The <physdesc> element is comparable to ISAD(G) data element 3.1.5 and MARC field 300.

May contain:

#PCDATA, abbr, archref, bibref, corpname, date, dimensions, emph, expan, extent, extptr, extref, famname, function, genreform, geogname, lb, linkgrp, name, occupation, persname, physfacet, ptr, ref, subject, title

May occur within:

archref, did

Attributes:

ALTRENDER	#IMPLIED, CDATA
AUDIENCE	#IMPLIED, external, internal
ENCODINGANALOG	#IMPLIED, CDATA
ID	#IMPLIED, ID
LABEL	#IMPLIED, CDATA
RULES	#IMPLIED, NMTOKEN
SOURCE	#IMPLIED, NMTOKEN

Examples:

1.
```
<c01 level="series">
   <did>
      <unittitle>Seizure Records, </unittitle>
      <unitdate>December 1908-January 1928.</unitdate>
      <physdesc>4 volumes and 1 folder.</physdesc>
   </did>
</c01>
```

2.
```
<c level="subseries">
   <did>
      <unittitle>Documentary Movies, </unittitle>
      <unitdate type="inclusive">1952-1964</unitdate>
      <physdesc><extent>2.5 linear ft.</extent></physdesc>
   </did>
</c>
```

<physfacet> Physical Facet

Description:

A <physdesc> subelement for information about an aspect of the appearance of the described materials, such as their color, style, marks, substances, materials, or techniques and methods of creation. It is used especially to note aspects of appearance that affect or limit use of the materials. It generally should not be used for aspects of physical description that are covered more directly by the <extent>, <dimensions>, and <genreform> elements, although use of <genreform> may be appropriate for further specification within some <physfacet> instances.

The TYPE attribute may be used to specify which aspect of the physical appearance is being designated, e.g.,

```
<physfacet type="color">red</physfacet>
```

May contain:

#PCDATA, abbr, archref, bibref, corpname, date, emph, expan, extptr, extref, famname, function, genreform, geogname, lb, linkgrp, name, occupation, persname, ptr, ref, subject, title

May occur within:

physdesc

Attributes:

ALTRENDER	#IMPLIED, CDATA
AUDIENCE	#IMPLIED, external, internal
ENCODINGANALOG	#IMPLIED, CDATA
ID	#IMPLIED, ID
LABEL	#IMPLIED, CDATA
RULES	#IMPLIED, NMTOKEN
SOURCE	#IMPLIED, NMTOKEN
TYPE	#IMPLIED, CDATA
UNIT	#IMPLIED, CDATA

Examples:

1.
```
<physdesc>
   <extent>3 </extent>
   <genreform>daguerreotypes, </genreform>
   <physfacet>hand colored</physfacet>
</physdesc>
```

<physfacet>

2.
```
<physdesc>
   <physfacet type="material">Paper</physfacet>
   <physfacet type="ruling">Ruled in red ink</physfacet>
   <physfacet type="watermarks">Briquet 1234</physfacet>
   <physfacet type="binding">Bound in 19th century red
      leather</physfacet>
</physdesc>
```

<physloc> Physical Location

Description:

Information identifying the place where the described materials are stored, such as the name or number of the building, room, stack, shelf, or other tangible area.

Do not confuse with <container>, which is used to identify the cartons, boxes, reels, folders, and other storage devices used to hold the described materials. Also do not confuse with <repository>, which is used to identify the institution or agency responsible for providing intellectual access to the described materials.

Like all Descriptive Identification <did> subelements, the <physloc> element has a LABEL attribute which may be used to provide a readily understandable heading for the element's content. The TYPE attribute may also be used to identify the nature of the storage location. For security reasons, the AUDIENCE attribute value may be set to "internal" to shield public access to storage location information.

The <physloc> element is comparable to MARC field 852.

May contain:

#PCDATA, abbr, archref, bibref, emph, expan, extptr, extref, lb, linkgrp, ptr, ref, title

May occur within:

archref, did

Attributes:

ALTRENDER	#IMPLIED, CDATA
AUDIENCE	#IMPLIED, external, internal
ENCODINGANALOG	#IMPLIED, CDATA
ID	#IMPLIED, ID
LABEL	#IMPLIED, CDATA
PARENT	#IMPLIED, IDREFS
TYPE	#IMPLIED, CDATA

<physloc>

Examples:

1.
```
<archdesc type="inventory" level="subgrp">
   <did>
      <head>Overview of the Records</head>
      <repository label="Repository:"><corpname>Minnesota
         Historical Society</corpname></repository>
      <origination label="Creator:">Minnesota. Game and Fish
         Department</origination>
      <unittitle label="Title:">Game laws violation records,
      </unittitle>
      <unitdate label="Dates:">1908-1928</unitdate>
      <abstract label="Abstract:">Records of prosecutions for and
         seizures of property resulting from violation of the
         state's hunting and fishing laws.</abstract>
      <physdesc label="Quantity:">2.25 cu. ft. (7 v. and 1 folder
         in 3 boxes)</physdesc>
      <physloc label="Location:">See Detailed Description section
         for box location</physloc>
   </did>
</archdesc>
```

2.
```
<c02 level="file">
   <did>
      <physloc>112.I.8.1B-2</physloc>
      <container type="box">2</container>
      <unittitle><unitdate type="inclusive">December 1908-July
         1917</unitdate></unittitle>
   </did>
</c02>
```

<phystech> Physical Characteristics and Technical Requirements

Description:

A description of important physical conditions or characteristics that affect the storage, preservation, or use of the materials described. This includes details of their physical composition or the need for particular hardware or software to preserve or access the materials.

The <phystech> element is comparable to ISAD(G) data element 3.4.4 and MARC fields 340 and 538.

May contain:

address, blockquote, chronlist, head, list, note, p, phystech, table

May occur within:

archdesc, archdescgrp, c, c01, c02, c03, c04, c05, c06, c07, c08, c09, c10, c11, c12, descgrp, phystech

Attributes:

ALTRENDER	#IMPLIED, CDATA
AUDIENCE	#IMPLIED, external, internal
ENCODINGANALOG	#IMPLIED, CDATA
ID	#IMPLIED, ID
TYPE	#IMPLIED, CDATA

Examples:

1.
```
<c04 level="item">
   <did>[...]</did>
   <phystech>
      <p>Some oxydization of the aluminum layer.</p>
   </phystech>
</c04>
```

2.
```
<c02 level="subseries">
   <did>[...]</did>
   <phystech>
      <head>System Requirements</head>
      <p>48K RAM; Apple Disk II with controller; colour
         monitor</p>
   </phystech>
</c02>
```

<prefercite> Preferred Citation

Description:

Information about how users should identify the described materials when referring to them in published credits. Generally the repository or agent responsible for providing intellectual access to the materials will supply users with a recommended wording or prescribed format for structuring references to the described materials in bibliographies, footnotes, screen credits, etc.

Do not confuse with <archref> or <bibref> which are used to cite and/or link to materials other than those described in the finding aid.

In EAD Version 1.0 <prefercite> was a subelement of Administrative Information <admininfo>, which has been deprecated in EAD 2002 (see Appendix B). The new Description Group <descgrp> element, which can group any of the <did>-level elements (except the Description of Subordinate Components <dsc>), may be used to wrap elements where a group heading is desirable. The <descgrp> element can be used to replace <admininfo> where it has been used as a wrapper when converting finding aids encoded in EAD V1.0 to EAD 2002.

The <prefercite> element is comparable to MARC field 524.

May contain:

address, blockquote, chronlist, head, list, note, p, prefercite, table

May occur within:

archdesc, archdescgrp, c, c01, c02, c03, c04, c05, c06, c07, c08, c09, c10, c11, c12, descgrp, prefercite

Attributes:

ALTRENDER	#IMPLIED, CDATA
AUDIENCE	#IMPLIED, external, internal
ENCODINGANALOG	#IMPLIED, CDATA
ID	#IMPLIED, ID

Examples:

1.
```
<prefercite>
   <head>Preferred Citation</head>
   <p>[Identification of item], Arequipa Sanatorium Records, BANC
      MSS 92/894c, The Bancroft Library, University of
      California, Berkeley.</p>
</prefercite>
```

2.
```
<prefercite>
   <p>item, folder title, box number, Charles Thomas, Jr. Papers,
      Bentley Historical Library, University of Michigan.</p>
</prefercite>
```

<processinfo> Processing Information

Description:

Information about accessioning, arranging, describing, preserving, storing, or otherwise preparing the described materials for research use. Specific aspects of each of these activities may be encoded separately within other elements, such as <acqinfo>, <arrangement>, <physloc>, etc.

In EAD Version 1.0 <processinfo> was a subelement of Administrative Information <admininfo>, which has been deprecated in EAD 2002 (see Appendix B). The new Description Group <descgrp> element, which can group any of the <did>-level elements (except the Description of Subordinate Components <dsc>), may be used to wrap elements where a group heading is desirable. The <descgrp> element can be used to replace <admininfo> where it has been used as a wrapper when converting finding aids encoded in EAD V1.0 to EAD 2002.

The <processinfo> element is comparable to ISAD(G) data element 3.7.1 and MARC field 583. A <date> within a <processinfo><p> element is comparable to ISAD(G) data element 3.7.3.

May contain:

address, blockquote, chronlist, head, list, note, p, processinfo, table

May occur within:

archdesc, archdescgrp, c, c01, c02, c03, c04, c05, c06, c07, c08, c09, c10, c11, c12, descgrp, processinfo

Attributes:

ALTRENDER	#IMPLIED, CDATA
AUDIENCE	#IMPLIED, external, internal
ENCODINGANALOG	#IMPLIED, CDATA
ID	#IMPLIED, ID
TYPE	#IMPLIED, CDATA

Example:

```
<processinfo>
   <head>Processing Information:</head>
   <p>These records were organized and cataloged in
      <date>1977</date> by Lydia Lucas.</p>
</processinfo>
```

<profiledesc> Profile Description

Description:

An optional subelement of the <eadheader> that bundles information about the creation of the encoded version of the finding aid, including the name of the agent, place, and date of encoding. The <profiledesc> element also designates the predominant and minor languages used in the finding aid.

Do not confuse with <filedesc>, which bundles such bibliographic information as the title, author, publisher, edition, and publishing series of the finding aid.

For newer finding aids, the author and encoder may be the same person or institution, but for most older finding aids, someone other than the author will be converting and encoding the document. The encoder should be listed in the <creation> subelement of <profiledesc>, while the author should be identified in the <titlestmt> subelement of <filedesc>.

Within <profiledesc> the Descriptive Rules <descrules> element can be used to specify the descriptive code or guidelines followed in creating the finding aid.

May contain:

creation, descrules, langusage

May occur within:

eadheader

Attributes:

ALTRENDER	#IMPLIED, CDATA
AUDIENCE	#IMPLIED, external, internal
ENCODINGANALOG	#IMPLIED, CDATA
ID	#IMPLIED, ID

<profiledesc>

Example:

```
<eadheader audience="internal" langencoding="iso639-2b">
   <eadid>[...]</eadid>
   <filedesc>[...]</filedesc>
   <profiledesc>
      <creation>Machine-readable finding aid and skeletal markup
         derived via a macro from WordPerfect file; markup
         checked and completed by Sarah Taylor. <date
         normal="19950423">April 23, 1995.</date>
      </creation>
      <langusage>Finding aid written in <language
         langcode="eng">English.</language></langusage>
      <descrules>Finding aid prepared using <title
         render="italic">Rules for Archival Description</title>
      </descrules>
   </profiledesc>
</eadheader>
```

<ptr> Pointer

Description:

An empty internal linking element that uses attributes to provide for movement from one place in a finding aid to another place in the same finding aid. Unlike the <ref> element, the <ptr> element cannot contain text and subelements to describe the referenced object.

Do not confuse with <extptr> which is used to connect the EAD document to an external electronic object, which is not part of the described materials.

See related linking elements <extptr>, <extptrloc>, <extref>, <extrefloc>, <linkgrp>, <ptrgrp>, <ptrloc>, <ref>, and <refloc>.

While XML Linking Language (XLink) Version 1.0, which is the basis for EAD linking elements, is a stable document, examples of EAD usage are hypothetical and have not been tested in real XLink-based applications. Those wishing to use XLink are encouraged to consult the specification available online at <http://www.w3.org/TR/xlink/>.

May contain:

EMPTY

May occur within:

abstract, addressline, archref, author, bibref, bibseries, container, corpname, creation, date, descrules, dimensions, edition, emph, entry, event, extent, extref, extrefloc, famname, function, genreform, geogname, head, head01, head02, imprint, indexentry, item, label, langmaterial, language, langusage, legalstatus, materialspec, name, num, occupation, origination, p, persname, physdesc, physfacet, physloc, ptrgrp, publisher, ref, refloc, repository, runner, sponsor, subarea, subject, subtitle, title, titleproper, unitdate, unitid, unittitle

Attributes:

ACTUATE	#IMPLIED, onload, onrequest, actuateother, actuatenone
ALTRENDER	#IMPLIED, CDATA
ARCROLE	#IMPLIED, CDATA
AUDIENCE	#IMPLIED, external, internal
HREF	#IMPLIED, CDATA
ID	#IMPLIED, ID
LINKTYPE	#FIXED, simple, simple
ROLE	#IMPLIED, CDATA
SHOW	#IMPLIED, new, replace, embed, showother, shownone
TARGET	#IMPLIED, IDREF
TITLE	#IMPLIED, CDATA
XPOINTER	#IMPLIED, CDATA

<ptr>

Example:

```
<appraisal>
   <p>This collection was re-appraised by repository staff in
      1992 in order to facilitate use by weeding the collection
      of materials no longed deemed as having evidential or
      informational value. A list of materials removed from the
      collection after the re-appraisal is provided at the end of
      this guide.<ptr linktype="simple" actuate="onrequest"
      show="replace" target="mss1982-062_add2"/>
   </p>
</appraisal>
```

<ptrgrp> Pointer Group

Description:

A wrapper element for two or more Pointer <ptr> or Reference <ref> elements used in an <indexentry>. Pointers and references are internal links that provide for movement from one place in the finding aid to another place in the same finding aid. When encoding an index in EAD, a name or entry is generally listed only once, followed by a <ptrgrp> containing the series of pointers and references that link the name or entry to the places in the finding aid where it appears. The <ptrgrp> prevents the name or entry from having to appear multiple times in the index.

May contain:

ptr, ref

May occur within:

indexentry

Attributes:

ALTRENDER	#IMPLIED, CDATA
AUDIENCE	#IMPLIED, external, internal
ID	#IMPLIED, ID

Example:

```
<index>
   <head>Correspondent Index</head>
   <indexentry>
      <persname>Adeltraud, Jerome</persname>
      <ptrgrp>
         <ref linktype="simple" target="corresp19730824"
            actuate="onrequest" show="replace"><date
            normal="19730824">1973 August 24</date></ref>
         <ref linktype="simple" target="corresp19740228"
            actuate="onrequest" show="replace"><date
            normal="19740228">1974 February 28</date></ref>
         <ref linktype="simple" target="corresp19750315"
            actuate="onrequest" show="replace"><date
            normal="19750315">1975 March 15</date></ref>
      </ptrgrp>
   </indexentry> . . .
</index>
```

<ptrloc> Pointer Location

Description:

The location of a pointer <ptr> that is a resource in an extended link.

While XML Linking Language (XLink) Version 1.0, which is the basis for EAD linking elements, is a stable document, examples of EAD usage are hypothetical and have not been tested in real XLink-based applications. Those wishing to use XLink are encouraged to consult the specification available online at <http://www.w3.org/TR/xlink/>.

May contain:

EMPTY

May occur within:

daogrp, linkgrp

Attributes:

ALTRENDER	#IMPLIED, CDATA
AUDIENCE	#IMPLIED, external, internal
HREF	#IMPLIED, CDATA
ID	#IMPLIED, ID
LABEL	#IMPLIED, NMTOKEN
LINKTYPE	#FIXED, locator, locator
ROLE	#IMPLIED, CDATA
TARGET	#IMPLIED, IDREF
TITLE	#IMPLIED, CDATA
XPOINTER	#IMPLIED, CDATA

<publicationstmt> Publication Statement

Description:

A wrapper element within the <filedesc> portion of <eadheader> for information concerning the publication or distribution of the encoded finding aid, including the publisher's name and address, the date of publication, and other relevant details. The <publicationstmt> may contain just text, laid out in Paragraphs <p>, or it may include the <publisher>, <address>, <date>, and <num> elements, which allow for more specific tagging of a publisher's name and address, the date of publication, and the number, if any, assigned to the published finding aid.

May contain:

address, date, num, p, publisher

May occur within:

filedesc

Attributes:

ALTRENDER	#IMPLIED, CDATA
AUDIENCE	#IMPLIED, external, internal
ENCODINGANALOG	#IMPLIED, CDATA
ID	#IMPLIED, ID

Examples:

```
<filedesc>
   <titlestmt>[...]</titlestmt>
   <publicationstmt>
      <date>1995</date>
      <publisher>Prints &amp; Photographs Division<lb/>Library of
         Congress</publisher>
      <address><addressline>Washington, D.C.
         20540</addressline></address>
   </publicationstmt>
</filedesc>
```

<publisher> Publisher

Description:

When used in the <publicationstmt> portion of <eadheader> and in the <titlepage> element in <frontmatter>, the <publisher> is the name of the party responsible for issuing or distributing the encoded finding aid. Often this party is the same corporate body identified in the <repository> element in the finding aid. When used in the <imprint> section of a Bibliographic Reference <bibref>, the <publisher> is the name of the party issuing a monograph or other bibliographic work cited in the finding aid.

May contain:

#PCDATA, emph, extptr, lb, ptr

May occur within:

imprint, publicationstmt, titlepage

Attributes:

ALTRENDER	#IMPLIED, CDATA
AUDIENCE	#IMPLIED, external, internal
ENCODINGANALOG	#IMPLIED, CDATA
ID	#IMPLIED, ID

Examples:

1.
```
<filedesc>
   <titlestmt>[...]</titlestmt>
   <publicationstmt>
      <date>1995</date>
      <publisher>Prints &amp; Photographs Division<lb/>Library of
         Congress</publisher>
      <address><addressline>Washington, D.C.
         20540</addressline></address>
   </publicationstmt>
</filedesc>
```

2.
```
<bibliography>
   <bibref>
      <persname role="author">Kinder, Dolores.</persname>
      <title >Once Upon a Lullaby.</title>
      <imprint><geogname>New York: </geogname>
      <publisher>Wells &amp; Sons, </publisher>
      <date type="publication">1931</date></imprint>
   </bibref>
</bibliography>
```

<ref> Reference

Description:

An internal linking element that provides for movement from one place in a finding aid to another place in the same finding aid. Unlike the internal Pointer <ptr> element, the <ref> element may contain text and subelements that identify or describe the referenced object. The <ref> element may be used in a variety of ways in an encoded finding aid. For example, a <ref> may provide a dynamic link from one Component <c> to another related Component <c> in the same way that *See* and *See also* references direct readers of paper-based finding aids. Or, a <ref> might be used to direct the reader from text in a scope and content note to a description of a Component <c> in a contents list.

While XML Linking Language (XLink) Version 1.0, which is the basis for EAD linking elements, is a stable document, examples of EAD usage are hypothetical and have not been tested in real XLink-based applications. Those wishing to use XLink are encouraged to consult the specification available online at <http://www.w3.org/TR/xlink/>.

May contain:

#PCDATA, abbr, address, archref, bibref, blockquote, chronlist, corpname, date, emph, expan, extptr, extref, famname, function, genreform, geogname, lb, list, name, note, num, occupation, origination, persname, ptr, repository, subject, table, title, unitdate, unittitle

May occur within:

abstract, archref, bibliography, bibref, container, creation, descrules, dimensions, emph, entry, event, extent, extref, indexentry, item, label, langmaterial, langusage, materialspec, origination, otherfindaid, p, physdesc, physfacet, physloc, ptrgrp, relatedmaterial, repository, separatedmaterial, unitdate, unitid, unittitle

Attributes:

ACTUATE	#IMPLIED, onload, onrequest, actuateother, actuatenone
ALTRENDER	#IMPLIED, CDATA
ARCROLE	#IMPLIED, CDATA
AUDIENCE	#IMPLIED, external, internal
HREF	#IMPLIED, CDATA
ID	#IMPLIED, ID
LINKTYPE	#FIXED, simple, simple
ROLE	#IMPLIED, CDATA
SHOW	#IMPLIED, new, replace, embed, showother, shownone
TARGET	#IMPLIED, IDREF
TITLE	#IMPLIED, CDATA
XPOINTER	#IMPLIED, CDATA

Example:

```
<index>
   <head>Index to Correspondents and Recipients</head>
   <indexentry>
      <corpname>Bach &amp; Bros.</corpname>
      <ref linktype="simple" target="NonC:21-2" show="replace"
         actuate="onrequest">(In non correspondence)</ref>
   </indexentry>
   <indexentry>
      <namegrp>
         <corpname>Bacon and Lewis, Ltd.</corpname>
         <persname>Levering, Alexander M.</persname>
         <persname>Windom, Lucious</persname>
      </namegrp>
      <ref linktype="simple" target="Cres:18610408"
         show="replace" actuate="onrequest">(1861 Apr. 8, ALS,
         to W.W., re: inquiry into what to do with unsold
         flour)</ref>
   </indexentry> . . .
</index>
```

<refloc> Reference Location

Description:

A linking element that provides the location of a reference <ref> that is a resource in an extended link.

While XML Linking Language (XLink) Version 1.0, which is the basis for EAD linking elements, is a stable document, examples of EAD usage are hypothetical and have not been tested in real XLink-based applications. Those wishing to use XLink are encouraged to consult the specification available online at <http://www.w3.org/TR/xlink/>.

May contain:

#PCDATA, abbr, address, blockquote, chronlist, corpname, date, emph, expan, extptr, famname, function, genreform, geogname, lb, list, name, note, num, occupation, origination, persname, ptr, repository, subject, table, unitdate, unittitle

May occur within:

daogrp, linkgrp

Attributes:

ALTRENDER	#IMPLIED, CDATA
AUDIENCE	#IMPLIED, external, internal
HREF	#IMPLIED, CDATA
ID	#IMPLIED, ID
LABEL	#IMPLIED, NMTOKEN
LINKTYPE	#FIXED, locator, locator
ROLE	#IMPLIED, CDATA
TARGET	#IMPLIED, IDREF
TITLE	#IMPLIED, CDATA
XPOINTER	#IMPLIED, CDATA

Example:

```
<archdesc level="collection">
   <did>[...]</did>
   <arrangement>
      <p>This collection is organized into two major sections.
         The Original Gift portion reflects the materials
         originally donated to the Society by Mr. Provenance,
         while the Additions portion contains records transferred
         following his death.  As these two groups of documents
         have not been physically interfiled, materials on any
         given topic may appear in either or both sections, each
         of which is divided into four parallel series.
         <linkgrp>
            <refloc target="a9"></refloc>
            <refloc target="s1"></refloc>
            <refloc target="s7"></refloc>
         </linkgrp>
      </p>
      <p id="a9">Personal Correspondence></p>
      <p id="a10">Financial Records</p>
      <p id="a11">Diaries</p>
      <p id="a12">Literary Manuscripts</p>
   </arrangement>
   <dsc type="combined">
      <head>Original Gift</head>
      <c01 id="s1">
         <did>
            <unittitle>Personal correspondence, </unittitle>
            <unitdate>1917-1965.</unitdate>
         </did>
      </c01> . . .
   </dsc>
   <dsc type="combined">
      <head>Additions</head>
      <c01 id="s7">
         <did>
            <unittitle>Personal correspondence, </unittitle>
            <unitdate>1922-1945.</unitdate>
         </did>
      </c01> . . .
   </dsc>
</archdesc>
```

<relatedmaterial> Related Material

Description:

Information about materials that are not physically or logically included in the material described in the finding aid but that may be of use to a reader because of an association to the described materials. Materials designated by this element are not related to the described material by provenance, accumulation, or use.

Do not confuse <relatedmaterial> with the element <separatedmaterial>, which provides information about materials that have been separated or physically removed from the described materials but that are related to them by provenance. Also do not confuse with <altformavail>, which encodes information about copies of the described materials, such as microforms, photocopies, and reproductions in digital formats. Do not confuse with <originalsloc>, which encodes information regarding the existence and location of the originals when the unit being described consists of copies.

In EAD Version 1.0 <relatedmaterial> was a subelement of Adjunct Descriptive data <add>, which has been deprecated in EAD 2002 (see Appendix B). The new Description Group <descgrp> element, which can group any of the <did>-level elements (except the Description of Subordinate Components <dsc>), may be used to wrap elements where a group heading is desirable. The <descgrp> element can be used to replace <add> when converting finding aids encoded in EAD V1.0 to EAD 2002.

The <relatedmaterial> element is comparable to ISAD(G) data element 3.5.3 and MARC field 544 with indicator 1.

May contain:

address, archref, bibref, blockquote, chronlist, extref, head, linkgrp, list, note, p, ref, relatedmaterial, table, title

May occur within:

archdesc, archdescgrp, c, c01, c02, c03, c04, c05, c06, c07, c08, c09, c10, c11, c12, descgrp, relatedmaterial

Attributes:

ALTRENDER	#IMPLIED, CDATA
AUDIENCE	#IMPLIED, external, internal
ENCODINGANALOG	#IMPLIED, CDATA
ID	#IMPLIED, ID
TYPE	#IMPLIED, CDATA

<relatedmaterial>

Examples:

1.
```
<relatedmaterial>
   <head>Related Correspondence</head>
   <p>Researchers should note that a significant amount of the
      correspondence between Franklin Wigglethorpe and Nellie
      Forbush is extant. In addition to the incoming letters in
      this collection from Mr. Wigglethorpe to Miss Forbush, the
      letters written to Mr. Wigglethorpe by Miss Forbush are
      available to researchers at the Mainline University Special
      Collections Library.</p>
   <archref><origination><persname>Wigglethorpe,
      Franklin.</persname></origination>
      <unittitle>Franklin Wigglethorpe Papers, <unitdate
      type="inclusive">1782-1809.</unitdate></unittitle>
      <unitid>MSS 00143</unitid>
   </archref>
   <p>An online guide to the Wigglethorpe Papers is available.
      <extptr actuate="onrequest" entityref="mu-scl-00143"
      show="new"></p>
</relatedmaterial>
```

2.
```
<separatedmaterial>
   <p>Photographs and sound recordings have been transferred to
      the appropriate custodial divisions of the Library where
      they are identified as part of these papers. Among the
      sound recordings are the following broadcasts:</p>
   <list>[...]</list>
</separatedmaterial>
<separatedmaterial>
   <p>Other papers of Earl Warren, which relate chiefly to his
      early years and public service in California, are held by
      the California State Archives in Sacramento.</p>
</separatedmaterial>
<relatedmaterial>
   <p>Records relating to the Warren Commission are held in the
      National Archives and Records Administration.</p>
</relatedmaterial>
```

<repository> Repository

Description:

The institution or agency responsible for providing intellectual access to the materials being described. The <corpname> element may be used within <repository> to encode the institution's proper name.

Although the repository providing intellectual access usually also has physical custody over the materials, this is not always the case. For example, an archives may assume responsibility for long-term intellectual access to electronic records, but the actual electronic data files or systems may continue to reside in the office where they were created and maintained, or they may be held for long-term storage by a unit such as a data library that is able to provide the appropriate technical facilities for storage and remounting. When it is clear that the physical custodian does not provide intellectual access, use <physloc> to identify the custodian and <repository> to designate the intellectual caretaker. When a distinction cannot be made, assume that the custodian of the physical objects also provides intellectual access to them and should be recognized as the <repository>.

The <repository> element is comparable to MARC field 852.

May contain:

#PCDATA, abbr, address, archref, bibref, corpname, emph, expan, extptr, extref, lb, linkgrp, name, ptr, ref, subarea, title

May occur within:

archref, did, entry, event, extref, extrefloc, item, label, p, ref, refloc

Attributes:

ALTRENDER	#IMPLIED, CDATA
AUDIENCE	#IMPLIED, external, internal
ENCODINGANALOG	#IMPLIED, CDATA
ID	#IMPLIED, ID
LABEL	#IMPLIED, CDATA

<repository>

Examples:

1.

```
<archdesc type="inventory" level="subgrp">
   <did>
      <head>Overview of the Records</head>
      <repository label="Repository:"><corpname>Minnesota
         Historical Society</corpname></repository>
      <origination label="Creator:">Minnesota. Game and Fish
         Department</origination>
      <unittitle label="Title:">Game laws violation records,
      </unittitle>
      <unitdate label="Dates:">1908-1928</unitdate>
      <abstract label="Abstract:">Records of prosecutions for and
         seizures of property resulting from violation of the
         state's hunting and fishing laws.</abstract>
      <physdesc label="Quantity:">2.25 cu. ft. (7 v. and 1 folder
         in 3 boxes)</physdesc>
      <physloc label="Location:">See Detailed Description section
         for box location</physloc>
   </did>
</archdesc>
```

2. Note: The Public Record Office of the United Kingdom uses a 7 level system of intellectual units devised specifically for that repository. In that system "lettercode" is the equivalent of "fonds" and "class" is the equivalent of "series."

```
<archdesc level="otherlevel" otherlevel="Lettercode">
   <did>
      <unitid>EW</unitid>
      <unittitle>Records of the Department of Economic
         Affairs</unittitle>
      <origination><corpname>Department of Economic
         Affairs</corpname></origination>
      <unitdate>1945-1979</unitdate>
      <physdesc><extent>28 </extent>
         <genreform>classes</genreform>
      </physdesc>
      <repository>Public Record Office, Kew</repository>
   </did>
</archdesc>
```

<resource> Resource

Description:

A linking element that specifies the local resource that participates in an extended link.

While XML Linking Language (XLink) Version 1.0, which is the basis for EAD linking elements, is a stable document, examples of EAD usage are hypothetical and have not been tested in real XLink-based applications. Those wishing to use XLink are encouraged to consult the specification available online at <http://www.w3.org/TR/xlink/>.

May contain:

#PCDATA, emph, lb

May occur within:

daogrp, linkgrp

Attributes:

ALTRENDER	#IMPLIED, CDATA
AUDIENCE	#IMPLIED, external, internal
ID	#IMPLIED, ID
LABEL	#IMPLIED, NMTOKEN
LINKTYPE	#FIXED, resource, resource
ROLE	#IMPLIED, CDATA
TITLE	#IMPLIED, CDATA

<resource>

Example:

```
<c02 level="file">
   <did>
      <unittitle>Photographs of John Smith and family
         members</unittitle>
      <unitdate type="inclusive" normal="1895/1928">1895-
         1928</unitdate>
      <daogrp linktype="extended">
         <daodesc>
            <p>Sample digitized image from this file: John Smith
               graduation portrait, <date normal="18950528">28
               May 1895</date>.</p>
         </daodesc>
         <resource linktype="resource" label="start"/>
         <daoloc entityref="f0042_1tmb" linktype="locator"
            label="thumb"/>
         <daoloc entityref="f0042_1ref" linktype="locator"
            label="reference"/>
         <arc linktype="arc" show="embed" actuate="onload"
            from="start" to="thumb"/>
         <arc linktype="arc" show="new" actuate="onrequest"
            from="thumb" to="reference"/>
      </daogrp>
   </did>
</c02>
```

<revisiondesc> Revision Description

Description:

An optional subelement of the <eadheader> for information about changes or alterations that have been made to the encoded finding aid. The revisions may be recorded as part of a <list> or as a series of <change> elements. Like much of the <eadheader>, the <revisiondesc> element is modeled on an element found in the Text Encoding Initiative (TEI) DTD. The TEI recommends that revisions be numbered and appear in reverse chronological order, with the most recent <change> first.

May contain:

change, list

May occur within:

eadheader

Attributes:

ALTRENDER	#IMPLIED, CDATA
AUDIENCE	#IMPLIED, external, internal
ENCODINGANALOG	#IMPLIED, CDATA
ID	#IMPLIED, ID

Example:

```
<eadheader audience="internal" langencoding="iso639-2b">
   <eadid>[...]</eadid>
   <filedesc>[...]</filedesc>
   <profiledesc>[...]</profiledesc>
   <revisiondesc>
      <change>
         <date normal="19970505">May 5, 1997</date>
         <item>This electronic finding aid was updated to current
            markup standards by Sarah Taylor using a perl script.
            Updates included: eadheader, eadid, arrangement of
            did elements and their labels.</item>
      </change>
   </revisiondesc>
</eadheader>
```

<row> Table Row

Description:

A formatting element that contains one or more <entry> elements (horizontal cells) in a table.

By convention, a rule specified by the ROWSEP attribute prints or displays below the row. Vertical rules are specified by the COLSEP attribute in <table> or one of its column-related subelements; external rules are specified by the FRAME attribute available on the <table> element.

See also related elements <table>, <tbody>, <tgroup>, and <thead>.

May contain:

entry

May occur within:

tbody, thead

Attributes:

ALTRENDER	#IMPLIED, CDATA
AUDIENCE	#IMPLIED, external, internal
ID	#IMPLIED, ID
ROWSEP	#IMPLIED, NMTOKEN
VALIGN	#IMPLIED, top, middle, bottom

Example:

```
<table frame="none">
   <tgroup cols="3">
      <colspec colnum="1" colname="1" align="left" colwidth="50pt"/>
      <colspec colnum="2" colname="2" align="left" colwidth="50pt"/>
      <colspec colnum="3" colname="3" align="left" colwidth="50pt"/>
      <thead>
         <row>
            <entry colname="1">Major Family Members</entry>
            <entry colname="2">Spouses</entry>
            <entry colname="3">Children</entry>
         </row>
      </thead>
      <tbody>
         <row>
            <entry colname="1">John Albemarle (1760-1806)</entry>
            <entry colname="2">Mary Frances Delaney (1769-
               1835)</entry>
            <entry colname="3">John Delaney Albemarle (1787-
               1848)</entry>
         </row> . . .
      </tbody>
   </tgroup>
</table>
```

<runner> Runner

Description:

An optional formatting element that provides for a header, footer, or watermark to appear on every page of a printed finding aid or throughout an electronic version. If a transparent image is desired as background, use <extptr> instead. The <runner> is available within <archdesc> and <archdescgrp> and must appear before the <did>. The PLACEMENT attribute specifies whether the <runner> should appear as a header, footer, or watermark.

May contain:

#PCDATA, emph, extptr, lb, ptr

May occur within:

archdesc, archdescgrp

Attributes:

ALTRENDER	#IMPLIED, CDATA
AUDIENCE	#IMPLIED, external, internal
ID	#IMPLIED, ID
PLACEMENT	#IMPLIED, footer, header, watermark
ROLE	#IMPLIED, CDATA

Example:

```
<runner placement="footer">Special Collections, University of
   Virginia Library, #5866-b</runner>
```

<scopecontent> Scope and Content

Description:

A prose statement summarizing the range and topical coverage of the described materials, often mentioning the form and arrangement of the materials and naming significant organizations, individuals, events, places, and subjects represented. The purpose of the <scopecontent> element is to assist readers in evaluating the potential relevance of the materials to their research. It may highlight particular strengths of, or gaps in, the described materials and may summarize in narrative form some of the descriptive information entered in other parts of the finding aid.

Additional <scopecontent> elements may be nested inside one another when a complex collection of materials is being described and separate headings are desired. For example, when a collection is received and processed in installments, individual scope and content notes may be created for each installment. EAD permits these separate narrative descriptions to be encoded as discrete <scopecontent> elements, but it also enables the encoder to gather the independent <scopecontent> notes within a single larger <scopecontent> reflective of the materials as a whole. Nested <scopecontent> elements might also occur when an institution encodes the first paragraph of a long scope and content note as a separate summary <scopecontent> with an ENCODINGANALOG attribute set to MARC field 520$a.

The <scopecontent> element is comparable to ISAD(G) data element 3.3.1 and MARC field 520.

May contain:

address, arrangement, blockquote, chronlist, dao, daogrp, head, list, note, p, scopecontent, table

May occur within:

archdesc, archdescgrp, c, c01, c02, c03, c04, c05, c06, c07, c08, c09, c10, c11, c12, descgrp, scopecontent

Attributes:

ALTRENDER	#IMPLIED, CDATA
AUDIENCE	#IMPLIED, external, internal
ENCODINGANALOG	#IMPLIED, CDATA
ID	#IMPLIED, ID

<scopecontent>

Examples:

1.
```
<archdesc level="fonds">
   <did>[...]</did>
   <scopecontent encodinganalog="520">
      <head>Scope and Content</head>
      <p>Fonds includes records relating to the Department of
         Plant Ecology's administration, teaching and research;
         extension work relating to the Saskatchewan Weed Survey;
         and correspondence with a variety of institutions and
         individuals. A series of minutes and correspondence
         relating to the Saskatchewan Committee on the Ecology
         and Preservation of Grasslands (established in 1935)
         documents the efforts to establish permanent reserves of
         significant grasslands in  Saskatchewan.</p>
   </scopecontent>
</archdesc>
```

2.
```
<dsc type="combined">
   <head>Detailed Description of the Collection</head>
   <c01 level="series">
      <did>
         <unittitle>Record of Prosecutions, </unittitle>
         <unitdate>1916-1927. </unitdate>
         <physdesc>3 volumes.</physdesc>
      </did>
      <scopecontent>
         <p>Information provided in each entry: date of report,
            name and address of person arrested, location where
            offense was committed, date of arrest, nature of
            offense, name of judge or justice, result of trial,
            amounts of fine and court costs, number of days
            served if jailed, name of warden, and occasional
            added remarks.  Types of offenses included hunting or
            fishing out of season or in unauthorized places,
            exceeding catch or bag limits, taking undersized
            fish, illegal fishing practices such as gill-netting
            or dynamiting, illegal hunting practices such as
            night-lighting, killing non-game birds, fishing or
            hunting without a license, and hunting-related
            offenses against persons such as fraud and
            assault.</p>
      </scopecontent>
   </c01>
</dsc>
```

3. **<scopecontent>**

```
<p>Papers of the Lewis family, 19th-20th cent., mainly letters
   to: Elizabeth, Lady Lewis (1844-1931), with a few to her
   husband Sir George Lewis, 1st Bart. (1833-1911); to one of
   their daughters, Katherine Elizabeth Lewis (d. 1961), with
   a few to their son Sir George Lewis, 2nd Bart. (1868-1927);
   and to their grand-daughter Elizabeth Lewis, later
   Wansbrough (d. 1995). Many of the letters are undated; some
   can be dated from the postmark on the envelope, but several
   letters were kept in the wrong envelopes; most of
   Paderewski's and Whistler's letters had become separated
   from their envelopes.</p>
```

</scopecontent>

<separatedmaterial> Separated Material

Description:

Information about materials that are associated by provenance to the described materials but that have been physically separated or removed. Items may be separated for various reasons, including the dispersal of special formats to more appropriate custodial units; the outright destruction of duplicate or nonessential material; and the deliberate or unintentional scattering of fonds among different repositories. Do not confuse with <relatedmaterial>, which is used to encode descriptions of or references to materials that are not physically or logically included in the material described in the finding aid but that may be of use to a reader because of an association to the described materials. Items encoded as <relatedmaterial> are not related to the described material by provenance, accumulation, or use.

In EAD Version 1.0 <separatedmaterial> was a subelement of Adjunct Descriptive Data <add>, which has been deprecated in EAD 2002 (see Appendix B). The new Description Group <descgrp> element, which can group any of the <did>-level elements (except the Description of Subordinate Components <dsc>), may be used to wrap elements where a group heading is desirable. The <descgrp> element can be used to replace <add> when converting finding aids encoded in EAD V1.0 to EAD 2002.

The <separatedmaterial> element is comparable to ISAD(G) data element 3.5.3 and MARC field 544 with indicator 0.

May contain:

address, archref, bibref, blockquote, chronlist, extref, head, linkgrp, list, note, p, ref, separatedmaterial, table, title

May occur within:

archdesc, archdescgrp, c, c01, c02, c03, c04, c05, c06, c07, c08, c09, c10, c11, c12, descgrp, separatedmaterial

Attributes:

ALTRENDER	#IMPLIED, CDATA
AUDIENCE	#IMPLIED, external, internal
ENCODINGANALOG	#IMPLIED, CDATA
ID	#IMPLIED, ID
TYPE	#IMPLIED, CDATA

Examples:

1.
```
<separatedmaterial>
   <head>Materials Cataloged Separately</head>
   <p>Photographs have been transferred to Pictorial Collections
      of The Bancroft Library.</p>
</separatedmaterial>
```

2.
```
<separatedmaterial>
   <p>Photographs and sound recordings have been transferred to
      the appropriate custodial divisions of the Library where
      they are identified as part of these papers. Among the
      sound recordings are the following broadcasts:</p>
   <list>[...]</list>
</separatedmaterial>
<separatedmaterial>
   <p>Other papers of Earl Warren, which relate chiefly to his
      early years and public service in California, are held by
      the California State Archives in Sacramento.</p>
</separatedmaterial>
<relatedmaterial>
   <p>Records relating to the Warren Commission are held in the
      National Archives and Records Administration.</p>
</relatedmaterial>
```

<seriesstmt> Series Statement

Description:

A wrapper element within the <filedesc> portion of <eadheader> that groups information about the published monographic series, if any, to which an encoded finding aid belongs. The <seriesstmt> may contain just text, laid out in Paragraphs <p>, or it may include the <titleproper> and <num> elements, which allow for more specific tagging of names or numbers associated with the series.

May contain:

num, p, titleproper

May occur within:

filedesc

Attributes:

ALTRENDER	#IMPLIED, CDATA
AUDIENCE	#IMPLIED, external, internal
ENCODINGANALOG	#IMPLIED, CDATA
ID	#IMPLIED, ID

Example:

```
<filedesc>
   <titlestmt>
      <titleproper>Inventory of the Alfred Harrison Joy Papers,
      <date>1910-1972</date></titleproper>
      <author>Processed by Ronald S. Brashear; machine-readable
         finding aid created by Xiuzhi Zhou</author>
   </titlestmt>
   <publicationstmt>
      &hdr-huntm;
      <date>&copy; 1998</date>
      <p>The Huntington Library. All rights reserved.</p>
   </publicationstmt>
   <seriesstmt>
      <p>Observatories of the Carnegie Institution of Washington
         Collection</p>
   </seriesstmt>
</filedesc>
```

<sponsor> Sponsor

Description:

Name(s) of institution(s) or individual(s) who endorsed, financed, or arranged the acquisition, appraisal, and processing of the described materials or the preparation and distribution of the finding aid. Because acknowledgment of such contributors often appears on title pages of finding aids, the <sponsor> element is available in both the optional <titlepage> element in <frontmatter> and in the required <titlestmt> portion of the <eadheader>. Do not confuse with <author>, which is used to denote the persons or institutions responsible for the intellectual content of the finding aid, or with <repository>, which is used to identify the institution or corporate body providing intellectual access to the described materials.

The <sponsor> element is comparable to MARC field 536.

May contain:

#PCDATA, emph, extptr, lb, ptr

May occur within:

titlepage, titlestmt

Attributes:

ALTRENDER	#IMPLIED, CDATA
AUDIENCE	#IMPLIED, external, internal
ENCODINGANALOG	#IMPLIED, CDATA
ID	#IMPLIED, ID

Example:

```
<filedesc>
   <titlestmt>
      <titleproper>Inventory of The Bruno Walter Papers,
      <date>ca. 1887-1966</date></titleproper>
      <author>Processed by Richard Koprowski, Fran Barulich, and
         Robert Kosovsky; machine-readable finding aid created by
         Robert Kosovsky</author>
      <sponsor>Encoding funded by the generous support of the
         Gladys Krieble Delmas Foundation.</sponsor>
   </titlestmt> . . .
</filedesc>
```

<subarea> Subordinate Area

Description:

A name or phrase that indicates a secondary or subsidiary administrative level within a repository or other corporate body; a specialized area of subject or other collecting emphasis within a larger unit; or an ancillary collecting area based on the physical form of the materials. This information may be included as plain text within the <repository> and <corpname> elements, or it may be encoded within <repository> and <corpname> as separately tagged <subarea> elements. The latter approach facilitates the filtering of finding aids by administrative division, department, or specialty. For <corpname>s other than <repository>, the <subarea> might help refine searches of large corporate entities, such as government agencies, which share common words, e.g., United States.

May contain:

#PCDATA, emph, extptr, lb, ptr

May occur within:

corpname, repository

Attributes:

ALTRENDER	#IMPLIED, CDATA
AUDIENCE	#IMPLIED, external, internal
ENCODINGANALOG	#IMPLIED, CDATA
ID	#IMPLIED, ID

Examples:

1.
```
<did>
   <repository><corpname>Library of Congress, <subarea>Manuscript
   Division</subarea></corpname></repository>
</did>
```

2.
```
<controlaccess>
   <head>Index Terms</head>
   <corpname>National Association for the Advancement of Colored
      People <subarea>Washington Bureau</subarea>
   </corpname>
</controlaccess>
```

<subject> Subject

Description:

A term that identifies a topic associated with or covered by the described materials. Personal, corporate, and geographic names behaving as subjects are tagged as <persname>, <corpname>, and <geogname>, respectively. The ROLE attribute can be set to "subject" when it is necessary to specify the relationship of the name to the materials being described.

All subjects mentioned in a finding aid do not have to be tagged. One option is to tag those subjects for which access other than basic, undifferentiated keyword retrieval is desired. Use of controlled vocabulary forms is recommended to facilitate access to the subjects within and across finding aid systems. The <subject> element may be used in text elements such as <p>. To indicate a subject with major representation in the materials being described, nest <subject> within the <controlaccess> element.

Use the SOURCE attribute to specify the vocabulary from which the term has been taken. The NORMAL attribute can be used to provide the authority form of a term that has been encoded with <subject> in narrative text, e.g., within a paragraph. The RULES attribute can be used to specify the descriptive rules followed when formulating the term. The AUTHFILENUMBER attribute can be used to identify a link to an authority file record that has more information about the subject or cross references for alternative forms of a subject term.

The <subject> element is comparable to MARC fields 650 and 69x.

May contain:

#PCDATA, emph, extptr, lb, ptr

May occur within:

controlaccess, entry, event, extref, extrefloc, indexentry, item, label, namegrp, p, physdesc, physfacet, ref, refloc, unittitle

Attributes:

ALTRENDER	#IMPLIED, CDATA
AUDIENCE	#IMPLIED, external, internal
AUTHFILENUMBER	#IMPLIED, CDATA
ENCODINGANALOG	#IMPLIED, CDATA
ID	#IMPLIED, ID
NORMAL	#IMPLIED, CDATA
RULES	#IMPLIED, NMTOKEN
SOURCE	#IMPLIED, NMTOKEN

<subject>

Example:

```
<controlaccess>
   <head>Selected Search Terms</head>
   <controlaccess>
      <head>Subjects:</head>
      <subject encodinganalog="650">Alien and Sedition laws,
         1798</subject>
      <subject encodinganalog="650">American Confederate
         voluntary exiles</subject>
      <subject encodinganalog="650">Kentucky and Virginia
         resolutions of 1798</subject>
   </controlaccess>
</controlaccess>
```

<subtitle> Subtitle

Description:

A secondary or subsidiary name of an encoded finding aid that is subordinate to the main name encoded in <titleproper>. The <subtitle> element is available only within <titlepage> and <titlestmt> to capture bibliographic aspects of the finding aid. Subtitles of monographs, serials, paintings, and other such works mentioned in the finding aid are not separately encoded, but they may be listed as part of the <title> element.

May contain:

#PCDATA, abbr, date, emph, expan, extptr, lb, num, ptr

May occur within:

titlepage, titlestmt

Attributes:

ALTRENDER	#IMPLIED, CDATA
AUDIENCE	#IMPLIED, external, internal
ENCODINGANALOG	#IMPLIED, CDATA
ID	#IMPLIED, ID

Example:

```
<filedesc>
   <titlestmt>
      <titleproper>Tom Stoppard</titleproper>
      <subtitle>An Inventory of His Papers at the Harry Ransom
         Humanities Research Center</subtitle>
      <author>Finding aid written by Katherine Mosley</author>
   </titlestmt>
   <publicationstmt>
      <publisher>The University of Texas at Austin, Harry Ransom
         Humanities Research Center</publisher>
      <date>2000</date>
   </publicationstmt>
</filedesc>
```

<table> Table

Description:

A wrapper element for formatting information in a row and column display.

The application of the <table> element is based on the XML Exchange Table Model, an XML expression of the Exchange subset of the full CALS table model DTD. This model is promulgated by the Organization for the Advancement of Structured Information Standards (OASIS) to promote interoperability among vendor products.

May contain:

head, tgroup

May occur within:

accessrestrict, accruals, acqinfo, altformavail, appraisal, arrangement, bibliography, bioghist, blockquote, controlaccess, custodhist, daodesc, descgrp, div, dsc, dscgrp, event, extref, extrefloc, fileplan, index, item, note, odd, originalsloc, otherfindaid, p, phystech, prefercite, processinfo, ref, refloc, relatedmaterial, scopecontent, separatedmaterial, titlepage, userestrict

Attributes:

ALTRENDER	#IMPLIED, CDATA
AUDIENCE	#IMPLIED, external, internal
COLSEP	#IMPLIED, NMTOKEN
FRAME	#IMPLIED, top, bottom, topbot, all, sides, none
ID	#IMPLIED, ID
PGWIDE	#IMPLIED, NMTOKEN
ROWSEP	#IMPLIED, NMTOKEN

Example:

```
<table frame="none">
   <tgroup cols="3">
      <colspec colnum="1" colname="1" align="left" colwidth="50pt"/>
      <colspec colnum="2" colname="2" align="left" colwidth="50pt"/>
      <colspec colnum="3" colname="3" align="left" colwidth="50pt"/>
      <thead>
         <row>
            <entry colname="1">Major Family Members</entry>
            <entry colname="2">Spouses</entry>
            <entry colname="3">Children</entry>
         </row>
      </thead>
      <tbody>
         <row>
            <entry colname="1">John Albemarle (1760-1806)</entry>
            <entry colname="2">Mary Frances Delaney (1769-
               1835)</entry>
            <entry colname="3">John Delaney Albemarle (1787-
               1848)</entry>
         </row> . . .
      </tbody>
   </tgroup>
</table>
```

<tbody> Table Body

Description:

A formatting element that contains one or more <row> elements, which in turn contain <entry> elements in a <table>. The <tbody> element identifies the body of the information in a <table>, as distinct from the column headings (Table Head <thead>).

See also related elements <entry>, <row>, <table>, <tgroup>, and <thead>.

May contain:

row

May occur within:

tgroup

Attributes:

ALTRENDER	#IMPLIED, CDATA
AUDIENCE	#IMPLIED, external, internal
ID	#IMPLIED, ID
VALIGN	#IMPLIED, top, middle, bottom

Example:

```
<table frame="none">
   <tgroup cols="3">
      <colspec colnum="1" colname="1" align="left" colwidth="50pt"/>
      <colspec colnum="2" colname="2" align="left" colwidth="50pt"/>
      <colspec colnum="3" colname="3" align="left" colwidth="50pt"/>
      <thead>
         <row>
            <entry colname="1">Major Family Members</entry>
            <entry colname="2">Spouses</entry>
            <entry colname="3">Children</entry>
         </row>
      </thead>
      <tbody>
         <row>
            <entry colname="1">John Albemarle (1760-1806)</entry>
            <entry colname="2">Mary Frances Delaney (1769-
               1835)</entry>
            <entry colname="3">John Delaney Albemarle (1787-
               1848)</entry>
         </row> . . .
      </tbody>
   </tgroup>
</table>
```

<tgroup> Table Group

Description:

A formatting element that bundles <table> subelements: <colspec>, <thead>, and <tbody>. Tables are comprised of one or more <tgroup>s, depending on the number of times the column specifications change. The <tgroup> element provides a subgrouping of rows within a table that all use the same column specifications.

Three attributes are used together to force horizontal alignment on a specific character, such as a decimal point. The ALIGN attribute must be set to "char" (align="char"). The CHAR attribute should be set to the specific character on which the text will align (for example the decimal point, char="."). The CHAROFF attribute controls the position of the alignment by naming the percentage of the current column width that is to the left of the alignment character (for example, charoff="30"). The required COLS attribute specifies the number of columns in the table.

By convention, any rule specified in COLSEP is printed or displayed to the right of the column. External rules are specified with the FRAME attribute of <table>; horizontal rules are specified with the <table> or <tgroup> ROWSEP attribute.

By convention, any rule specified in ROWSEP prints or displays below the row. Vertical rules are specified by a COLSEP attribute; external rules are specified by the FRAME attribute of the <table> element.

See also related elements <colspec>, <table>, <tbody>, <thead>.

May contain:

colspec, tbody, thead

May occur within:

table

Attributes:

ALIGN	#IMPLIED, left, right, center, justify, char
ALTRENDER	#IMPLIED, CDATA
AUDIENCE	#IMPLIED, external, internal
COLS	#REQUIRED, NMTOKEN
COLSEP	#IMPLIED, NMTOKEN
ID	#IMPLIED, ID
ROWSEP	#IMPLIED, NMTOKEN

<tgroup>

Example:

```
<odd>
   <head>Appendix: Chronological List of the Names of Major Family
      Members, Their Spouses, and Children</head>
   <p>Papers of the individuals listed here make up the greater part
      of the Albemarle Family Papers.  Names of children who are
      known not to have survived to adulthood are omitted.</p>
   <table frame="none">
      <tgroup cols="3">
         <colspec colnum="1" colname="1" align="left" colwidth="50pt">
         <colspec colnum="2" colname="2" align="left" colwidth="50pt">
         <colspec colnum="3" colname="3" align="left" colwidth="50pt">
         <thead>
            <row>
               <entry colname="1">Major Family Members</entry>
               <entry colname="2">Spouses</entry>
               <entry colname="3">Children</entry>
            </row>
         </thead>
         <tbody>
            <row>
               <entry colname="1">John Albemarle (1760-1806)</entry>
               <entry colname="2">Mary Frances Delaney (1769-
                  1835)</entry>
               <entry colname="3">John Delaney Albemarle (1787-
                  1848)</entry>
            </row>
            <row>
               <entry colname="3">Lucretia Albemarle Goodrich (1788-
                  1823)</entry>
            </row>
            <row>
               <entry colname="3">Porter Breckinridge Albermarle
                  (1790-1831)</entry>
            </row>
            <row>
               <entry colname="3">Joseph Fairfax Albemarle (1792-
                  1856)</entry>
            </row>
            <row>
               <entry colname="1">John Delaney Albemarle (1787-
                  1848)</entry>
               <entry colname="2">Martha Mary Adams (1795-
                  1862)</entry>
               <entry colname="3">John Adams Albemarle (1814-
                  1867)</entry></row>
            <row>
               <entry colname="3">Mary Delaney Albemarle (1818-
                  1880)</entry>
            </row> . . .
         </tbody>
      </tgroup>
   </table>
</odd>
```

<thead> Table Head

Description:

A formatting element that contains the heading information in a <table>, usually column heads, that appears at the top of the table and may appear again at the top of any physical break in rows in the body. The <thead> element is used inside an ordinary structural <table> and to provide column headings for Components <c> or the Description of Subordinate Components <dsc>.

See related elements <table> and <tgroup> for general table information.

May contain:

row

May occur within:

c, c01, c02, c03, c04, c05, c06, c07, c08, c09, c10, c11, dsc, tgroup

Attributes:

ALTRENDER	#IMPLIED, CDATA
AUDIENCE	#IMPLIED, external, internal
ID	#IMPLIED, ID
VALIGN	#IMPLIED, top, middle, bottom

Example:

```
<table frame="none">
   <tgroup cols="3">
      <colspec colnum="1" colname="1" align="left" colwidth="50pt">
      <colspec colnum="2" colname="2" align="left" colwidth="50pt">
      <colspec colnum="3" colname="3" align="left" colwidth="50pt">
      <thead>
         <row>
            <entry colname="1">Major Family Members</entry>
            <entry colname="2">Spouses</entry>
            <entry colname="3">Children</entry>
         </row>
      </thead>
      <tbody>[. . .]</tbody>
   </tgroup>
</table>
```

<title> Title

Description:

The formal name of a work, such as a monograph, serial, or painting, listed in a finding aid. Subtitles of such works are not separately encoded but may instead be listed as part of the <title> element.

Do not confuse with <titleproper>, which is used for the title of the encoded finding aid. Also do not confuse with <unittitle>, which is used to encode the name of the described materials, such as the title of a collection, record group, fonds, series, file, or item. Do not confuse with the TITLE attribute which is found in several linking elements. The <title> element may be used inside of <unittitle>, and it is possible that a <unittitle> may contain no text other than that which is further specified by the <title> element. (See example below.)

The RULES attribute can be used to specify the descriptive rules followed when forming the title, such as AACR2R. The ENTITYREF or HREF attributes may be used to name either the entity or pointer when linking to a machine-readable version of the cited <title>. The RENDER attribute permits specification of how the content of a particular <title> element should be displayed or printed, e.g., bold, italics, quoted, etc.

The <title> element is comparable to MARC fields 130, 240, 245, 630, 730, and 740.

While XML Linking Language (XLink) Version 1.0, which is the basis for EAD linking elements, is a stable document, examples of EAD usage are hypothetical and have not been tested in real XLink-based applications. Those wishing to use XLink are encouraged to consult the specification available online at <http://www.w3.org/TR/xlink/>.

May contain:

#PCDATA, date, emph, extptr, lb, num, ptr

May occur within:

abstract, archref, bibliography, bibref, bibseries, container, controlaccess, creation, descrules, dimensions, emph, entry, event, extent, extref, indexentry, item, label, langmaterial, langusage, materialspec, namegrp, origination, otherfindaid, p, physdesc, physfacet, physloc, ref, relatedmaterial, repository, separatedmaterial, unitdate, unitid, unittitle

Attributes:

ACTUATE	#IMPLIED, onload, onrequest, actuateother, actuatenone
ALTRENDER	#IMPLIED, CDATA
ARCROLE	#IMPLIED, CDATA
AUDIENCE	#IMPLIED, external, internal
AUTHFILENUMBER	#IMPLIED, CDATA
ENCODINGANALOG	#IMPLIED, CDATA
ENTITYREF	#IMPLIED, ENTITY
HREF	#IMPLIED, CDATA
ID	#IMPLIED, ID
LINKTYPE	#FIXED, simple, simple
NORMAL	#IMPLIED, CDATA
RENDER	#IMPLIED, altrender, bold, bolddoublequote, bolditalic, boldsinglequote, boldsmcaps, boldunderline, doublequote, italic, nonproport, singlequote, smcaps, sub, super, underline
ROLE	#IMPLIED, CDATA
RULES	#IMPLIED, NMTOKEN
SHOW	#IMPLIED, new, replace, embed, showother, shownone
SOURCE	#IMPLIED, NMTOKEN
TITLE	#IMPLIED, CDATA
TYPE	#IMPLIED, CDATA
XPOINTER	#IMPLIED, CDATA

Examples:

1.
```
<c01>
   <did>
      <unittitle>Short stories, </unittitle>
      <unitdate>1946-1954</unitdate>
   </did>
   <c02>
      <did>
         <unittitle><title render="italic">The Lottery</title>
         </unittitle>
      </did>
   </c02>
</c01>
```

2.
```
<bibref>
   <title render="italic">Library of Congress Acquisitions:
      Manuscript Division, <date>1982,</date></title> p. 29.
</bibref>
```

<titlepage> Title Page

Description:

A wrapper element within <frontmatter> that groups bibliographic information about an encoded finding aid, including its name, author, and other aspects of its creation and publication. It contains much of the same information found in the <filedesc> portion of the <eadheader>, such as the <titleproper>, <subtitle>, <author>, <sponsor>, <publisher>, and <date> of the finding aid. Although it is possible to generate an electronic or printed title page directly from the <eadheader>, use of the <titlepage> may be more accommodating of local preferences, including displays of photographic illustrations, institutional logos, or other graphic images.

May contain:

address, author, bibseries, blockquote, chronlist, date, edition, list, note, num, p, publisher, sponsor, subtitle, table, titleproper

May occur within:

frontmatter

Attributes:

ALTRENDER	#IMPLIED, CDATA
AUDIENCE	#IMPLIED, external, internal
ID	#IMPLIED, ID

Example:

```
<frontmatter>
   <titlepage>
      <titleproper>Inventory of The Arequipa Sanatorium Records,
         <date>1911&ndash;1958</date></titleproper>
      <num type="Collection number:">BANC MSS 92/894 c</num>
      <publisher>The Bancroft Library<lb/>University of
         California, Berkeley<lb/>Berkeley, California
      </publisher>
      <list type="deflist">
         <defitem>
            <label>Processed by:</label>
            <item>Lynn Downey</item>
         </defitem>
         <defitem>
            <label>Completed by:</label>
            <item>Mary Morganti and Katherine Bryant</item>
         </defitem>
         <defitem>
            <label>Date Completed:</label>
            <item><date>May 1994</date></item>
         </defitem>
         <defitem>
            <label>Encoded by:</label>
            <item>Gabriela A. Montoya</item>
         </defitem>
      </list>
      <p>&copy; 1996 The Regents of the University of California.
         All rights reserved.</p>
   </titlepage>
</frontmatter>
```

<titleproper> Title Proper of the Finding Aid

Description:

The name of the finding aid or finding aid series. The <titleproper> element is required within the <titlestmt> subelement of <filedesc>, part of the <eadheader>. It may also be optionally used in the <titlepage> subelement of <frontmatter>. To encode the name of a finding aid series, <titleproper> may be used in the optional <seriesstmt> subelement of <filedesc>.

The <titlestmt> relates to the finding aid and should not be confused with Title <title>, used to encode the formal names of works such as monographs, serials, paintings, etc., listed in the finding aid, or with Title of the Unit <unittitle>, used to encode the name of the described materials.

May contain:

#PCDATA, abbr, date, emph, expan, extptr, lb, num, ptr

May occur within:

seriesstmt, titlepage, titlestmt

Attributes:

ALTRENDER	#IMPLIED, CDATA
AUDIENCE	#IMPLIED, external, internal
ENCODINGANALOG	#IMPLIED, CDATA
ID	#IMPLIED, ID
RENDER	#IMPLIED, altrender, bold, bolddoublequote, bolditalic, boldsinglequote, boldsmcaps, boldunderline, doublequote, italic, nonproport, singlequote, smcaps, sub, super, underline
TYPE	#IMPLIED, CDATA

Examples:

1.
```
<filedesc>
   <titlestmt>
      <titleproper>Inventory of the Kingsley Amis Papers,
      <date>1941-1995</date></titleproper>
      <author>Processed by Sara S. Hodson; machine-readable
      finding aid created by Xiuzhi Zhou</author>
   </titlestmt> . . .
</filedesc>
```

2.
```
<frontmatter>
   <titlepage>
      <titleproper> Inventory of The Arequipa Sanatorium Records,
         <date>1911&ndash;1958</date></titleproper>
      <num type="Collection number:">BANC MSS 92/894 c</num>
      <publisher>The Bancroft Library<lb/>University of
         California, Berkeley<lb/>Berkeley, California
      </publisher>
      <p>&copy; 1996 The Regents of the University of California.
         All rights reserved.</p>
   </titlepage>
</frontmatter>
```

<titlestmt> Title Statement

Description:

A required wrapper element within the <filedesc> portion of <eadheader> that groups information about the name of an encoded finding aid and those responsible for its intellectual content. Like much of the <eadheader>, the <titlestmt> element is modeled on an element found in the Text Encoding Initiative (TEI) DTD, and its subelements must adhere to the following prescribed sequence: a required <titleproper>, followed by an optional <subtitle>, optional <author>, and optional <sponsor>.

The <titlestmt> relates to the finding aid and should not be confused with Title <title>, used to encode the formal names of works such as monographs, serials, paintings, etc., listed in the finding aid. Also do not confuse with Title of the Unit <unittitle>, used to encode the name of the described materials.

May contain:

author, sponsor, subtitle, titleproper

May occur within:

filedesc

Attributes:

ALTRENDER	#IMPLIED, CDATA
AUDIENCE	#IMPLIED, external, internal
ENCODINGANALOG	#IMPLIED, CDATA
ID	#IMPLIED, ID

Example:

```
<filedesc>
   <titlestmt>
      <titleproper>Inventory of the Kingsley Amis Papers,
      <date>1941-1995</date></titleproper>
      <author>Processed by Sara S. Hodson; machine-readable
      finding aid created by Xiuzhi Zhou</author>
   </titlestmt> . . .
</filedesc>
```

<unitdate> Date of the Unit

Description:

The creation year, month, or day of the described materials. The <unitdate> may be in the form of text or numbers, and may consist of a single date or range of dates. As an important subelement of the Descriptive Identification <did>, the <unitdate> is used to tag only the creation and other relevant dates of the materials described in the encoded finding aid. Do not confuse it with the <date> element, which is used to tag all other dates.

A standard numeric form of the date (YYYYMMDD, etc.) can be specified with the NORMAL attribute to facilitate machine comparison of dates for search purposes. The TYPE attribute may be used to indicate whether the <unitdate> represents inclusive dates or bulk (predominant) dates. The CERTAINTY attribute may be applied to indicate if the date has been supplied or estimated by the archivist. The DATECHAR attribute can be used to supply a term characterizing the nature of the dates, such as creation or accumulation. The CALENDAR attribute, which has a default value of "gregorian," specifies the calendar from which the date stems. The value "ce" (common or Christian era) is the default for the ERA attribute.

The <unitdate> may be nested within the <unittitle> or used independently of that element.

This element is comparable to ISAD(G) element 3.1.3, and MARC fields 245 subfield f for inclusive dates, 245 subfield g for bulk dates, or 260 subfield c.

May contain:

#PCDATA, abbr, archref, bibref, emph, expan, extptr, extref, lb, linkgrp, ptr, ref, title

May occur within:

archref, did, entry, event, extref, extrefloc, item, label, p, ref, refloc, unittitle

<unitdate>

Attributes:

ALTRENDER	#IMPLIED, CDATA
AUDIENCE	#IMPLIED, external, internal
CALENDAR	gregorian, NMTOKEN
CERTAINTY	#IMPLIED, CDATA
DATECHAR	#IMPLIED, CDATA
ENCODINGANALOG	#IMPLIED, CDATA
ERA	ce, NMTOKEN
ID	#IMPLIED, ID
LABEL	#IMPLIED, CDATA
NORMAL	#IMPLIED, CDATA
TYPE	#IMPLIED, bulk, inclusive

Examples:

1.
```
<archdesc level="collection">
   <did>
      <head>Collection Summary</head>
      <origination label="Creator"><corpname
         encodinganalog="110">National Association for the
         Advancement of Colored People</corpname>
      </origination>
      <unittitle label="Title" encodinganalog="245">Visual
         Materials from the National Association for the
         Advancement of Colored People Records (Library of
         Congress)</unittitle>
      <unitdate label="Dates" type="inclusive"
         encodinganalog="260">ca. 1838-1969, </unitdate>
         <unitdate type="bulk">bulk 1944-1955</unitdate>
   </did>
</archdesc>
```

2.
```
<dsc type="analyticover">
   <c level="subseries">
      <did>
         <unittitle>Documentary Movies, </unittitle>
         <unitdate type="inclusive" normal="1952/1964">1952-
            1964</unitdate>
         <physdesc><extent>2.5 linear ft.</extent></physdesc>
         <abstract>Includes scores, arranged alphabetically by
            movie title, and some correspondence, arranged
            chronologically.</abstract>
      </did>
   </c> . . .
</dsc>
```

<unitid> ID of the Unit

Description:

Any alpha-numeric text string that serves as a unique reference point or control number for the described material, such as a lot number, an accession number, a classification number, or an entry number in a bibliography or catalog. An important subelement of the Descriptive Identification <did>, the <unitid> is primarily a logical designation, which sometimes secondarily provides location information, as in the case of a classification number. Use other <did> subelements, such as <physloc> and <container>, to designate specifically the physical location of the described materials.

Do not confuse <unitid>, which relates to the archival materials, with <cadid>, which is used to designate a unique identification string for the finding aid.

Although not required, the COUNTRYCODE and REPOSITORYCODE attributes should be used in <unitid> at the <archdesc><did> level to comply with ISAD(G) element 3.1.1. REPOSITORYCODE specifies the ISO 15511 code for the institution that has custody of the materials described, while COUNTRYCODE provides the ISO 3166-1 code for the country in which that institution is located. IDENTIFIER should contain a machine-readable unique identifier, containing a value similar to the text in the <unitid> element. The TYPE attribute may be used to indicate the system from which the <unitid> was derived, e.g., accessioning system, record group classification scheme, records retention scheduling system, etc.

May contain:

#PCDATA, abbr, archref, bibref, emph, expan, extptr, extref, lb, linkgrp, ptr, ref, title

May occur within:

archref, did

Attributes:

ALTRENDER	#IMPLIED, CDATA
AUDIENCE	#IMPLIED, external, internal
COUNTRYCODE	#IMPLIED, NMTOKEN
ENCODINGANALOG	#IMPLIED, CDATA
ID	#IMPLIED, ID
IDENTIFIER	#IMPLIED, CDATA
LABEL	#IMPLIED, CDATA
REPOSITORYCODE	#IMPLIED, NMTOKEN
TYPE	#IMPLIED, CDATA

<unitid>

Example:

```
<archdesc level="collection">
   <did>
      <head>Descriptive Summary</head>
      <unittitle label="Title">Donald C. Stone, Jr. Papers,
         </unittitle>
      <unitdate type="inclusive">1971-1983</unitdate>
      <unitid countrycode="us" repositorycode="cbgtu"
         label="Accession number">GTU 2001-8-03</unitid>
      <origination label="Creator"><persname source="lcnaf">
         Stone, Donald C., Jr.</persname></origination>
      <physdesc label="Extent"><extent>4 boxes,
         </extent><extent>4 linear ft.</extent> </physdesc>
      <repository label="Repository">The <corpname>Graduate
         Theological Union</corpname>
         <address><addressline>Berkeley,
         California</addressline></address></repository>
      <abstract label="Abstract">The papers document Donald C.
         Stone's work with Ornstein and Swencionis on the <emph
         render="italic">est</emph> Outcome Project, and the
         development of his doctoral research, including his
         various publications on the human potential movement, up
         to the completion of his doctoral
         dissertation.</abstract>
      <physloc label="Shelf location">5/D/4-5</physloc>
   </did> . . .
</archdesc>
```

<unittitle> Title of the Unit

Description:

The name, either formal or supplied, of the described materials. May consist of a word, phrase, character, or group of characters. As an important subelement of the Descriptive Identification <did>, the <unittitle> encodes the name of the described materials at both the highest unit or <archdesc> level (e.g., collection, record group, or fonds) and at all the subordinate Component <c> levels (e.g., subseries, files, items, or other intervening stages within a hierarchical description).

Do not confuse <unittitle> with Title <title>, a more general element used to encode the formal names of works such as monographs, serials, paintings, etc. Also do not confuse with Title Proper of the Finding Aid <titleproper>, used to designate the name of a finding aid, or a finding aid series encoded in EAD.

The <unittitle> element is comparable to ISAD(G) element 3.1.2 and MARC field 245.

May contain:

#PCDATA, abbr, archref, bibref, bibseries, corpname, date, edition, emph, expan, extptr, extref, famname, function, genreform, geogname, imprint, lb, linkgrp, name, num, occupation, persname, ptr, ref, subject, title, unitdate

May occur within:

archref, did, entry, event, extref, extrefloc, item, label, p, ref, refloc

Attributes:

ALTRENDER	#IMPLIED, CDATA
AUDIENCE	#IMPLIED, external, internal
ENCODINGANALOG	#IMPLIED, CDATA
ID	#IMPLIED, ID
LABEL	#IMPLIED, CDATA
TYPE	#IMPLIED, CDATA

<unittitle>

Example:

```
<c level="subseries">
   <did>
      <unittitle>Documentary Movies, </unittitle>
      <unitdate type="inclusive">1952-1964</unitdate>
      <physdesc><extent>2.5 linear ft.</extent></physdesc>
      <abstract label="Summary:">Includes scores, arranged
         alphabetically by movie title, and some correspondence,
         arranged chronologically.</abstract>
   </did>
</c>
```

<userestrict> Conditions Governing Use

Description:

Information about conditions that affect use of the described materials after access has been granted. May indicate limitations, regulations, or special procedures imposed by a repository, donor, legal statute, or other agency regarding reproduction, publication, or quotation of the described materials. May also indicate the absence of restrictions, such as when copyright or literary rights have been dedicated to the public. Do not confuse with Conditions Governing Access <accessrestrict>, which designates information about conditions affecting the availability of the described materials. Preferred Citation <prefercite> may be used in conjunction with <userestrict> to encode statements specifying how the described materials should be referenced when reproduced, published, or quoted by patrons.

In EAD Version 1.0 <userestrict> was a subelement of Administrative Information <admininfo>, which has been deprecated in EAD 2002 (see Appendix B). The new Description Group <descgrp> element, which can group any of the <did>-level elements (except the Description of Subordinate Components <dsc>), may be used to wrap elements where a group heading is desirable. The <descgrp> element can be used to replace <admininfo> where it has been used as a wrapper when converting finding aids encoded in EAD V1.0 to EAD 2002.

The <userestrict> element is comparable to ISAD(G) data element 3.4.2 and MARC field 540.

May contain:

address, blockquote, chronlist, head, list, note, p, table, userestrict

May occur within:

archdesc, archdescgrp, c, c01, c02, c03, c04, c05, c06, c07, c08, c09, c10, c11, c12, descgrp, userestrict

Attributes:

ALTRENDER	#IMPLIED, CDATA
AUDIENCE	#IMPLIED, external, internal
ENCODINGANALOG	#IMPLIED, CDATA
ID	#IMPLIED, ID
TYPE	#IMPLIED, CDATA

<userestrict>

Examples:

1.
```
<userestrict>
   <p>Until 2015 permission to photocopy some materials from this
      collection has been limited at the request of the donor.
      Please ask repository staff for details if you are
      interested in obtaining photocopies from Series 1:
      Correspondence.</p>
</userestrict>
```

2.
```
<userestrict>
   <p>Copyright to the collection has been transferred to the
      Regents of the University of Michigan.</p>
</userestrict>
```

Appendix A

EAD CROSSWALKS

This appendix includes three "crosswalks" intended to enable comparison of EAD elements with the data elements defined in two related metadata standards or frameworks: ISAD(G)[4] and MARC21. Use of these crosswalks may facilitate mapping of data between and among these metadata tools, such as for exporting data from EAD finding aids to create MARC21 records. Further information about the relationship between EAD and these other standards is contained in various sections of the *EAD Application Guidelines.*

The three crosswalks are these:

A.1. ISAD(G) to EAD
A.2. EAD to ISAD(G)
A.3. MARC21 to EAD

A conservative approach was taken in compiling these crosswalks. In other words, only clear equivalencies between data elements were included. Other roughly compatible elements that may be identifiable by users were omitted because the match was felt to be ambiguous or uncertain.

Listing of two EAD elements side by side in the following tables indicates that the second element is a subelement of the first. For example, "<controlaccess><persname>" indicates that the <persname> element should be nested within <controlaccess>.

Listing of different EAD elements on separate lines within a table cell indicates that all of the listed elements can be mapped to the matching data element from the corresponding metadata tool.

[4] This crosswalk is to the second edition of ISAD(G), published by the International Council on Archives in 2000.

Appendix A

A.1. ISAD(G) to EAD

ISAD(G)	EAD
3.1.1 Reference code(s)	<eadid> with COUNTRYCODE and MAINAGENCYCODE attributes <unitid> with COUNTRYCODE and REPOSITORYCODE attributes
3.1.2 Title	<unittitle>
3.1.3 Dates	<unitdate>
3.1.4 Level of description	<archdesc> and <c> LEVEL attribute
3.1.5 Extent and medium of the unit	<physdesc> and subelements <extent>, <dimensions>, <genreform>, <physfacet>
3.2.1 Name of creator	<origination>
3.2.2 Administrative/Biographical history	<bioghist>
3.2.3 Archival history	<custodhist>
3.2.4 Immediate source of acquisition	<acqinfo>
3.3.1 Scope and content	<scopecontent>
3.3.2 Appraisal, destruction and scheduling	<appraisal>
3.3.3 Accruals	<accruals>
3.3.4 System of arrangement	<arrangement>
3.4.1 Conditions governing access	<accessrestrict>
3.4.2 Conditions governing reproduction	<userestrict>
3.4.3 Language/scripts of material	<langmaterial>
3.4.4 Physical characteristics and technical requirements	<phystech>
3.4.5 Finding aids	<otherfindaid>
3.5.1 Existence and location of originals	<originalsloc>
3.5.2 Existence and location of copies	<altformavail>
3.5.3 Related units of description	<relatedmaterial> <separatedmaterial>
3.5.4 Publication note	<bibliography>
3.6.1 Note	<odd> <note>
3.7.1 Archivist's note	<processinfo>
3.7.2 Rules or conventions	<descrules>
3.7.3 Date(s) of descriptions	<processinfo><p><date>

A.2. EAD to ISAD(G)

EAD	ISAD (G)
<accessrestrict>	3.4.1 Conditions governing access
<accruals>	3.3.3 Accruals
<acqinfo>	3.2.4 Immediate source of acquisition
<altformavail>	3.5.2 Existence and location of copies
<appraisal>	3.3.2 Appraisal, destruction and scheduling
<archdesc> LEVEL attribute	3.1.4 Level of description
<arrangement>	3.3.4 System of arrangement
<bibliography>	3.5.4 Publication note
<bioghist>	3.2.2 Administrative/Biographical history
<c> LEVEL attribute	3.1.4 Level of description
<custodhist>	3.2.3 Archival history
<descrules>	3.7.2 Rules or conventions
<eadid> with MAINAGENCYCODE and COUNTRYCODE attributes	3.1.1 Reference code(s)
<langmaterial> with <language> LANGCODE and SCRIPTCODE attributes	3.4.3 Language/scripts of material
<legalstatus>	3.4.1 Conditions governing access
<note>	3.6.1 Note
<odd>	3.6.1 Note
<originalsloc>	3.5.1 Existence and location of originals
<origination>	3.2.1 Name of creator
<otherfindaid>	3.4.5 Finding aids
<physdesc> and subelements <extent>, <dimensions>, <genreform>, <physfacet>	3.1.5 Extent and medium of the unit
<phystech>	3.4.4 Physical characteristics and technical requirements
<processinfo>	3.7.1 Archivist's note
<processinfo><p><date>	3.7.3 Date(s) of descriptions
<relatedmaterial>	3.5.3 Related units of description
<scopecontent>	3.3.1 Scope and content
<separatedmaterial>	3.5.3 Related units of description
<unitdate>	3.1.3 Dates
<unitid> with COUNTRYCODE and REPOSITORYCODE attributes	3.1.1 Reference code(s)
<unittitle>	3.1.2 Title
<userestrict>	3.4.2 Conditions governing reproduction

A.3. MARC21 to EAD

Table A.3 does not include all possible MARC21 fields to which EAD elements might be mapped to generate a partial MARC21 record for the collection; it instead focuses on the most significant and useful fields. In addition, MARC21 fields that contain coded data, such as Leader and Directory fields, are not included, because it is unlikely that such information would be provided in a finding aid in a format that could be directly ported into a MARC21 record (or vice versa).

Note that this mapping is between an EAD finding aid and a MARC21 record describing that same collection, not to a MARC21 record describing the finding aid per se. The table only includes MARC21 fields for which there is a direct, logical analog to an EAD element.

The right-hand column listing EAD elements specifies the use of a subelement within another element in some situations. In other cases, this column provides a list of optional elements, leaving it to the archivist to determine which one best fits the data being encoded.

It is most useful to map to MARC21 the EAD data that is encoded in the high-level <did> or in other <did>-level elements such as <bioghist>, <scopecontent>, and <controlaccess> to their field equivalencies in MARC21 records. Since most repositories create MARC21 records only at the "collection level," mapping from more detailed components of EAD finding aids, while theoretically feasible, is less likely to be useful in practical terms.

Note that EAD data being mapped to MARC21 fields that require authority-controlled data must be in controlled access form in order to be imported into a valid MARC21 record.

MARC21	EAD
041 Language	LANGCODE attribute in <language>
100 Main entry—personal name	<origination><persname> <origination><famname>
110 Main entry—corporate name	<origination><corpname>
111 Main entry—meeting name	<origination><corpname>
130 Main entry—uniform title	<unittitle>
240 Uniform title	<controlaccess><title>
245 Title statement	<unittitle>
245$f Title statement/inclusive dates	<unitdate type="inclusive">
245$g Title statement/bulk dates	<unitdate type="bulk">
254 Musical presentation statement	<materialspec>
255 Cartographic mathematical data	<materialspec>
256 Computer file characteristics	<materialspec>
260$c Date	<unitdate>
300 Physical description	<physdesc> and subelements <extent>, <dimensions>, <genreform>, <physfacet>
340 Physical medium	<phystech>
351 Organization and arrangement	<arrangement>
351$c Hierarchical level	<archdesc> LEVEL attribute
355 Security classification control	<legalstatus>
500 General note	<odd> <note>
506 Restrictions on access note	<accessrestrict> <legalstatus>
510 Citation/references	<bibliography>
520 Summary, etc.	<scopecontent>
524 Preferred citation of described materials	<prefercite>
530 Additional physical form available	<altformavail>
535 Location of Originals/Duplicates	<originalsloc>
536 Funding information	<sponsor>
538 System Details	<phystech>
540 Terms governing use and reproduction	<userestrict>
541 Immediate source of acquisition	<acqinfo>
544 Location of other archival materials	<relatedmaterial> <separatedmaterial>
545 Biographical or historical data	<bioghist>
546 Language	<langmaterial>
555 Cumulative index/finding aids	[5]
561 Ownership and custodial history	<custodhist>

[5] In a MARC21 record a note in the 555 field would mention the existence of the EAD-encoded finding aid, but no specific EAD element maps to this field. The existence of other finding aids can be noted in <otherfindaid>.

Appendix A

581 Publications about described materials	<bibliography>
583 Action	<appraisal> <processinfo>
584 Accumulation and frequency of use	<accruals>
600 Subject—personal name	<controlaccess><persname role="subject"> <controlaccess><famname role="subject">
610 Subject—corporate name	<controlaccess><corpname role="subject">
611 Subject—meeting	<controlaccess><corpname role="subject">
630 Subject—uniform title	<controlaccess><title role="subject">
650 Subject—topical	<controlaccess><subject>
651 Subject—geographic name	<controlaccess><geogname role="subject">
655 Genre/form	<controlaccess><genreform>
656 Occupation	<controlaccess><occupation>
657 Function	<controlaccess><function>
69x Local subject access	<controlaccess><subject source="local">
700 Added entry—personal name	<controlaccess><persname> <controlaccess><famname>
710 Added entry—corporate name	<controlaccess><corpname>
711 Added entry—meeting name	<controlaccess><corpname>
720 Added entry—uncontrolled	<name>
730 Added entry—uniform title	<controlaccess><title>
740 Added entry—uncont./related anal. title	<title>
752 Added entry—hierarchical place name	<geogname>
852 Location	<repository> <physloc>

Appendix B

Deprecated and Obsolete Elements and Attributes

What are deprecated elements and attributes?

The EAD Working Group, in response to submissions for changes to the DTD in 2001, is recommending that certain elements no longer be used by encoders. Deprecation means that an element or attribute is not included in the distributed "default" version of the DTD. While it is possible to "switch on" these elements, encoders use them at their own risk, as deprecated elements and attributes will be made obsolete in the next version. While the Working Group will supply transformation scripts mapping deprecated elements and attributes from version 1.0 to version 2002, it will not supply scripts that map deprecated version 1.0 elements to the version that supercedes EAD2002. Deprecated elements can be switched on by making the following change to the DTD:

<!ENTITY % deprecate 'IGNORE' >	to	<!ENTITY % deprecate 'INCLUDE' >

Following is a list of deprecated elements and attributes, which is in turn followed by their descriptions from the *EAD Tag Library Version 1.0*. Adjunct Descriptive Data <add> and Administrative Information <admininfo> were wrappers for a number of subelements that in EAD 2002 have been "unbundled" and made available at the same level as <did> and <scopecontent>. The rationale for this is that these wrapper elements simply represented tagging overhead, particularly when used at the component level. If element grouping is desirable in some instances, the new element Description Group <descgrp> may be used. The distinction between <organization> and <arrangement> was never very clear to archivists, so the two meanings have been combined in <arrangement> and brought in line with ISAD(G) element 3.3.4 System of Arrangement.

Tabular display elements Display Row <drow>, Display Entry <dentry>, and Table Specification <tspec> (which also had to be switched on in Version 1.0) are deprecated in favor of using style sheets to control the display of container and folder lists. However, if the use of these elements is desired, the following change must be made in the DTD:

<!ENTITY % tabular 'IGNORE' >	to	<!ENTITY % tabular 'INCLUDE' >

The deprecated attributes LANGMATERIAL and LEGALSTATUS have been replaced by <langmaterial> and <legalstatus> elements. The absence of LEGALSTATUS made the OTHERLEGALSTATUS attribute unnecessary.

Appendix B

Deprecated Elements
<add> Adjunct Descriptive Data
<admininfo> Administrative Information
<dentry> Display Entry
<drow> Display Row
<organization> Organization
<tspec> Table Specification

Deprecated Attributes
LANGMATERIAL
LEGALSTATUS
OTHERLEGALSTATUS

What are obsolete elements and attributes?
Inquiries to the archival community indicated that some of the tabular display elements were not being used or their use was being phased out, indicating that the Working Group could eliminate them from the DTD without first deprecating them. Obsolete elements and attributes are not available and cannot be switched on in the DTD.

A number of linking attributes were added to EAD Version 1.0 elements in anticipation of the XLink standard reaching a recommendation phase. XLink has changed substantially since that time and these attributes are no longer part of the specification. Other attributes made obsolete were available only in the tabular elements also made obsolete, or have been replaced by other attributes. In the case of OTHERSOURCE, the elimination of the semi-closed list in the SOURCE attribute has made it unnecessary.

Obsolete Elements
<spanspec> Spanned Column Specification
<tfoot> Table Foot

Obsolete Attributes
BEHAVIOR
CONTENT-ROLE
CONTENT-TITLE
EXTENT
INLINE
NUMBERED
ORIENT
OTHERSOURCE
PUBSTATUS
ROTATE
SHORTENTRY
SPANNAME
SYSTEMID
TABSTYLE
TARGETTYPE
TGROUPSTYLE
TOCENTRY
XLINK:FORM

Deprecated Elements

<add> Adjunct Descriptive Data

Description:

A wrapper element for supplemental information that facilitates use of the materials described in the finding aid. This includes additional access tools, such as indexes, file plans, and other finding aids, as well as descriptions or lists of materials separated from or related to those described in the finding aid. The main role of the <add> element is to distinguish supplemental information from the core description of the materials.

When information in <add> supplements information contained throughout the <archdesc>, the <add> might be used once as the last <archdesc> element near the end of the finding aid. When <add> information refers to a single Component <c>, it might be used at the end of the <c>, e.g., to mention a card index to a single series. Brief statements about other finding aids, separated materials, or bibliographical references that might appear, for example, in a scope and contents note do not usually need to be tagged as <add>.

May contain:

add, address, bibliography, blockquote, chronlist, fileplan, head, index, list, note, otherfindaid, p, relatedmaterial, separatedmaterial, table

May occur within:

add, archdesc, c, c01, c02, c03, c04, c05, c06, c07, c08, c09, c10, c11, c12, dentry

Attributes:

ALTRENDER	#IMPLIED, CDATA
AUDIENCE	#IMPLIED, external, internal
ENCODINGANALOG	#IMPLIED, CDATA
ID	#IMPLIED, ID
TYPE	#IMPLIED, CDATA

<admininfo> Administrative Information

Description:

A wrapper element for descriptive background information that helps readers of the finding aid know how to approach the archival materials and make use of the information they find. Includes information about acquisition source and custodial history, availability of microform or digital surrogates, processing method, preferred citation, restrictions on use or reproduction, and other kinds of administrative information.

The <admininfo> element may present text as a series of Paragraphs <p>, or it may feature content-specific elements: <accessrestrict>, <accruals>, <acqinfo>, <altformavail>, <appraisal>, <custodhist>, <prefercite>, <processinfo>, and <userestrict>. Both examples below illustrate the second approach.

May contain:

accessrestrict, accruals, acqinfo, address, admininfo, altformavail, appraisal, blockquote, chronlist, custodhist, head, list, note, p, prefercite, processinfo, table, userestrict

May occur within:

admininfo, archdesc, archdescgrp, c, c01, c02, c03, c04, c05, c06, c07, c08, c09, c10, c11, c12, dentry

Attributes:

ALTRENDER	#IMPLIED, CDATA
AUDIENCE	#IMPLIED, external, internal
ENCODINGANALOG	#IMPLIED, CDATA
ID	#IMPLIED, ID
TYPE	#IMPLIED, CDATA

<dentry> Display Entry

Description:

A formatting element that designates a single cell in a complex tabular layout by using the SPANNAME attribute to specify which columns the cell spans. The layout for a printed finding aid is often a multicolumn display with varying column widths. Four table elements work together to preserve the hierarchically indented appearance of printed finding aid container lists and descriptions of series: <tspec>, <thead>, <drow>, and <dentry>. Many online finding aids do not need to preserve these strict layouts and can rely on indented Component <c> elements to distinguish subordinate parts of Components <c> and associate them with the appropriate <container> or <unitid> elements.

The table layout is first specified in the Table Specification <tspec> element, which uses the subelements <colspec> and <spanspec> to spell out the column characteristics. A Table Head <thead> contains the column heads. The Display Row <drow> is part of a Component <c> and groups information that constitutes a row in the table. The Display Entry <dentry> identifies one cell in the tabular display, and is followed by elements that designate the cell's content, for example, <unittitle> or <unitid>.

The tabular display features that may be used within <dsc>, such as Display Entry <dentry>, are not included in the default version of the DTD. To "switch on" these elements, change the value of the parameter entity "%tabular" in the ead.dtd and eadgrp.dtd files from IGNORE to INCLUDE and the value of the parameter entity "%nontabular" from INCLUDE to IGNORE.

For additional information about using these specialized tabular elements, consult the *EAD Retrospective Conversion Guidelines* at the University of California, Berkeley:
<http://sunsite.berkeley.edu/amher/upguide.html>.

May contain:

abstract, accessrestrict, accruals, acqinfo, add, admininfo, altformavail, appraisal, arrangement, bibliography, bioghist, container, controlaccess, custodhist, dao, daogrp, descgrp, fileplan, index, langmaterial, materialspec, note, odd, organization, originalsloc, origination, otherfindaid, physdesc, physloc, phystech, prefercite, processinfo, relatedmaterial, repository, scopecontent, separatedmaterial, unitdate, unitid, unittitle, userestrict

May occur within:

drow

Attributes:

ALIGN	#IMPLIED, left, right, center, justify, char
ALTRENDER	#IMPLIED, CDATA
AUDIENCE	#IMPLIED, external, internal
CHAR	#IMPLIED, CDATA
CHAROFF	#IMPLIED, NMTOKEN
COLNAME	#IMPLIED, NMTOKEN
COLSEP	#IMPLIED, NMTOKEN
ID	#IMPLIED, ID
MOREROWS	#IMPLIED, NMTOKEN
NAMEEND	#IMPLIED, NMTOKEN
NAMEST	#IMPLIED, NMTOKEN
ROWSEP	#IMPLIED, NMTOKEN
VALIGN	#IMPLIED, top, middle, bottom

<drow> Display Row

Description:

A formatting element that designates one row of information in a complex tabular layout for a Component <c> element. The <drow> contains one or more <dentry> cells with subelements that contain descriptive text. The layout for a printed finding aid is often a multi-column display with varying column widths. Four table elements work together to preserve the hierarchically indented appearance of printed finding aid container lists and descriptions of series. Many online finding aids do not need to preserve these strict layouts and can rely on indented Component <c> elements to distinguish subordinate parts of Components <c> and associate them with the appropriate <container> or <unitid> elements.

The table layout is first specified in the Table Specification <tspec> element, which uses the subelements <colspec> and <spanspec> to spell out the column characteristics. A Table Head <thead> contains the column heads. The Display Row <drow> is part of a Component <c> and groups information that constitutes a row in the table. The Display Entry <dentry> identifies one cell in the tabular display, and is followed by elements that designate the cell's content, for example, <unittitle> or <unitid>.

The tabular display features that may be used within <dsc>, such as Display Row <drow>, are not included in the default version of the DTD. To "switch on" these elements, change the value of the parameter entity "%tabular" in the ead.dtd and eadgrp.dtd files from IGNORE to INCLUDE and the value of the parameter entity "%nontabular" from INCLUDE to IGNORE.

For additional information about using these specialized tabular elements, consult the *EAD Retrospective Conversion Guidelines* at the University of California, Berkeley:
<http://sunsite.berkeley.edu/amher/upguide.html>.

May contain:

dentry

May occur within:

c, c01, c02, c03, c04, c05, c06, c07, c08, c09, c10, c11, c12

Attributes:

ALTRENDER	#IMPLIED, CDATA
AUDIENCE	#IMPLIED, external, internal
ID	#IMPLIED, ID
ROWSEP	#IMPLIED, NMTOKEN
VALIGN	#IMPLIED, top, middle, bottom

<organization> Organization

Description:

Information on how the described materials have been subdivided into smaller units, e.g., record groups into series. It is used to identify the logical or physical groupings of the described materials within a hierarchical structure. Do not confuse with <arrangement>, which is for information on the filing sequence of the described materials within each grouping, e.g., alphabetical, chronological, geographical, office of origin, etc.

The <organization> element may occur within <archdesc> and <c> or as a subelement of <scopecontent>.

The <organization> element is comparable to MARC field 351$a.

May contain:

address, blockquote, chronlist, head, list, note, organization, p, table

May occur within:

archdesc, archdescgrp, c, c01, c02, c03, c04, c05, c06, c07, c08, c09, c10, c11, c12, descgrp, organization, scopecontent

Attributes:

ALTRENDER	#IMPLIED, CDATA
AUDIENCE	#IMPLIED, external, internal
ENCODINGANALOG	#IMPLIED, CDATA
ID	#IMPLIED, ID

<tspec> Table Specification

Description:

A formatting element that contains subelements that describe how the columns will be arranged in a complex tabular finding aid layout. The Table Specification <tspec> element has at least one Column Specification <colspec> for each column in the table. The <colspec> can be followed by one or more optional <spanspec> elements to specify columns formed by spanning more than one column.

Four specialized tabular elements work together to preserve the hierarchically indented appearance of printed container lists and descriptions of series. Many online finding aids do not need to preserve these strict layouts and can rely on indented Component <c> elements to distinguish subordinate parts of Components <c> and associate them with the appropriate <container> or <unitid>. Table Specification <tspec> contains the column setting elements <colspec> and <spanspec> that comprise the basic layout. Table Head <thead> contains the column heads. Display Row <drow> is part of a Component <c> and groups information that constitutes a row in the table. The Display Entry <dentry> element is part of a <drow> and identifies one cell in the tabular display by containing elements that designate the cell's content, for example, <unittitle> or <unitid>.

The <tpsec> element has no attributes.

The tabular display features that may be used within <dsc>, such as Table Specification <tspec>, are not included in the default version of the DTD. To "switch on" these elements, change the value of the parameter entity "%tabular" in the ead.dtd and eadgrp.dtd files from IGNORE to INCLUDE and the value of the parameter entity "%nontabular" from INCLUDE to IGNORE.

For additional information about using these specialized tabular elements, consult the *EAD Retrospective Conversion Guidelines* at the University of California, Berkeley:
<http://sunsite.berkeley.edu/amher/upguide.html>.

May contain:

colspec

May occur within:

dsc

Attributes:

None

Deprecated Attributes

LANGMATERIAL

The language of the collection materials described in <archdesc>, <c>, and <c01-12>. The value of the LANGMATERIAL attribute should be set using the three-letter codes for the appropriate language from ISO 639-2 (e.g., "eng" for English). If two or more codes are needed, separate them by a space, e.g.

```
<archdesc langmaterial="eng fre ger">
```

LEGALSTATUS

The statutorily-defined status of the materials being described in the encoded finding aid, as, for example, defined by the Public Records Act of 1958 in the United Kingdom. If not "public" or "private," an explanation may be provided in the OTHERLEGALSTATUS attribute. Available only in <archdesc>, <c>, and <c01> through <c12> elements. Values are:

- public
- private
- otherlegalstatus

OTHERLEGALSTATUS

The legal status of the materials being described in the encoded finding aid, other than the "public" or "private" choices from the semi-closed list in the LEGALSTATUS attribute.

Obsolete Elements

<spanspec> Spanned Column Specification

Description:

An empty formatting element that names and describes a column that is formed by combining (spanning) several other columns within a <table>. The <spanspec> element provides the formatting for this horizontal span and can be used to create a "cross head," in which a row contains a heading that flows across many columns and acts as a title for the cells below the row.

Three attributes are used together to force horizontal alignment on a specific character, such as a decimal point. The ALIGN attribute must be set to "char" (align="char"). The CHAR attribute should be set to the specific character on which the text will align (for example the decimal point, char="."). The CHAROFF attribute controls the position of the alignment. CHAROFF names the percentage of the current column width that is to the left of the alignment character (for example, charoff="30").

The extent of a horizontal span is determined by naming the first column (NAMEST) and the last column (NAMEEND) in the span.

By convention, any rule specified in COLSEP is printed or displayed to the right of the column. External rules are specified with the FRAME attribute of <table>; horizontal rules are specified with the <spanspec>, <table> or <tgroup> ROWSEP attribute.

By convention, any rule specified in ROWSEP prints or displays below the row. Vertical rules are specified by a COLSEP attribute; external rules are specified by the FRAME attribute of <table>.

See also related elements <colspec>, <table>, <tgroup>, and <tspec>.

May contain:

EMPTY

May occur within:

tgroup, tspec

Attributes:

ALIGN	#IMPLIED, left, right, center, justify, char
CHAR	#IMPLIED, CDATA
CHAROFF	#IMPLIED, CDATA
COLSEP	#IMPLIED, CDATA
NAMEEND	#REQUIRED, NMTOKEN
NAMEST	#REQUIRED, NMTOKEN
ROWSEP	#IMPLIED, CDATA
SPANNAME	#REQUIRED, NMTOKEN

<tfoot> Table Foot

Description:

A formatting element that contains information that usually appears at the bottom of the table, like a footer. This information may follow the <tbody> or may be repeated to provide a footer <row> at the bottom of any physical break in <row>s in the body of the table.

See also related elements <entry>, <row>, <table>, <tfoot>, <tgroup>, and <thead>.

May contain:

colspec, row

May occur within:

tgroup

Attributes:

ALTRENDER	#IMPLIED, CDATA
AUDIENCE	#IMPLIED, external, internal
ID	#IMPLIED, ID
VALIGN	top, top, middle, bottom

Obsolete Attributes

BEHAVIOR

Detailed instructions about the behavior of a link that are beyond the scope of the controls provided by the SHOW and ACTUATE attributes.

CONTENT-ROLE

Information that explains to application software the part that a local resource plays in a link.

CONTENT-TITLE

Information that serves as a viewable caption which explains to the user the part that a local resource plays in an extended link.

EXTENT

The information in a <title> or <titleproper> element may refer to the entire bibliographic work, part of the work, or an unknown portion of the work. Values are:

- all
- part
- unknown-extent

INLINE

Specification defining whether or not the element containing the link serves as one of the resources for the link. Values are:

- true (the element containing the link serves as one of the resources, i.e., is the local resource, for the link. Most simple links are inline. This is the default value for the attribute.)
- false (the element containing the link does not serve as one of the resources for the link. This is the case with the following elements used with extended links: <daoloc>, <extptrloc>, <extrefloc>, <ptrloc>, and <refloc>. It is also possible, though uncommon, to have simple links that are not inline).

NUMBERED

The presence or absence of enumerated materials, as in a bibliographic citation. Values are:

- yes
- no

ORIENT — The orientation of the table relative to the page or screen. Values are:

- port (portrait—the top of the table is at the top of the page, which is the short edge of the paper)
- land (landscape—the top of the table is on one of the long edges of the paper, thus on the side of the page)

OTHERSOURCE — The source of the content of the element or rules for creating the controlled vocabulary term can be specified when the name of the appropriate thesaurus, term list, or set of rules is not present in the semi-closed list in the SOURCE attribute.

PUBSTATUS — The information given in the <title> may represent a published work, an unpublished work, or the publication status may not be known. Values are:

- pub
- unpub
- unknown-pub

ROTATE — Is the entry rotated 90 degrees to the orientation of the whole table? Possible values are (default is 1):

- 1 (entry is oriented 90 degrees counterclockwise to the table orientation)
- 0 (entry orientation is the same as the table orientation)

SHORTENTRY — Is the head used in the table of contents a shortened version? Values are:

- 1 (yes)
- 0 (no)

SPANNAME — Name of the previously specified horizontal span of columns in which the entry will be placed. The value must be a column name, as defined by the SPANNAME attribute on a Span Specification <spanspec> element.

SYSTEMID — An alphabetic or numeric representation of the automated system in which the <eadid> value is valid. When the <eadid> SOURCE attribute would be equivalent to the SYSTEMID attribute, the SOURCE attribute is sufficient.

TABSTYLE — The unique style of the table. This attribute can be used to reference a style in a stored library of table styles.

TARGETTYPE — A description of the characteristics of the resource to which a TARGET attribute links in a <ptr> or <ref> element.

TGROUPSTYLE — Unique table group style in the output specification, this is analogous to a table's tabstyle. Value is one "word" made up of letters and numbers with no spaces inside it.

TOCENTRY — Does the head appear in a list of tables? Values are:

- 1 (yes)
- 0 (no)

XLINK:FORM — The type of XML link being employed. Values are:

- simple (a uni-directional, inline link. This is the default value for the following linking elements: <dao>, <extptr>, <extref>, <ptr>, and <ref>. For most simple links, the value of the attribute INLINE is "true".)
- locator (an extended, multi-directional link. This is the default value for the following linking elements: <daoloc>, <extptrloc>, <extrefloc>, <ptrloc>, and <refloc>. For most extended links, the value of the attribute INLINE is "false".)

Appendix C

The following finding aids were originally encoded in EAD Version 1.0 and modified to conform to EAD 2002. One displays a minimal level of markup, while the other makes extensive use of attributes. Neither should be considered normative, as the archival community continues to experiment with the "optimal" level of markup.

Example 1

Guide to the Mildred Davenport Dance Programs and Dance School Materials

Example 1 describes a collection of personal papers at the collection and file levels, using the "combined" <dsc> approach to emphasize the hierarchical nature of this archival description. It utilizes the LEVEL attribute throughout in order to record unambiguously how, in several cases, multiple nested components are used to describe a single "file," and to clearly mark for server-side processing the boundaries between "file" and "item" levels of description. Further, it encodes physical housing information using a single <container> element within each <c0x> component.

Choices for the minimum set of EAD elements and usage of LABEL attributes and <head> elements were made using the *Online Archive of California Best Practice Guidelines Version 1.0: Encoding New Finding Aids Using Encoded Archival Description* (available online at <http://www.cdlib.org/libstaff/sharedcoll/oac/>). These Guidelines will be updated by a subcommittee of the Online Archive of California Working Group shortly after EAD 2002 documentation is released, and are based, where appropriate, on ISAD(G), APPM, AACR2, and other national and international standards for data content and values.

```
<?xml version="1.0"?>
<!DOCTYPE EAD PUBLIC "+//ISBN 1-931666-00-8//DTD ead.dtd (Encoded Archival
Description (EAD) Version 2002)//EN" [
<!ENTITY hdr-cu-i-spcoll PUBLIC "-//University of California,
Irvine::Library::Special Collections and Archives//TEXT (eadheader: name and
address)//EN" "hdrcuisp.sgm">
<!ENTITY tp-cu-i-spcoll PUBLIC "-//University of California,
Irvine::Library::Special Collections and Archives//TEXT (titlepage: name and
address)//EN" "tpcuisp.sgm">
<!ENTITY ucseal PUBLIC "-//University of California, Berkeley::Library//NONSGML
(University of California seal)//EN" NDATA GIF>
]>

<ead>
   <eadheader audience="internal" countryencoding="iso3166-1"
      dateencoding="iso8601" langencoding="iso639-2b"
      repositoryencoding="iso15511">
      <eadid countrycode="us" mainagencycode="cu-i" publicid="-//us::cu-i//TEXT
         us::cu-i::p29.sgm//EN">Mildred Davenport Dance Programs and Dance
         School Materials, MS-P29
      </eadid>
      <filedesc>
         <titlestmt>
            <titleproper>Guide to the Mildred Davenport Dance Programs and Dance
               School Materials</titleproper>
            <author>Processed by Adrian Turner; machine-readable finding aid
               created by Adrian Turner</author>
         </titlestmt>
```

```
      <publicationstmt>&hdr-cu-i-spcoll;
         <date>&copy; 2001</date>
         <p>The Regents of the University of California. All rights
            reserved.</p>
      </publicationstmt>
      <notestmt>
         <note>
            <p>
               <subject source="cdl">Arts and Humanities--Dance--Dance
                  Performance</subject>
               <subject source="cdl">Arts and Humanities--Dance--Dance
                  History and Criticism</subject>
               <subject source="cdl">Area, Interdisciplinary, and Ethnic
                  Studies--African American Studies</subject>
            </p>
         </note>
      </notestmt>
   </filedesc>
   <profiledesc>
      <creation>Machine-readable finding aid derived from MS Word.  Date of
         source: <date>2001.</date></creation>
      <langusage>Description is in <language>English.</language></langusage>
   </profiledesc>
</eadheader>

<frontmatter>
   <titlepage>
      <titleproper>Guide to the Mildred Davenport Dance Programs and Dance
         School Materials</titleproper>
      <num>Collection number: MS-P29</num>
      <publisher>Special Collections and Archives
         <lb>The UCI Libraries
         <lb><extptr actuate="onload" show="embed" entityref="ucseal">
         <lb>University of California
         <lb>Irvine, California</publisher>
         &tp-cu-i-spcoll;
      <list type="deflist">
         <defitem>
            <label>Processed by: </label>
            <item>Adrian Turner</item>
         </defitem>
         <defitem>
            <label>Date Completed: </label>
            <item>2001</item>
         </defitem>
         <defitem>
            <label>Encoded by: </label>
            <item>Adrian Turner</item>
         </defitem>
      </list>
      <p>&copy; 2001 The Regents of the University of California. All rights
         reserved.</p>
   </titlepage>
</frontmatter>
```

```
<archdesc level="collection">
  <did>
    <head>Descriptive Summary</head>
    <unittitle label="Title">Mildred Davenport dance programs and dance
      school materials</unittitle>
    <unitdate type="inclusive" normal="1934/1942">1934-1942</unitdate>
    <unitid countrycode="us" repositorycode="cu-i" label="Collection
      number">MS-P29</unitid>
    <origination label="Creator"><persname rules="aacr2">Davenport,
      Mildred, 1900-1990</persname></origination>
    <physdesc label="Extent">
      <extent>0.3 linear feet (1 box and 1 oversize folder)</extent>
    </physdesc>
    <repository label="Repository">
      <corpname>University of California, Irvine. Library. Special
        Collections and Archives.</corpname>
      <address>
        <addressline>Irvine, California 92623-9557</addressline>
      </address>
    </repository>
    <abstract label="Abstract">This collection comprises dance programs,
      dance school materials, photographs, and ephemera documenting the
      early career of the Boston-based African-American dancer, dance
      instructor, and civic official Mildred Davenport. The bulk of this
      collection consists of dance programs and dance school materials.
      The collection also contains 29 photographs of Davenport, her
      students in various performances, and friends or individual
      students. Dance programs from 1925 to 1942 feature her solo
      performances and group performances with her students. The
      collection includes a complete run of programs for Bronze Rhapsody,
      an annual performance series choreographed, staged, and directed by
      Davenport. Her personal copy of a typescript of stage directions for
      a 1934 performance is included with these programs. Her dance
      schools, Davenport School of the Dance and Silver Box Studio, are
      documented in course brochures and applications. Biographical and
      academic materials include a 1939 newspaper article on
      Davenport.</abstract>
  </did>

  <descgrp>
    <head>Important Information for Users of the Collection</head>
    <accessrestrict>
      <head>Access</head>
      <p>Collection is open for research.</p>
    </accessrestrict>
    <userestrict>
    <head>Publication Rights</head>
      <p>Property rights reside with the University of California.
        Literary rights are retained by the creators of the records and
        their heirs. For permissions to reproduce or to publish, please
        contact the Head of Special Collections and Archives.</p>
    </userestrict>
```

```
   <prefercite>
      <head>Preferred Citation</head>
      <p>Mildred Davenport Dance Programs and Dance School Materials. MS-
         P29. Special Collections and Archives, The UC Irvine Libraries,
         Irvine, California.</p>
   </prefercite>
   <acqinfo>
      <head>Acquisition Information</head>
      <p>Acquired, 1998.</p>
   </acqinfo>
   <processinfo>
      <head>Processing History</head>
      <p>Processed by Adrian Turner, 2001.</p>
   </processinfo>
</descgrp>

<bioghist>
   <bioghist>
      <head>Biography</head>
      <p>Mildred Ellen Davenport was a noted civic official and military
         officer with an extensive career as a dancer and dance instructor
         in Boston in the 1930s and 1940s. She was born in Boston on
         November 12, 1900. She began her dance studies at C.C. Perkins
         Grade School and Prince School as a teenager, and graduated from
         Boston Girls' High School in 1918. In the 1920s she studied at
         the Sargent School for Physical Culture and at Harvard, and
         opened her first dance school, the Davenport School of Dance.
         Over the next ten years she studied under Ted Shawn and taught
         dance in Boston. She was also progressively more involved in road
         show performances such as Hot Chocolates. From 1930 to 1935 she
         performed in a number of African-American musical productions on
         Broadway, including Fast and Furious, Flying Colors, and Black
         Birds. In 1932 she established her second dance school, the
         Silver Box Studio, in the South End of Boston. She became the
         first African American woman to perform with the Arthur Fiedler
         Pops unit of the Boston Symphony Orchestra at this time.</p>
      <p>During World War II, Davenport enlisted in the Army as a captain.
         She produced musical shows for military bases and later served as
         a special service officer, library officer, and advisor in the
         Office of Racial Affairs. In 1950, she served as an executive
         board member for the N.A.A.C.P. office in Boston. From 1947 to
         1968 she worked for the Massachusetts Commission Against
         Discrimination, founded in 1944 to enforce fair employment
         practices. Davenport died in Boston in 1990.</p>
   </bioghist>

   <bioghist>
      <head>Chronology</head>
      <chronlist>
         <chronitem>
            <date>1900</date>
            <event>Born in Boston.</event>
         </chronitem>
```

```
<chronitem>
   <date>Ca. 1914</date>
   <event>Student at C.C. Perkins Grade School and Prince
      School.</event>
</chronitem>
<chronitem>
   <date>1918</date>
   <event>Graduates from Boston Girls' High School.</event>
</chronitem>
<chronitem>
   <date>Ca. 1920s</date>
   <event>Establishes Davenport School of Dance in
      Boston.</event>
</chronitem>
<chronitem>
   <date>1921</date>
   <event>Student at Sargent School for Physical Culture.</event>
</chronitem>
<chronitem>
   <date>1921-1922</date>
   <event>Physical training instructor at Tuskegee Institute,
      Alabama.</event>
</chronitem>
<chronitem>
    <date>1923</date>
    <event>Student at Harvard Summer School.</event>
</chronitem>
<chronitem>
   <date>1925-ca. 1930</date>
   <event>Staff member with the Department of Public Welfare,
      Boston.</event>
</chronitem>
<chronitem>
   <date>Ca. 1930-1935</date>
   <event>Performs on Broadway.</event>
</chronitem>
<chronitem>
   <date>1932</date>
   <event>Establishes Silver Box Studio in Boston.</event>
</chronitem>
<chronitem>
   <date>1946-1947</date>
   <event>U.S. Army, civilian defense instructor.</event>
</chronitem>
<chronitem>
   <date>1947</date>
   <event>U.S. Army Office of Racial Affairs, assistant special
      service officer, library officer, and advisor.</event>
</chronitem>
<chronitem>
   <date>1950</date>
   <event>Executive board member of N.A.A.C.P., Boston.  Member
      of Women's Service Club and League of Women for Community
      Service, Boston.</event>
</chronitem>
```

```
            <chronitem>
               <date>1947-1968</date>
               <event>Staff member with the Massachusetts Commission Against
                  Discrimination.</event>
            </chronitem>
            <chronitem>
               <date>1973</date>
               <event>Receives Sojourner Truth Award of the National
                  Association of Negro Business and Professional Women's
                  Clubs, Boston and Vicinity Club.</event>
            </chronitem>
            <chronitem>
               <date>1990</date>
               <event>Dies in Boston.</event>
            </chronitem>
         </chronlist>
      </bioghist>
   </bioghist>

   <scopecontent>
      <head>Collection Scope and Content Summary</head>
      <p>This collection comprises dance programs, dance school materials,
         photographs, and ephemera documenting the early career of the
         Boston-based African-American dancer, dance instructor, and civic
         official Mildred Davenport. The bulk of this collection consists of
         dance programs and dance school materials. The collection also
         contains 29 photographs of Davenport, her students in various
         performances, and friends or individual students. Dance programs
         from 1925 to 1942 feature her solo performances and group
         performances with her students. The collection includes a complete
         run of programs for Bronze Rhapsody, an annual performance series
         choreographed, staged, and directed by Davenport. Her personal copy
         of a typescript of stage directions for a 1934 performance is
         included with these programs. Her dance schools, Davenport School of
         the Dance and Silver Box Studio, are documented in course brochures
         and applications. Biographical and academic materials include a 1939
         newspaper article on Davenport.</p>
      <p>The collection is arranged topically. Materials are arranged
         chronologically within each topical grouping whenever possible.</p>
   </scopecontent>

   <controlaccess>
      <head>Indexing Terms</head>
      <p>The following terms have been used to index the description of this
         collection in the library's online public access catalog.</p>
      <controlaccess>
         <head>Subjects</head>
         <persname encodinganalog="600" rules="aacr2" role="subject">Davenport,
            Mildred, 1900-1990--Archives.</persname>
         <subject encodinganalog="650" source="lcsh">Dance schools--
            Massachusetts--Boston--Archival resources.</subject>
         <subject encodinganalog="650" source="lcsh">Dance--Archival
            resources.</subject>
         <subject encodinganalog="650" source="lcsh">Modern dance--United
            States--Archival resources.</subject>
         <subject encodinganalog="650" source="lcsh">Dance, Black--Archival
            resources.</subject>
```

```
        <subject encodinganalog="650" source="lcsh">African American
           dancers--Archival resources.</subject>
     </controlaccess>
     <controlaccess>
        <head>Genres and Forms of Materials</head>
        <genreform encodinganalog="655" source="local">Dance
           programs.</genreform>
        <genreform encodinganalog="655" source="gmgpc">Photographic
           prints.</genreform>
        <genreform encodinganalog="655" source="gmgpc">Posters.</genreform>
     </controlaccess>
     <controlaccess>
        <head>Occupations</head>
        <occupation encodinganalog="656" source="aat">Dancers.</occupation>
        <occupation encodinganalog="656" source="lcsh">Dance
           teachers.</occupation>
     </controlaccess>
  </controlaccess>

  <dsc type="combined">
     <head>Collection Contents</head>
     <c01 level="file">
        <did>
           <container type="box-folder" label="Box ">1 : 1</container>
           <unittitle>Biographical and academic materials</unittitle>
        </did>
        <c02 level="file">
           <did>
              <container type="box-folder" label="Box ">FB-21 :
                 1</container>
              <unittitle>Boston Girls' High School, commencement
                 program</unittitle>
              <unitdate normal="1918">1918</unitdate>
           </did>
        </c02>
        <c02 level="file">
           <did>
              <container type="box-folder" label="Box ">1 : 1</container>
              <unittitle>George Peabody College for Teachers, School of the
                 Dance, schedule of courses offered by Ted Shawn</unittitle>
              <unitdate normal="1938">1938</unitdate>
           </did>
        </c02>
        <c02 level="file">
           <did>
              <container type="box-folder" label="Box ">1 : 1</container>
              <unittitle>"Boston teacher called evangelist of the dance,"
                 newspaper clipping</unittitle>
              <unitdate normal="1939">1939</unitdate>
           </did>
        </c02>
     </c01>
```

```
<c01 level="file">
   <did>
      <container type="box-folder" label="Box ">1 : 2-4</container>
      <unittitle>Dance programs</unittitle>
   </did>
   <c02 level="item">
      <did>
         <container type="box-folder" label="Box ">1 : 4</container>
         <unittitle>The Feast of Apollo, Brattle Hall,
            Massachusetts</unittitle>
         <unitdate normal="1925">1925</unitdate>
      </did>
   </c02>
   <c02 level="item">
      <did>
         <container type="box-folder" label="Box ">1 : 4</container>
         <unittitle>Mildred Davenport and her pupils, Brattle Hall,
            Massachusetts</unittitle>
         <unitdate normal="1928">1928</unitdate>
      </did>
   </c02>
   <c02 level="item">
      <did>
         <container type="box-folder" label="Box ">1 : 4</container>
         <unittitle>Recital of dance poems and songs, Allied Art
            Studio, Boston</unittitle>
         <unitdate normal="1928">1928</unitdate>
      </did>
   </c02>
   <c02 level="item">
      <did>
         <container type="box-folder" label="Box ">1 : 4</container>
         <unittitle>Mildred Davenport and Sepia Beauties in revue,
            Challengers Club, Boston</unittitle>
         <unitdate normal="1933">1933</unitdate>
      </did>
   </c02>
   <c02 level="file">
      <did>
         <container type="box-folder" label="Box ">1 : 2-3</container>
         <unittitle>Bronze rhapsody</unittitle>
      </did>
      <c03 level="file">
         <did>
            <container type="box-folder" label="Box ">1 : 2</container>
            <unittitle><unitdate normal="1934">1934</unitdate>
            </unittitle>
         </did>
```

```
                <c04 level="item">
                   <did>
                      <container type="box-folder" label="Box ">1 :
                         2</container>
                      <unittitle>Typescript of stage directions, with
                         holograph note "Miss Davenport (personal)" on first
                         leaf</unittitle>
                      <unitdate normal="1934">1934</unitdate>
                   </did>
                </c04>
             </c03>
             <c03 level="file">
                <did>
                   <container type="box-folder" label="Box ">1 : 3</container>
                   <unittitle><unitdate type="inclusive"
                      normal="1935/1941">1935-1941</unitdate></unittitle>
                </did>
             </c03>
             <c03 level="file">
                <did>
                   <container type="box-folder" label="Box ">1 : 3</container>
                   <unittitle><unitdate
                      normal="1942">1942</unitdate></unittitle>
                </did>
                <c04 level="item">
                   <did>
                      <container type="box-folder" label="Box ">FB-21 :
                         1</container>
                      <unittitle>Hand-colored poster (partial) </unittitle>
                      <unitdate normal="1942">1942</unitdate>
                   </did>
                </c04>
             </c03>
          </c02>
          <c02 level="file">
             <did>
                <container type="box-folder" label="Box ">1 : 4</container>
                <unittitle>Classic, John Hancock Hall, Boston</unittitle>
                <unitdate normal="1938">1938</unitdate>
             </did>
          </c02>
          <c02 level="file">
             <did>
                <container type="box-folder" label="Box ">1 : 4</container>
                <unittitle>Shadowland Ball Room performances, Boston,
                   undated.</unittitle>
                <physdesc><extent>2 items.</extent></physdesc>
             </did>
          </c02>
       </c01>

       <c01 level="file">
          <did>
             <container type="box-folder" label="Box ">1 : 5</container>
             <unittitle>Dance school materials</unittitle>
          </did>
```

```
<c02 level="item">
   <did>
      <container type="box-folder" label="Box ">1 : 5</container>
      <unittitle>Davenport School of the Dance application,
         undated</unittitle>
   </did>
</c02>
<c02 level="file">
   <did>
      <container type="box-folder" label="Box ">1 : 5</container>
      <unittitle>Silver Box Studio</unittitle>
   </did>
   <c03 level="file">
      <did>
         <container type="box-folder" label="Box ">1 : 5</container>
         <unittitle>Course brochures and applications,
            undated.</unittitle>
         <physdesc><extent>3 items.</extent></physdesc>
      </did>
   </c03>
   <c03 level="file">
      <did>
         <container type="box-folder" label="Box ">1 : 5</container>
         <unittitle>Event invitation and greeting card</unittitle>
         <unitdate normal="1939">1939 and undated.</unitdate>
         <physdesc><extent>2 items.</extent></physdesc>
      </did>
   </c03>
</c02>
</c01>

<c01 level="file">
   <did>
      <container type="box-folder" label="Box ">1 : 6-11</container>
      <unittitle>Photographs</unittitle></did>
   <c02 level="file">
      <did>
         <container type="box-folder" label="Box ">1 : 6-7</container>
         <unittitle>Personal</unittitle>
      </did>
      <c03 level="item">
         <did>
            <container type="box-folder" label="Box ">FB-21 :
               1</container>
            <unittitle>Prince School class, photographic
               print</unittitle>
            <unitdate normal="1914">1914</unitdate>
         </did>
      </c03>
      <c03 level="file">
         <did>
            <container type="box-folder" label="Box ">1 : 6</container>
            <unittitle>Teenage performances, undated.</unittitle>
            <physdesc><extent>5 items.</extent></physdesc>
         </did>
      </c03>
```

```
        <c03 level="file">
          <did>
            <container type="box-folder" label="Box ">1 : 7</container>
            <unittitle>Portraits, undated.</unittitle>
            <physdesc><extent>3 items.</extent></physdesc>
          </did>
        </c03>
      </c02>
      <c02 level="file">
        <did>
          <container type="box-folder" label="Box ">1 : 8-10</container>
          <unittitle>Performances by students</unittitle>
        </did>
        <c03 level="item">
          <did>
            <container type="box-folder" label="Box ">1 : 8</container>
            <unittitle>Piggilly wiggily</unittitle>
            <unitdate normal="1942">ca. 1942</unitdate>
          </did>
        </c03>
        <c03 level="item">
          <did>
            <container type="box-folder" label="Box ">1 : 8</container>
            <unittitle>Top hat</unittitle>
            <unitdate normal="1942">ca. 1942</unitdate>
          </did>
        </c03>
        <c03 level="file">
          <did>
            <container type="box-folder" label="Box ">1 : 8-
              10</container>
            <unittitle>Unidentified, undated.</unittitle>
            <physdesc><extent>15 items.</extent></physdesc>
          </did>
        </c03>
      </c02>
      <c02 level="file">
        <did>
          <container type="box-folder" label="Box ">1 : 11</container>
          <unittitle>Other individuals</unittitle>
        </did>
        <c03 level="file">
          <did>
            <container type="box-folder" label="Box ">1 :
              11</container>
            <unittitle>Hall, Tom</unittitle>
            <unitdate normal="1930">1930</unitdate>
          </did>
        </c03>
        <c03 level="file">
          <did>
            <container type="box-folder" label="Box ">1 :
              11</container>
            <unittitle>Purcell, Barbara</unittitle>
            <unitdate normal="1942">ca. 1942</unitdate>
          </did>
        </c03>
```

```
            <c03 level="file">
               <did>
                  <container type="box-folder" label="Box ">1 :
                     11</container>
                  <unittitle>Stokes, Bernice</unittitle>
                  <unitdate normal="1942">ca. 1942</unitdate>
               </did>
            </c03>
            <c03 level="file">
               <did>
                  <container type="box-folder" label="Box ">1 :
                     11</container>
                  <unittitle>Roberts, Francine</unittitle>
                  <unitdate normal="1942">ca. 1942</unitdate>
               </did>
            </c03>
         </c02>
      </c01>
   </dsc>
 </archdesc>
</ead>
```

Example 2

Minnesota Territorial Archives
Records of Territorial Governor Willis A. Gorman

Example 2 describes a series of government records that has been minimally encoded. It uses the "combined" <dsc> model to emphasize the hierarchical nature of the archival description.

```
<?xml version="1.0" encoding="utf-8"?>
<!DOCTYPE EAD PUBLIC "+//ISBN 1-931666-00-8//DTD ead.dtd (Encoded Archival
Description (EAD) Version 2002)//EN">

<ead>
   <eadheader countryencoding="iso3166-1" repositoryencoding="iso15511"
   langencoding="iso639-2b" relatedencoding="marc">
      <eadid countrycode="us" repositorycode="mnhi">terr06</eadid>
      <filedesc>
         <titlestmt>
            <titleproper>MINNESOTA TERRITORIAL ARCHIVES. Territorial
               Governor:</titleproper>
            <subtitle> An Inventory of Territorial Governor Willis A.
               Gorman</subtitle>
            <author>Finding aid prepared by Lydia Lucas.</author>
         </titlestmt>
      </filedesc>
      <profiledesc>
         <creation>Finding aid encoded by Lyda Morehouse,
         <date>July 17, 2002.</date></creation>
      </profiledesc>
   </eadheader>

   <archdesc level="series">
      <did id="a1">
         <head>OVERVIEW OF THE RECORDS</head>
         <repository label="Repository:">Minnesota Historical
            Society</repository>
         <origination label="Creator:">Agency:Minnesota. Governor (1853-1857 :
            Gorman).</origination>
         <unittitle label="Title:">Series Records of territorial governor Willis
            A. Gorman,</unittitle>
         <unitdate label="Date:">1852-1857.</unitdate>
         <abstract label="Abstract:">Subject files, correspondence,
            appointments, pardon records, reports from territorial officers,
            requests for return of fugitives, and miscellany.</abstract>
         <physdesc label="Quantity:">0.75 cu. ft. (23 folders in 2 partial
            boxes).</physdesc>
         <physloc label="Location:">See Detailed Description section for box
            locations.</physloc>
      </did>
```

```
<bioghist>
   <head id="a2">BIOGRAPHICAL SKETCH OF GOVERNOR WILLIS A. GORMAN</head>
   <p>Willis Arnold Gorman was born in Kentucky on January 12, 1816. His
      early career was as a lawyer and state legislator (Democrat) in
      Indiana. During the Mexican War he raised and commanded an Indiana
      rifle battalion and an infantry regiment, and subsequently was
      elected to two terms in the U.S. Congress. President Franklin Pierce
      appointed him Governor of Minnesota in May 13, 1853, and he served
      in that office until 1857. He was subsequently a delegate to the
      state constitutional convention (1857) and was elected to the first
      state legislature (1858).</p>
   <p>At the outset of the Civil War he commanded the First Minnesota
      Infantry Volunteers (April-October, 1861) until his promotion to
      brigadier general. Following his discharge from military service in
      1864, he practiced law in St. Paul in partnership with Cushman K.
      Davis. In 1869 he was appointed St. Paul city attorney, and held
      that office until his death on May 20, 1876.</p>
   <p>Sources: <emph render="italic">Minnesota Biographies</emph>, pp.
      267-268; <emph render="italic">Minnesota in the Civil and Indian
      Wars</emph>, Vol. I, p. 14; William Watts Folwell, <emph
      render="italic">A History of Minnesota</emph> (St. Paul, rev. 1956),
      Vol. I, pp. 377-383; Theodore C. Blegen, <emph
      render="italic">Minnesota, A History of the State</emph> (1963), pp.
      171, 240-242, 293.</p>
</bioghist>

<scopecontent>
   <head id="a3">SCOPE AND CONTENTS OF THE RECORDS</head>
   <p>Subject files and correspondence of territorial governor Gorman. A
      large proportion relate to territorial officers' appointments and
      commissions. Letters received and sent address the following topics:
      concerns of federal civilian agencies, military and Indian affairs
      in general, the 1855 treaty with the Winnebago Indians, land sales,
      the Minnesota and Northwestern Railroad Company, and other
      territorial affairs. Also present are a legislative diary (Jan. 27-
      March 6, 1857), pardon records, petitions regarding local government
      organization, reports from territorial officers, and requests from
      other states for return of fugitives.</p>
   <p>Gorman's governorship spanned a period of both tangible and
      speculative growth in the state's infrastructure and economy, with
      numerous railroads, educational institutions, and corporations being
      chartered, new counties established, new towns incorporated, and
      several Indian treaties ratified. The surviving records contain only
      sketchy information on these developments, and do not appear to
      contain any significant documentation on an abortive 1857 scheme to
      remove the state capital from St. Paul to St. Peter.</p>
</scopecontent>

<arrangement>
   <head id="a4">ARRANGEMENT OF THE RECORDS</head>
   <p>Arranged alphabetically by topic; thereunder chronologically within
      each folder.</p>
</arrangement>
```

```
<controlaccess>
   <head id="a7">INDEX TERMS</head>
   <p> <emph render="italic">This collection is indexed under the
      following headings in the catalog of the Minnesota Historical
      Society. Researchers desiring materials about related topics,
      persons or places should search the catalog using these
      headings.</emph></p>
   <controlaccess>
      <head>Topics:</head>
      <subject>Civil-military relations--Minnesota.</subject>
      <subject>Extraditions--Minnesota.</subject>
      <subject>Federal government--Minnesota.</subject>
      <subject>Indians of North America—Government relations--1789-
         1869.</subject>
      <subject>Land titles--Minnesota--Registration and
         transfer.</subject>
      <subject>Pardons--Minnesota.</subject>
      <subject>Winnebago Indians--Treaties.</subject>
   </controlaccess>
   <controlaccess>
      <head>Places:</head>
      <geogname>Minnesota--Officials and employees--Selection and
         appointment.</geogname>
      <geogname>Minnesota--Politics and government--1849-1858.</geogname>
   </controlaccess>
   <controlaccess>
      <head>Persons:</head>
      <persname>Gorman, Willis Arnold, 1816-1876.</persname>
   </controlaccess>
   <controlaccess>
      <head>Organizations:</head>
      <corpname>Minnesota Territory.</corpname>
   </controlaccess>
   <controlaccess>
      <head>Types of Documents:</head>
      <genreform>Diaries--Minnesota.</genreform>
      <genreform>Petitions--Minnesota.</genreform>
      <genreform>Proclamations--Minnesota.</genreform>
      <genreform>Territorial records--Minnesota.</genreform>
   </controlaccess>
</controlaccess>

<prefercite>
   <head>Preferred Citation:</head>
   <p><emph render="italic">[Indicate the cited volume and page or item
      and folder title here].</emph> Minnesota Territorial Archives.
      Records of territorial governor Willis Gorman. Minnesota Historical
      Society. State Archives.</p>
   <p><emph render="italic">See the Chicago Manual of Style for additional
      examples.</emph></p>
</prefercite>

<acqinfo>
   <head>Accession Information:</head>
   <p>Accession number(s): none; 2001-46</p>
</acqinfo>
```

```
<processinfo>
   <head>Processing Information:</head>
   <p>PALS ID No.: 0800011304</p>
   <p>RLIN ID No.: MNHV90-A1172</p>
</processinfo>

<dsc type="combined" id="fruin" audience="external">
   <head id="a9">DETAILED DESCRIPTION OF THE RECORDS</head>
   <p id="MHSLoc"> <emph render="italic">Note to Researchers: To request
      materials, please note both the location and box numbers shown
      below.</emph></p>
   <c01>
      <did>
         <physloc>115.I.19.8F</physloc> <container>[1]</container>
         <unittitle>Appointments: Commission of Deeds, </unittitle>
         <unitdate>1853-1857. </unitdate>
         <physdesc>1 folder.</physdesc>
      </did>
      <scopecontent>
         <p>For each individual, may include any of the following:
            application, petition, recommendations, letter of
            resignation.</p>
      </scopecontent>
   </c01>

   <c01>
      <did>
         <unittitle>Appointments: Counties, </unittitle>
         <unitdate>1853-1857. </unitdate>
         <physdesc>1 folder.</physdesc>
      </did>
      <scopecontent>
         <p>For each individual, may include any of the following:
            application, petition, recommendations, letter of resignation.
            Arranged alphabetically by county.</p>
      </scopecontent>
   </c01>

   <c01>
      <did>
         <unittitle>Appointments: Notary Public, </unittitle>
         <unitdate>undated and 1853-1857. </unitdate>
         <physdesc>4 folders. </physdesc>
      </did>
      <scopecontent>
         <p>For each individual, may include any of the following:
         application, petition, recommendations, letter of
         resignation.</p>
      </scopecontent>
   </c01>
```

```
<c01>
   <did>
      <unittitle>Appointments: Territorial Offices, </unittitle>
      <unitdate>1853-1857. </unitdate>
   </did>
   <scopecontent>
      <p>May include any of the following: application, petition,
         recommendations, letter of resignation, for commissioner of
         emigration, librarian, superintendent of common schools,
         auditor, treasurer, building commissioner, supreme court
         reporter, militia, and land office.</p>
   </scopecontent>
</c01>

<c01>
   <did>
      <unittitle>Commissions, </unittitle>
      <unitdate>1855-1857. </unitdate>
      <physdesc>5 items.</physdesc>
   </did>
   <scopecontent>
      <p>For notary public, justice of the peace, and building
         commissioner.</p>
   </scopecontent>
</c01>

<c01>
   <did>
      <unittitle>Document Transmittals, Receipts, and Requests,
         </unittitle>
      <unitdate>1853-1857. </unitdate>
      <physdesc>1 folder. </physdesc>
   </did>
</c01>

<c01>
   <did>
      <unittitle>Legislative Diary, 1</unittitle>
      <unitdate>1857. </unitdate>
      <physdesc>1 volume </physdesc>
   </did>
   <scopecontent>
      <p>Fragmentary entries, January 27 - March 6, showing numbers and
         titles of bills.</p>
   </scopecontent>
</c01>
```

```
<c01>
   <did>
      <unittitle>Letters Received: Federal Civilian Agencies,
         18</unittitle>
      <unitdate>1853-1857. </unitdate>
      <physdesc>1 folder. </physdesc>
   </did>
   <scopecontent>
      <p>Letters and circulars from federal civilian agencies,
         including the General Land Office, the Post Office Department,
         and the Treasury Department.</p>
   </scopecontent>
</c01>

<c01>
   <did>
      <physloc>115.I.19.8F</physloc> <container>[1]</container>
      <unittitle>Letters Received: Indian and Military Affairs,
         </unittitle>
      <unitdate>1853-1857. </unitdate>
      <physdesc>1 folder. </physdesc>
   </did>
   <scopecontent>
      <p>Letters, reports, and orders relating to Indian and military
         affairs, from the commanding officers at Fort Snelling and
         Fort Ridgely; from legislative district representatives about
         the Winnebago treaty, with a copy of Governor Gorman's reply
         (January 1854); and petitions and requests for defense against
         the Indians.</p>
      <p>Includes a letter written by Henry B. Smythe on behalf of the
         Winnebago Indians (8 Jan. 1856) requesting the transfer of
         $806 from tribal funds to the superintendent of the Winnebago
         School. It may refer to funds available to the tribe under the
         1855 U.S. Treaty with the Winnebago; it is signed by many of
         the Winnebago signatories to that treaty.</p>
   </scopecontent>
</c01>

<c01>
   <did>
      <unittitle>Letters Received: Land Sales, </unittitle>
      <unitdate>1853-1857. </unitdate>
      <physdesc>9 items.</physdesc>
   </did>
   <scopecontent>
      <p>Letters about land sales and occupancy.</p>
   </scopecontent>
</c01>
```

```
<c01>
   <did>
      <unittitle>Letters Received: Other Territorial Affairs,
         </unittitle>
      <unitdate>1853-1857. </unitdate>
      <physdesc>16 items.</physdesc>
   </did>
   <scopecontent>
      <p>Letters from Senator Henry M. Rice and others about a variety
         of territorial affairs.</p>
   </scopecontent>
</c01>

<c01>
   <did>
      <physloc>115.I.19.9B</physloc> <container>[2]</container>
      <unittitle>Pardon Records, </unittitle>
      <unitdate>1852-1857. </unitdate>
      <physdesc>21 items.</physdesc>
   </did>
   <scopecontent>
      <p>Requests and petitions for pardons and commutations;
         governor's pardon; orders for release and related court
         records; letters for persons convicted and sentenced for
         various offenses, including murder, assault with intent to
         kill, assault and battery, simple assault, and resisting an
         officer; and letters asking for the release of an Indian
         hostage.</p>
   </scopecontent>
</c01>

<c01>
   <did>
      <unittitle>Petitions, </unittitle>
      <unitdate>1853-1855. </unitdate>
      <physdesc>10 items.</physdesc>
   </did>
   <scopecontent>
      <p>Various requests and petitions for the establishment of
         election precincts in Portsmouth and the Sioux Agency, for the
         organization of local governments in Rice County and Steele
         County, for a town organization in Bangor, for a vigilance
         committee to suppress liquor traffic at Traverse des Sioux,
         and for a certification of election districts in Carver
         County.</p>
   </scopecontent>
</c01>
```

```
<c01>
   <did>
      <unittitle>Proclamations, </unittitle>
      <unitdate>1854-1855. </unitdate>
      <physdesc>2 items.</physdesc>
   </did>
   <scopecontent>
      <p>Designating November 21, 1854, and November 20, 1855 as days
         of Thanksgiving.</p>
   </scopecontent>
</c01>

<c01>
   <did>
      <unittitle>Records Relating to the Minnesota and Northwestern
         Railroad Company, </unittitle>
      <unitdate>1854-1856. </unitdate>
      <physdesc>31 items.</physdesc>
   </did>
   <scopecontent>
      <p>Bills, correspondence, and reports dealing with its
         incorporation and with the political maneuverings surrounding
         its proposed land grant.</p>
   </scopecontent>
</c01>

<c01>
   <did>
      <physloc>115.I.19.9B</physloc> <container>[2]</container>
      <unittitle>Reports: Board of Inspectors of the Territorial
         Prison, </unittitle>
      <unitdate>1853-1856. </unitdate>
      <physdesc>1 folder. </physdesc>
   </did>
   <scopecontent>
      <p>Reports that include activities of the board and minutes of
         board meetings.</p>
   </scopecontent>
</c01>

<c01>
   <did>
      <unittitle>Reports: Commissioner of Emigration, </unittitle>
      <unitdate>1854-1857. </unitdate>
      <physdesc>1 folder. </physdesc>
   </did>
   <scopecontent>
      <p>Reports of activities, and financial reports including lists
         of expenditures and various receipts.</p>
   </scopecontent>
</c01>
```

```
          <c01>
             <did>
                <unittitle>Reports: Other Territorial Officers, </unittitle>
                <unitdate>1853-1855. </unitdate>
                <physdesc>7 items.</physdesc>
             </did>
             <c02>
                <did>
                   <unittitle>- Agent to select university lands (December 12,
                      1855).</unittitle>
                </did>
             </c02>
             <c02>
                <did>
                   <unittitle>- Commissioner for the Crystal Palace Exhibition
                      (1853, 1854).</unittitle>
                </did>
             </c02>
             <c02>
                <did>
                   <unittitle>- Superintendent of common schools (December 25,
                      1854).</unittitle>
                </did>
             </c02>
             <c02>
                <did>
                   <unittitle>- Territorial auditor (December 30, 1854; December
                      26, 1855).</unittitle>
                </did>
             </c02>
          </c01>

          <c01>
             <did>
                <unittitle>Requests for Return of Fugitives, </unittitle>
                <unitdate>1854-1857. </unitdate>
                <physdesc>2 folders. </physdesc>
             </did>
             <scopecontent>
                <p>Both to and from various states.</p>
             </scopecontent>
          </c01>
       </dsc>
    </archdesc>
</ead>
```

Appendix D

Index by Element Name

The following list of Encoded Archival Description data elements indicates the formal element name followed by its EAD tag.

Abbreviation <abbr>

Abstract <abstract>

Accruals <accruals>

Acquisition Information <acqinfo>

Address <address>

Address Line <addressline>

Alternative Form Available <altformavail>

Appraisal Information <appraisal>

Arc <arc>

Archival Description <archdesc>

Archival Description Group <archdescgrp>

Archival Reference <archref>

Arrangement <arrangement>

Author <author>

Bibliographic Reference <bibref>

Bibliographic Series <bibseries>

Bibliography <bibliography>

Biography or History <bioghist>

Block Quote <blockquote>

Change <change>

Chronology List <chronlist>

Chronology List Item <chronitem>

Component (Eighth Level) <c08>

Component (Eleventh Level) <c11>

Component (Fifth Level) <c05>

Component (First Level) <c01>

Component (Fourth Level) <c04>

Component (Ninth Level) <c09>

Component (Second Level) <c02>

Component (Seventh Level) <c07>

Component (Sixth Level) <c06>

Component (Tenth Level) <c10>

Component (Third Level) <c03>

Component (Twelfth Level) <c12>

Component (Unnumbered) <c>

Conditions Governing Access <accessrestrict>

Appendix D

Conditions Governing Use <userestrict>

Container <container>

Controlled Access Headings <controlaccess>

Corporate Name <corpname>

Creation <creation>

Custodial History <custodhist>

Date <date>

Date of the Unit <unitdate>

Definition List Item <defitem>

Description Group <descgrp>

Description of Subordinate Components <dsc>

Description of Subordinate Components Group <dscgrp>

Descriptive Identification <did>

Descriptive Rules <descrules>

Digital Archival Object <dao>

Digital Archival Object Description <daodesc>

Digital Archival Object Group <daogrp>

Digital Archival Object Location <daoloc>

Dimensions <dimensions>

EAD Group <eadgrp>

EAD Header <eadheader>

EAD Identifier <eadid>

Edition <edition>

Edition Statement <editionstmt>

Emphasis <emph>

Encoded Archival Description <ead>

Event <event>

Event Group <eventgrp>

Expansion <expan>

Extended Pointer <extptr>

Extended Pointer Location <extptrloc>

Extended Reference <extref>

Extended Reference Location <extrefloc>

Extent <extent>

Family Name <famname>

File Description <filedesc>

File Plan <fileplan>

First Heading <head01>

Front Matter <frontmatter>

Function <function>

Genre/Physical Characteristic <genreform>

Geographic Name <geogname>

Heading <head>

ID of the Unit <unitid>

Imprint <imprint>

Index <index>

Index Entry <indexentry>

Item <item>

Label <label>

Language <language>

Language of the Material <langmaterial>

Language Usage <langusage>

Legal Status <legalstatus>

Line Break <lb>

Linking Group <linkgrp>

List <list>

List Heading <listhead>

Location of Originals <originalsloc>

Material Specific Details <materialspec>

Name <name>

Name Group <namegrp>

Note <note>

Note Statement <notestmt>

Number <num>

Occupation <occupation>

Origination <origination>

Other Descriptive Data <odd>

Other Finding Aid <otherfindaid>

Paragraph <p>

Personal Name <persname>

Physical Characteristics and Technical Requirements <phystech>

Physical Description <physdesc>

Physical Facet <physfacet>

Physical Location <physloc>

Pointer <ptr>

Pointer Group <ptrgrp>

Pointer Location <ptrloc>

Preferred Citation <prefercite>

Processing Information <processinfo>

Profile Description <profiledesc>

Publication Statement <publicationstmt>

Publisher <publisher>

Reference <ref>

Reference Location <refloc>

Related Material <relatedmaterial>

Repository <repository>

Resource <resource>

Revision Description <revisiondesc>

Runner <runner>

Appendix D

Scope and Content <scopecontent>

Second Heading <head02>

Separated Material <separatedmaterial>

Series Statement <seriesstmt>

Sponsor <sponsor>

Subject <subject>

Subordinate Area <subarea>

Subtitle <subtitle>

Table <table>

Table Body <tbody>

Table Column Specification <colspec>

Table Entry <entry>

Table Group <tgroup>

Table Head <thead>

Table Row <row>

Text Division <div>

Title <title>

Title of the Unit <unittitle>

Title Page <titlepage>

Title Proper of the Finding Aid <titleproper>

Title Statement <titlestmt>